# Photography
## Reinvented

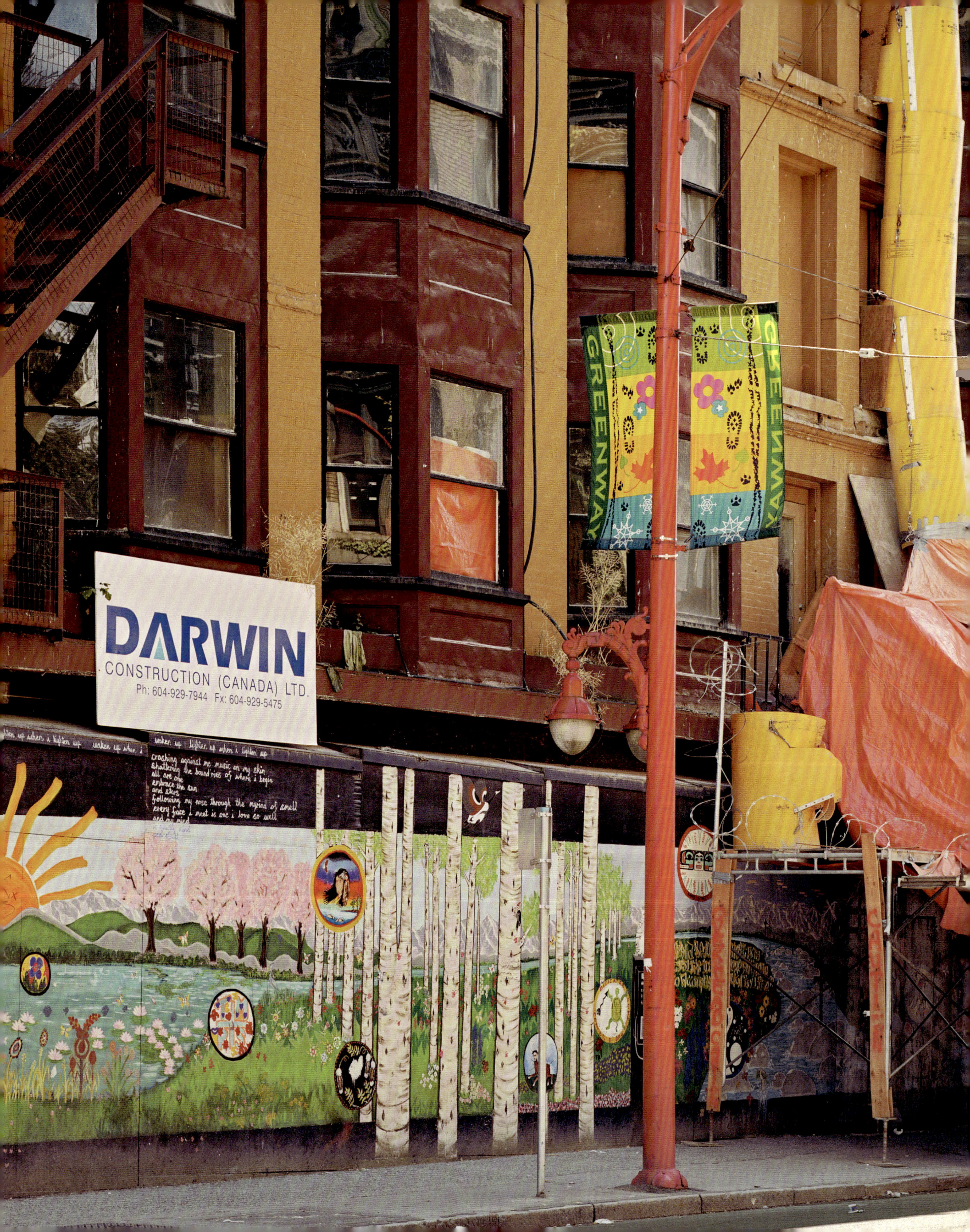

GREENWAY
GREENWAY
DARWIN
CONSTRUCTION (CANADA) LTD.
Ph: 604-929-7944  Fx: 604-929-5475

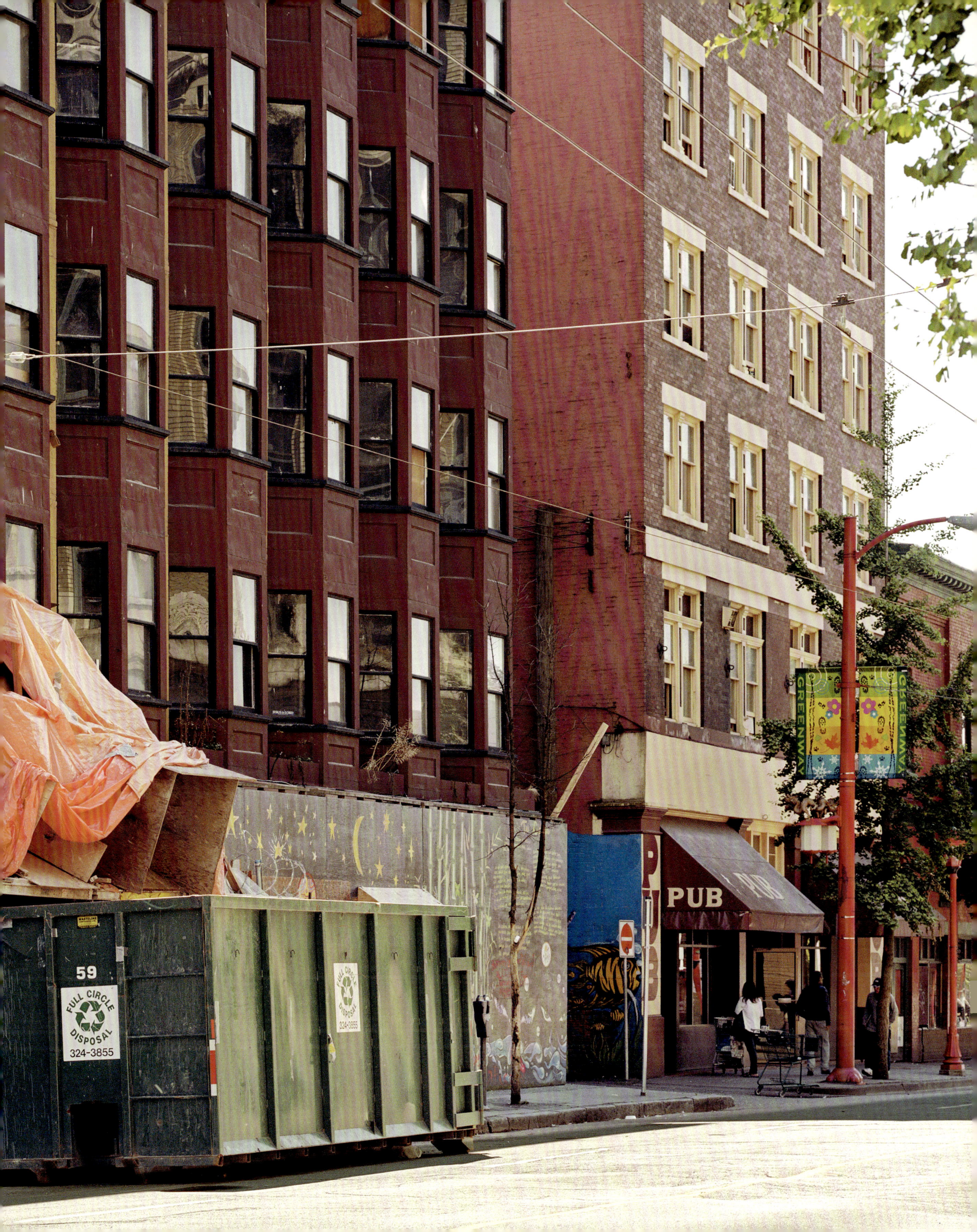
PUB
59
FULL CIRCLE
DISPOSAL
324-3855
GREENWAY

Sarah Greenough

with

Philip Brookman

Andrea Nelson

Leslie Ureña

Diane Waggoner

# Photography Reinvented

## The Collection of Robert E. Meyerhoff and Rheda Becker

NATIONAL GALLERY OF ART, WASHINGTON

PRINCETON UNIVERSITY PRESS, PRINCETON AND OXFORD

*Exhibition Dates*
September 30, 2016 – March 5, 2017



Produced by the Publishing Office,
National Gallery of Art, Washington
www.nga.gov

Judy Metro, *editor in chief*
Chris Vogel, *deputy publisher and
production manager*

Designed by Wendy Schleicher
Edited by Caroline Weaver

Sara Sanders-Buell, *image manager*
John Long, *print and digital production associate*
Mariah Shay, *production assistant*

Typeset in Scala Sans Pro and Scala Pro.
Printed on 115# Utopia Premium Silk Text by
Brilliant Graphics, Exton, Pennsylvania

10 9 8 7 6 5 4 3 2 1

Hardcover edition published in 2016
by the National Gallery of Art, Washington,
and Princeton University Press, Princeton
and Oxford

41 William Street
Princeton, NJ 08540

6 Oxford Street
Woodstock, Oxfordshire OX20 1TR
press.princeton.edu

*Library of Congress*
Control Number: 2016017053

ISBN 978-0-691-17287-3

Dimensions are given in centimeters, with
inches following, height preceding width,
which precedes depth. Dimensions refer to
the framed work of art.

*Divider images*
pp. ii–iii: Jeff Wall, *Hotels, Carrall St., Vancouver,
summer 2005* (detail, pl. 32); p. viii: Vik Muniz,
*Noon Rush Hour on Fifth Avenue, 1949, After
Andreas Feininger (Pictures of Paper)* (pl. 31);
p. xiii: Robert E. Meyerhoff and Rheda Becker,
photograph by Maximilian Franz; pp. xvi–1:
Thomas Struth, *Pergamon Museum 6, Berlin
1996* (detail, pl. 3); pp. 16–17: Candida Höfer,
*Musée du Louvre Paris VIII* (detail, pl. 10);
p. 100: Hiroshi Sugimoto, *Anne Boleyn* (pl. 22)

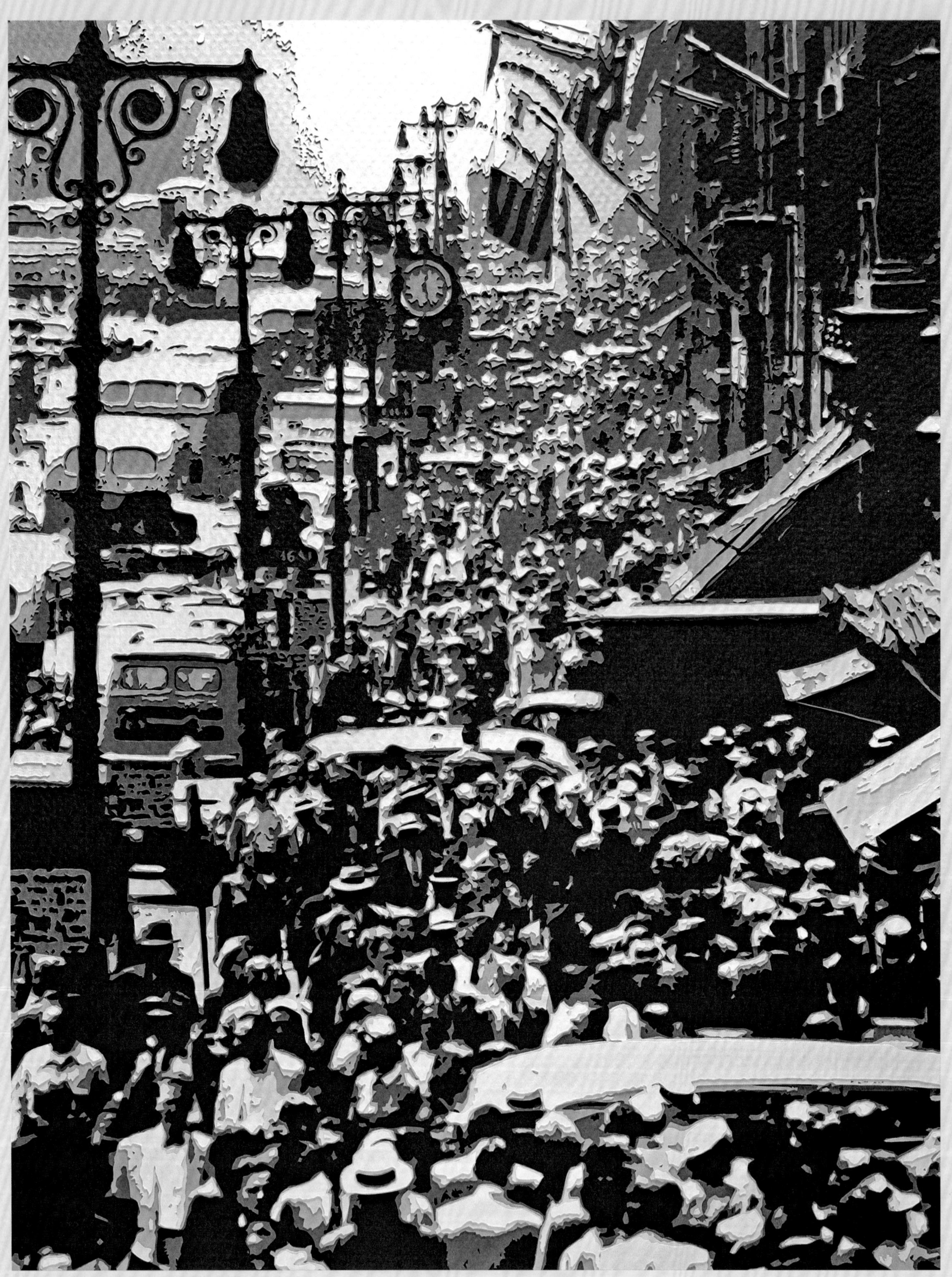

MOST OF US WOULD COUNT OURSELVES LUCKY if we excelled at one endeavor in life, and perhaps even more fortunate if others recognized our skills, wisdom, acumen, and foresight. Robert Meyerhoff and Rheda Becker are two people who have accomplished this and much more. Starting in 1958, Bob and his late wife, Jane, assembled one of the finest collections of mid-twentieth-century art in existence. Without using advisors and relying solely on their own eyes and knowledge, they collected more than three hundred works by fifty artists from Grace Hartigan, Hans Hofmann, and Mark Rothko to Jasper Johns, Ellsworth Kelly, Roy Lichtenstein, Brice Marden, Robert Rauschenberg, and Frank Stella. Yet they did more than amass an exceptional collection; elevating themselves to an entirely different class of collectors, they decided to share it with others, and in 1987 pledged their collection to the National Gallery of Art. In addition, they funded the Gallery's purchase of Barnett Newman's masterpiece, *The Stations of the Cross*, and a related painting, *Be II*. More recently, Bob designated their home and galleries near Baltimore as part of the donation to the Gallery to be used as an off-site facility for the study and display of art.

After Jane Meyerhoff's untimely death in 2004, Bob stopped collecting art; they had formed the collection as a couple, and it had been a central component in their life together. But he did not stop enjoying art, nor did he cease visiting museums and galleries. Shortly thereafter, he and Rheda Becker discovered their shared love of art and their growing interest in photography. Rheda is a celebrated musical narrator who has delighted audiences around the country with her performances. Like Bob, she has spent her life immersed in art, visiting museums wherever she traveled. In 2007, their mutual interests prompted Bob to change course after a lifetime of collecting painting and sculpture and begin to build a collection of photographs with Rheda. Perhaps even more remarkable is that the couple did not look to the well-established old masters of photography such as Alfred Stieglitz, Edward Steichen, or Edward Weston. Instead, they turned to the most innovative contemporary work that challenged accepted conventions of the nature of photography—in scale, subject matter, and method of creation—and helped to ensure the medium's prominence in the contemporary art arena. Bob and Rheda have now acquired thirty-five photographs by nineteen artists, including ones associated with the loosely knit group of artists known as the "Pictures Generation," such as Cindy Sherman, Louise Lawler, and John Baldessari, who appropriated images from the mainstream media, as well as several members of the Düsseldorf school of photography, such as Bernd and Hilla Becher, Andreas Gursky, Candida Höfer, Thomas Struth, and Thomas Ruff, and other leading artists such as Marina Abramović, Thomas Demand, Anselm Kiefer, Vera Lutter, Vik Muniz, Catherine Opie, Hiroshi Sugimoto, Jeff Wall, and James Welling. Bob and Rheda have collected only what they love: pictures that move them visually, intellectually, and even viscerally. In yet another sign of their exceptional generosity, they have pledged these photographs to the National Gallery of Art.

Taken together, these donations are acts of extraordinary philanthropy, ones that benefit the entire nation and are among the most significant gifts ever bestowed on the museum. Numerous exhibitions at the National Gallery of Art and elsewhere have confirmed the importance of the Robert and Jane Meyerhoff Collection and demonstrated that this donation forms the cornerstone of the Gallery's collection of twentieth-century painting. *Photography Reinvented: The Collection of Robert E. Meyerhoff and Rheda Becker* is our first opportunity to showcase this important group of pictures and reveal how it significantly enhances our collection of contemporary photographs.

With all that Bob and now Rheda have done to enrich the Gallery's collection of modern and contemporary art, it is fitting that *Photography Reinvented: The Collection of Robert E. Meyerhoff and Rheda Becker* is one of the exhibitions that celebrates the reopening of the East Building. In recent years our photography collection and program have grown markedly, making it patently clear that the presence of modern and contemporary photographs in the East Building will do much to augment the public's understanding of the development of modern art more broadly. This exhibition was organized by Sarah Greenough, senior curator and head of the department of photographs, who has led our initiative for photography for many years. I wish to express our great gratitude to her and to Harry Cooper, curator and head of the department of modern art, for his stewardship of the Robert and Jane Meyerhoff Collection.

On behalf of the Trustees of the National Gallery of Art, I extend the museum's profound thanks to Bob and Rheda. The Gallery is a collection formed from the fertile amalgamation of many personal collections, each one created by gifted, philanthropic collectors, and each one helping to define the standards of excellence for which the museum is justly celebrated. The Collection of Robert E. Meyerhoff and Rheda Becker will take its place in this distinguished lineage, where it will be enjoyed by our visitors for generations to come and will enhance appreciation of the vitality and complexity of modern and contemporary art and photography.

# Acknowledgments

Sarah Greenough

THE NATIONAL GALLERY OF ART is particularly fortunate to have a team of highly skilled professionals who work on the complex task of organizing exhibitions with exceptional dedication, creativity, efficiency, and good cheer. Each one of these people is committed to completing their job with nothing short of perfection and each one deserves to be thanked for their contributions. I would like to begin by thanking Earl A. Powell III, director, Franklin Kelly, deputy director, and D. Dodge Thompson, chief of exhibitions, who have witnessed the formation and growth of this collection over the last nine years and have guided this exhibition from its inception to installation with unswerving support. I am especially indebted to my colleague Harry Cooper, curator and head of modern art, for his invaluable assistance and perceptive insights as we worked on the installation of *Photography Reinvented: The Collection of Robert E. Meyerhoff and Rheda Becker* in the East Building. I also wish to extend my deepest thanks to Mark Leithauser, senior curator and chief of design, and Donna Kirk, senior architect and designer, who have worked tirelessly to create the elegant installation and have demonstrated, once again, why the National Gallery of Art is unsurpassed in its cogently beautiful displays of the works of art in its care.

In the department of photographs, I would like to thank my colleagues Philip Brookman, consulting curator, and Andrea Nelson and Diane Waggoner, both associate curators, along with Leslie Ureña, formerly curatorial research associate and now assistant curator at the Smithsonian National Portrait Gallery, for their astute essays and assistance with innumerable details related to both the catalog and exhibition. Anne Davis, curatorial assistant, and Anna Wieck, intern, also deserve special recognition for their superb organizational skills and adept help with all aspects of this endeavor, as does Lex Lancaster for her thorough research assistance.

While every exhibition poses its own set of issues, *Photography Reinvented* was especially challenging because of the size, fragility, and often experimental nature of the photographs themselves. Numerous individuals throughout the museum worked together to determine the best possible solutions for transport, handling, and display. I would particularly like to thank Lehua Fisher in the office of the registrar, who coordinated the movement and installation, as well as David Smith and Carson Murdach, who led the team of art handlers who installed the exhibition. Many conservators in various departments lent invaluable advice and aid to this project, including Connie McCabe and Sarah Wagner in the photograph conservation department, Bethann Heinbaugh and James Gleason in the department of preventive conservation, and Jenny Ritchie in the department of paper conservation. I would also like to thank Alan Newman, chief of digital media, along with Lorene Emerson, Lee Ewing, Denis Doorly, Ken Fleisher, and Kate Mayo for their superb scans of these large and complex photographs, as well as Barbara Wood for securing image permissions. Also to be thanked are Gordon Anson and Elizabeth Parr in the department of design; Wendy Battaglino in the department of exhibitions; Susan Arensberg in the department of exhibition programs; Faya Causey and Ali Peil in the department of academic programs for their assistance with the organization of the exhibition and its educational programs; and Jacqueline Protka in the interlibrary loan office. Carol Kelley in the department of special events should also be thanked for expertly arranging the events surrounding this exhibition, as should Anabeth Guthrie, chief of communications-converged media.

The talented team in our publishing office, led by Judy Metro, editor in chief, and Chris Vogel, deputy publisher, also deserve special recognition for creating and producing this beautiful catalog. Wendy Schleicher, design manager, is responsible for its stunning design, which faithfully conveys the power of the photographs themselves, and Caroline Weaver, editor, gave clarity and precision to our writing. In addition, I would like to thank John Long, print and digital production associate; Mariah Shay, production assistant; Sara Sanders-Buell, image manager, who secured images and permissions for works in the exhibition; and Bob Tursack of Brilliant Graphics for his excellent separations and printing of the catalog.

We were extremely fortunate that this exhibition enabled us to work with so many gifted artists and their studios and representatives, who generously gave of their time and expertise. We would particularly like to thank Erin Harris, Richard Avedon Foundation; Ester Dörring, Thomas Demand Studio; Kelsey Tyler and Robin Vousden, Gagosian Gallery; Catherine Belloy and Leslie Nolen, Marian Goodman Gallery; Annette Völker, Andreas Gursky Studio; Christine McMonagle, Anjuli Netram, and Mallory Roark, Sean Kelly Gallery; Ariel Fishman and Sean Logue, Matthew Marks Gallery; Allison Card, Pericles Kolias, Helene Winer, and James Woodward, Metro Pictures: Erica Benincasa, Vik Muniz Studio; Lindsay McGuire, Pace Gallery; Lauren Panzo, Pace/MacGill Gallery; Jose Luis G. Lopez, Regen Projects; Barbara de Palmenaer, Galerie Thaddaeus Ropac; Antonio Homem and Queenie Wong, Sonnabend Gallery; Susanne Partoll, Thomas Struth Studio; Alex Clarke and Kevin Doherty, Jeff Wall Studio; and Liz De Mase and Chris Rawson, David Zwirner.

Throughout our work on this exhibition and publication, we have also been aided immeasurably by Jeanette Preston, Charles Schlauch, Kevin Reithlingshoefer, and Dewey Matthews, who work with Bob Meyerhoff. They have answered innumerable questions and assisted us on multiple occasions, always with great professionalism and geniality.

Finally, I extend my deepest thanks to Bob Meyerhoff and Rheda Becker. During the last few years, it has been an immense pleasure to watch the collection's growth, to look at it with them, and to learn from them. As we have organized this exhibition and publication, we have repeatedly intruded on their lives and they have unfailingly responded with kindness and patience. I thank them for parting with these treasures for the six months the exhibition is on view, but most especially I thank them for their generosity in donating these exceptional photographs to the National Gallery of Art and for their passionate recognition of the power of great art to transform our lives.

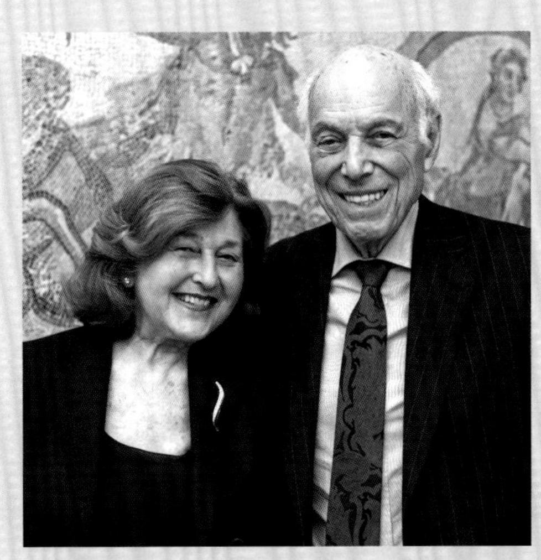

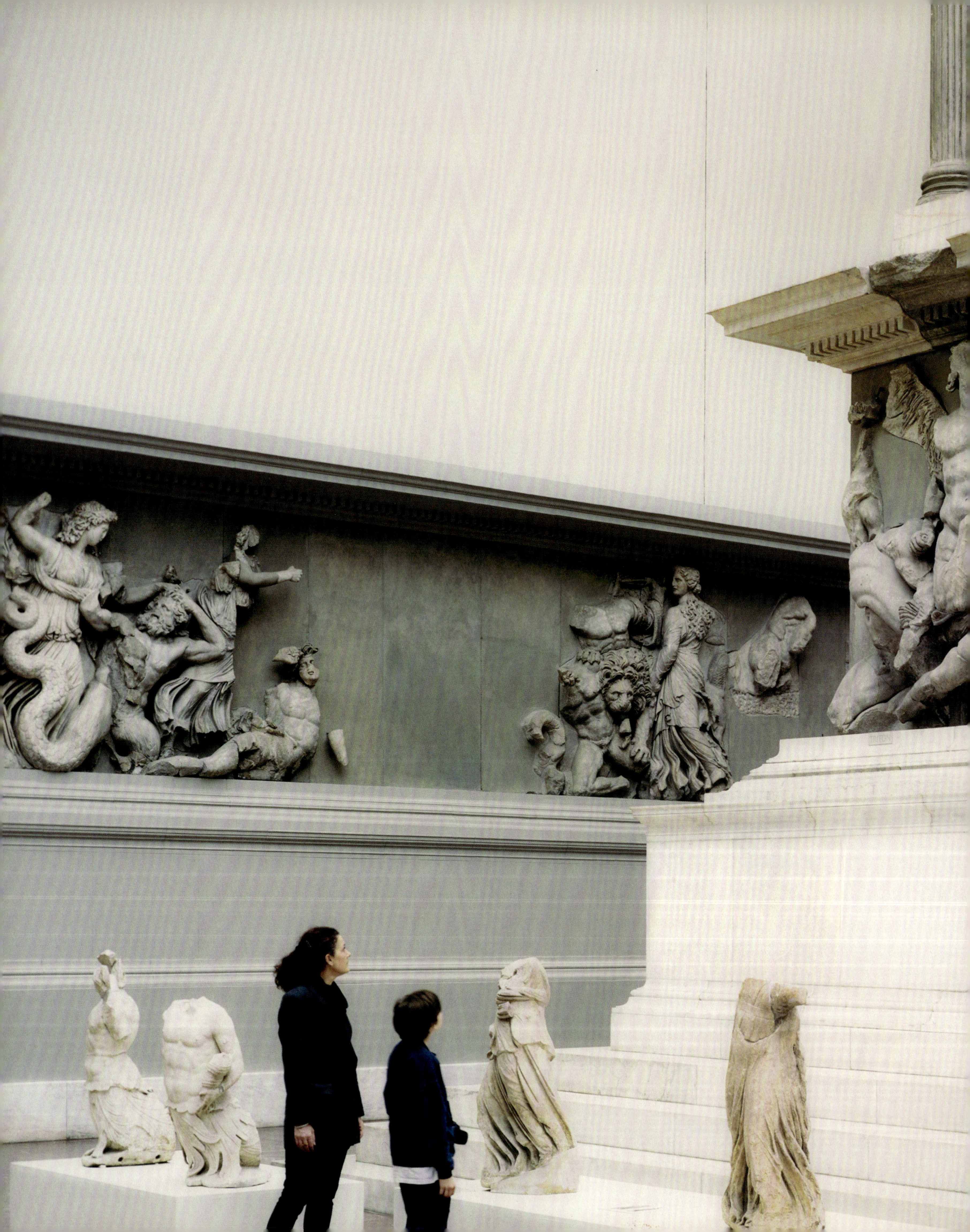

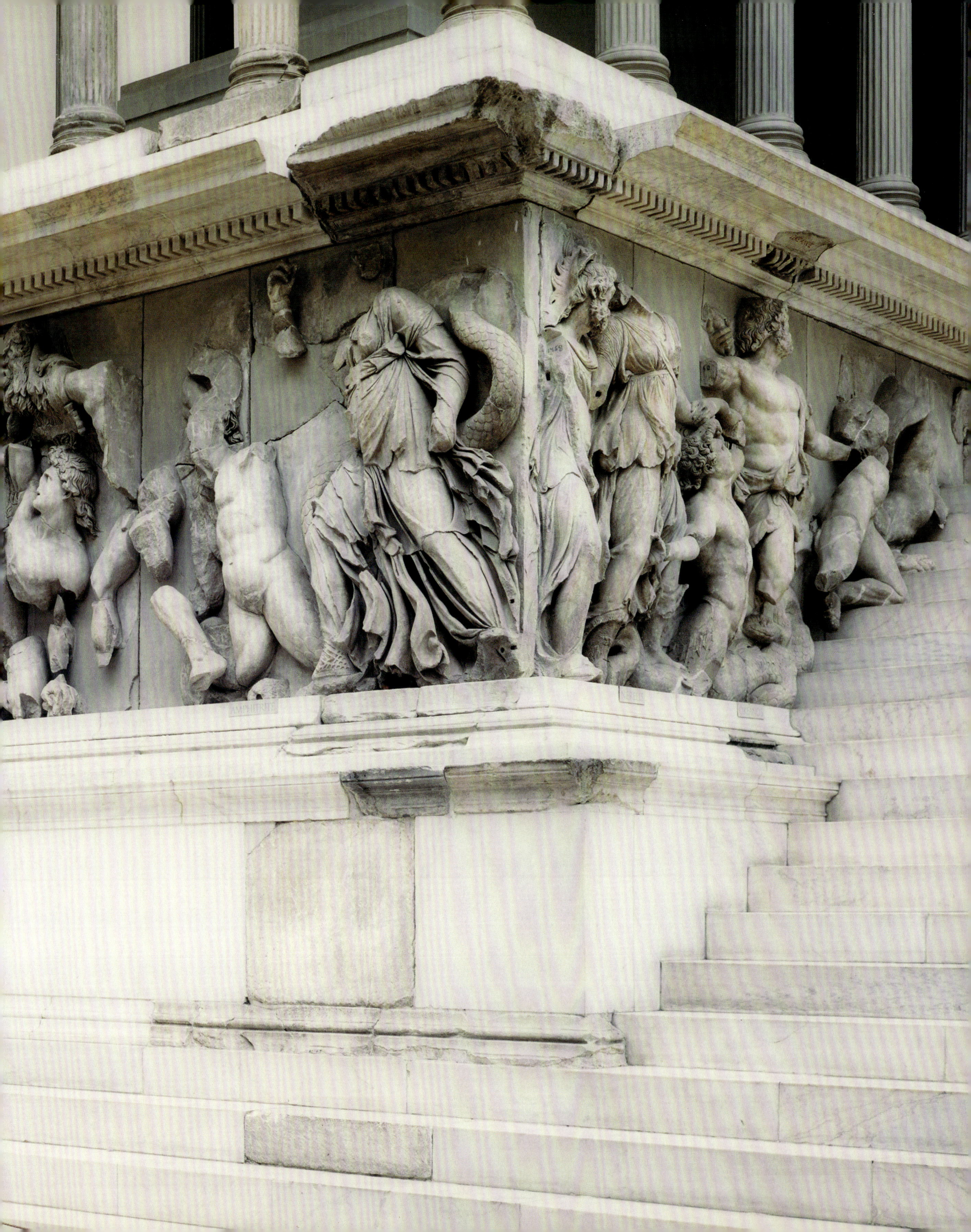

# Picturing a Collection
# Presenting a History

Sarah Greenough

THE COLLECTION OF ROBERT E. MEYERHOFF AND RHEDA BECKER IS A RICH group of pictures that traverses a swiftly changing and complex period in the history of photography. Consisting of thirty-five photographs, it includes celebrated works by nineteen artists: Marina Abramović, Richard Avedon, John Baldessari, Bernd and Hilla Becher, Thomas Demand, Andreas Gursky, Candida Höfer, Anselm Kiefer, Louise Lawler, Vera Lutter, Vik Muniz, Catherine Opie, Thomas Ruff, Cindy Sherman, Thomas Struth, Hiroshi Sugimoto, Jeff Wall, and James Welling. It was formed by two people, Robert Meyerhoff and Rheda Becker, who have immersed themselves in the arts for their entire lives. Rheda is a distinguished musical narrator who has worked with the Baltimore Symphony Orchestra and numerous other symphonies and chamber ensembles around the country for more than four decades. Bob is a businessman who, with his first wife, Jane, spent more than forty years assembling one of the finest collections of postwar American art in existence, with deep, unrivaled holdings of work by Jasper Johns, Ellsworth Kelly, Roy Lichtenstein, Brice Marden, Robert Rauschenberg, and Frank Stella, as well as exceptional paintings, prints, and drawings by Hans Hofmann, Franz Kline, Agnes Martin, Jackson Pollock, Clyfford Still, and many others. After Jane's untimely death in 2004, Bob stopped collecting, yet he continued to be deeply engaged with art.

Bob and Rheda began to collect photographs somewhat accidentally. Like so many others, Rheda was greatly moved when she first saw Albrecht Dürer's *Self-Portrait* hanging in the Alte Pinakothek in Munich in 2004. Yet she was startled when she went from there to the Pinakothek der Moderne and saw Thomas Struth's photograph *Alte Pinakothek, Self-Portrait, Munich 2000*, in which he presented himself admiring the same painting she had seen only moments before (pl. 5). In 2006, when Rheda told Bob of her experience and her delight in Struth's perceptive examination of the spectator's place in the museum, he remembered seeing this same photograph on display in New York. Shifting gears from decades of collecting paintings and drawings, Bob resolved to acquire it and together they embarked on a new passion. Although it took them more than a year to find a print of Struth's photograph, that visit to the Alte Pinakothek sparked their interest in forming a collection of photographs.

Every collection, especially a private one, bears the imprint, interests, and values of the personalities who formed it. On the most superficial level, we might assume that Rheda's love of music and performance helps to explain the inclusion of Baldessari's *Conductor/Pianist/Orchestra (Red/Yellow/Blue)* (pl. 19) and Sugimoto's pictures of a movie theater, *Tampa, Florida* (pl. 21), and Anne Boleyn holding a lute (pl. 22). Bob's degree in engineering, his knowledge of architecture, and his business in real estate might also suggest why Wall's *Hotels, Carrall St., Vancouver, summer 2005* (pl. 32),

Struth's *Notre Dame, Paris 2000* (pl. 7), and Welling's *0467* (pl. 24) would appeal to him. The numerous references to other artists and works of art — from obscure Renaissance portraits to celebrated paintings such as Diego Velázquez's *Las Meninas* — that appear in many of the photographs, especially those by Lawler, Struth, and Sugimoto (pls. 20, 2 – 6, 22), must surely have intrigued and delighted both of them, who have spent their lives going to museums and looking at art. But more fundamentally, every collection also grows out of a profound love of the objects themselves, and thus each picture was chosen primarily because of its individual power. They "fell in love" with each work of art, as Rheda explained, and "decided quickly with mutual enthusiasm and the desire to acquire it."[1]

The Meyerhoff-Becker Collection, though, is more than just a group of pictures with personal meanings to their owners; it is an intriguingly complex and telling collection of photographs. Perhaps one of the first things we notice on looking at it as a whole is that it has a remarkable diversity. Reflecting our new global society, nine of the artists were born in Germany and six in the United States, with one each born in Serbia, Brazil, Japan, and Canada. Ranging in age from fifty-two to eighty-five, four were born before World War II, six during or immediately after it, and nine in the 1950s or 1960s. Thus they matured during different periods in the tumultuous twentieth century: either in the mayhem of the war, its bleak aftermath, or the chaotic social and political unrest of the late 1960s and 1970s. Unlike earlier photographers who were often self-taught or served as apprentices to learn their craft, all but one attended art schools, and not all were trained as photographers; indeed, not all would consider themselves as such. Several studied painting, sculpture, or film, while those who went to school during the experimental 1960s and 1970s — when conceptual and performance art reigned supreme — often taught themselves how to photograph to record their other work. For almost all of these artists, photography made "an entrance by a sort of side door," as Wall has phrased his own embrace of the medium.[2]

Several of them, including Gursky, Höfer, Ruff, and Struth, are closely associated with the Düsseldorf school of photography, a group who studied with Bernd and Hilla Becher at the Kunstakademie Düsseldorf and were deeply inspired by their sober, unsentimental pictures of industrial architecture and the conceptual rigor of their typologies. Others, such as Lawler and Sherman, with Baldessari as a predecessor, are part of the "Pictures Generation," whose name derives from a 1977 exhibition at Artists Space in New York City of a fundamentally different group of artists who appropriated images from the mainstream media and often staged recreations of them. Several more, such as Abramović, Demand, Lutter, Opie, Sugimoto, Wall, and Welling, while influenced by the ideas of these two groups, were not part of either one, nor do they easily coalesce into another unit of their own. And even the members of the Düsseldorf school, the group with the largest presence in the Meyerhoff-Becker Collection, have matured into artists patently different from one another and from their teachers, the Bechers. Moreover, many other prominent members of both the Düsseldorf school (Elger Esser, Axel Hütte, Simone Nieweg, Jörg Sasse, or Petra Wunderlich) and the Pictures Generation (Barbara Kruger, Sherrie Levine, Robert Longo, Richard Prince, David Salle, Laurie Simmons, or Michael Zwack) are not represented in the collection.

The history of the formation of the collection is instructive. Bob and Rheda acquired the thirty-five photographs over the last nine years, purchasing from two to seven per year. Demonstrating a purposeful, methodical, and studious approach, they obtained multiple works by certain photographers — Demand, Struth, and Sugimoto, for example — deliberately and over time, rather than all at once. They also maintained a consistent breadth of focus instead of concentrating first on one school or group before moving on to another. In 2007, for example, the first year they began collecting photographs, they acquired four works by members of the Düsseldorf school (Höfer, Ruff, and two Struths) and three by artists unaffiliated with that group (Baldessari, Sugimoto, and Wall). Another year, 2010, saw the purchase of an equal number of pictures, again almost evenly split between the Düsseldorf school and others (two by Struth and one by Ruff, with one each by Abramović, Demand, Kiefer, and Muniz). With two-thirds of the pictures made in the last fifteen years, the Meyerhoff-Becker Collection is especially rich in contemporary photographs. But Bob and Rheda also reached back in time, grounding their most recent art with important precedents from the past. Almost every year since they began to collect, they have added works from the 1970s (by Sherman and Sugimoto), 1980s (Sherman, Struth, and Sugimoto), or 1990s (Baldessari, Demand, Ruff, Struth, and Sugimoto). Each year also saw the acquisition of pictures with a range of subjects from architectural studies, cityscapes, landscapes, portraits, and still lifes to pictures by Lutter and Welling, whose subjects can best be described as meditations on the practice of photography itself. And, although Bob and Rheda met some of the artists and befriended a few (such as Höfer, whose work they helped to arrange at the George Peabody Library and the Walters Art Museum in Baltimore), they did not seek to make the acquaintance of all the artists in the collection, nor did they purchase only the work of their friends. All of these factors make clear their intense focus and their determination to acquire specific works by specific artists.

In reflecting on the collection, we should also remember that both Bob and Rheda know that the cumulative power of a group of pictures is far greater and can tell us far more about the art and culture of the time than any single object by itself. The Robert and Jane Meyerhoff Collection also evidences a similar catholic approach, with works by both those dedicated to abstraction, such as Ellsworth Kelly, Brice Marden, and Frank Stella, as well as those who almost always included the figure in their paintings, like Jasper Johns, Roy Lichtenstein, and Robert Rauschenberg.[3] Yet together, those pictures provide an exceptionally rich account of the evolution of mid-twentieth-century painting. Rheda, too, from her work as a narrator performing scores that merge music and words to bring forth the beauty of both media, is keenly aware of the ways in which seemingly disparate works of art can enhance one another when they are brought together in new groupings.

What, then, ties these artists and this collection together? What are the ideas, as the symbolist poet Stéphane Mallarmé once wrote, that "split up into a number of equal motifs [and] rhyme" throughout the collection, binding it into a cohesive whole? And what do these concepts and concerns tell us about the evolution of contemporary photography? We might start to answer these questions by looking at several pictures made at key moments in the last forty years. Through them, we can begin to get a sense of the deep engagement that the artists in the Meyerhoff-Becker Collection have with history and see how they have drawn on the art of the past to invent a new course for contemporary photography in the twenty-first century.

Bernd and Hilla Becher's *Water Towers* (1972–2009, pl. 1) and Cindy Sherman's *Untitled Film Still #4* (1977, pl. 17) succinctly illustrate the two ideas that dominated photography in the late 1970s and 1980s: the photograph as a document, a record of the world, a trace and direct imprint of it, and the photograph as a picture, a work of art unto itself. This understanding of the dual nature of photography has, of course, existed since the medium's invention in the late 1830s, as artists, scientists, and others examined its nature and sought to determine its most appropriate use. Was it, to use phrases borrowed from two seminal historical figures, the "Pencil of Nature"—a process that faithfully documented the wonders of the world, as championed by one of its inventors, William Henry Fox Talbot — or the "Hand of Man," a tool that enabled the creation of pictures in which form and content could merge to create new meanings, as proclaimed by ardent proponent Alfred Stieglitz at the turn of the twentieth century? This debate percolated throughout the twentieth century, and was reignited in the 1960s and 1970s when artists associated with two new movements began to use photography in entirely new ways. The first to do so were conceptual and minimalist artists who sought to throw off centuries-old traditions of painting and sculpture as well as the heroicizing tendencies of art of the mid-twentieth century. Ed Ruscha, Sol LeWitt, and Dan Graham, all key proponents of conceptual art, and minimalist artists such as Carl Andre, prized photography for what they saw as its anti-art properties, democratic nature, and ease, as well as its cool, systematic, and seemingly anonymous mechanical nature. Photography, they thought, enabled them to create neutral, archival records of their ephemeral practices. Exploiting photography in a wide variety of new ways, some conceptual artists projected photographic imagery onto their canvases, others used it in their books or slide shows, while still more transformed photography into three-dimensional sculpture or folded it into their multimedia projects. But all infused the practice with new ideas.

The conceptual and minimalist artists saw a kindred approach in the work and practice of the German photographers Bernd and Hilla Becher. Beginning in the late 1960s, they championed the Bechers' objective, archival use of photography, often exhibiting or reproducing the couple's photographs alongside their own art. For more than fifty years, starting in the late 1950s and continuing until their deaths, the Bechers systematically photographed anonymous industrial architecture — blast furnaces, gas tanks, winding towers — and always depicted their subjects frontally, from an elevated vantage point, and with a gray or overcast sky. Deeply inspired by the methodical approach and cool objectivity of earlier German documentary photographers such as August Sander and Albert Renger-Patzsch, the Bechers did not turn their back on history but rethought earlier precedents by grouping multiple pictures of the same subject, made over several years, into series for publications and grids for exhibitions, as in *Water Towers*. They called these groupings typologies, a concept that would inform not only their own and their students' work but that of many others for years to come. Using the camera as a tool of empirical verification, they constructed their typologies in order to facilitate comparisons between similar types of structures, often revealing their exceptional diversity as well as the extensive impact they have had on the modern landscape. Many of the objects the Bechers recorded were no longer in use and had been slated for destruction by the time they photographed them, and thus their pictures form an important archive of vernacular architecture of the late industrial era. Yet they also insisted that the objects they photographed were "Anonymous Sculpture" (Anonyme Skulpturen), as they began to call them in the late 1960s. In so doing they linked their work to Marcel Duchamp's concept of the "readymade" and simultaneously indicated that their focus centered more on the thing they depicted than the picture they created, more on the knowledge to be garnered from their images than the pictures as works of art unto themselves.

The liberating example of conceptual art helped to invigorate and transform photography itself, prompting others to explore new paths. As Jeff Wall, who began his career as a conceptual artist, noted many years later, "when people came from outside the classic domain of photography and started practicing photography…they unlocked many aspects of photography that weren't readily available or had been blocked in a way."[4] One of those aspects that had been blocked was explored in the Artists Space show, organized by Douglas Crimp, of the Pictures Generation photographers. "Our experience is governed by pictures," Crimp asserted in the exhibition catalog, "pictures in newspapers and magazines, on television and in the cinema. Next to these pictures firsthand experience begins to retreat, to seem more trivial. While it once seemed that pictures had the function of interpreting reality, it now seems that they have usurped it."[5] As has been frequently noted, the artists whom Crimp exhibited in 1977, as well as others who came to be called the Pictures Generation, were the first to have been raised on television and bombarded from their youth with mass-media images that celebrated the new consumer society and showed them how to dress, what to buy and eat, and how to live their lives. Moreover, these artists emerged during a time when not only photography was changing, but identity itself was being rethought. Roland Barthes, Michel Foucault, and other theorists suggested it was not inborn and innate, but inculcated and deeply influenced by mass media and societal expectations.[6]

Although Cindy Sherman was not a part of the 1977 show of the artists who would come to be called the Pictures Generation, her photographs, especially those derived from cinema, such as *Untitled Film Still #4* (pl. 17), encapsulate many of their ideas and concerns. Drawing on indeterminate imagery that reminds us of movie stills or publicity shots, Sherman staged herself in sixty-nine pictures as a fictitious character in scenarios that resemble scenes from a movie. Wearing vintage clothing, wigs, and makeup, she presented herself in clichéd roles: a smartly dressed young secretary in the big city, a lonely girl on the run. As in *Untitled Film Still #4*, her female protagonist was almost always shown alone and in seemingly unguarded, reflective moments, as if considering the nature of her life and present situation. Sherman was hardly the first photographer to stage photographs inspired by other pictures. Throughout the nineteenth century, as photography sought to claim its place among the other arts, numerous photographers openly quoted paintings in their own pictures. Oscar Gustave Rejlander, a Swedish-born British painter and photographer, for example, based his photograph

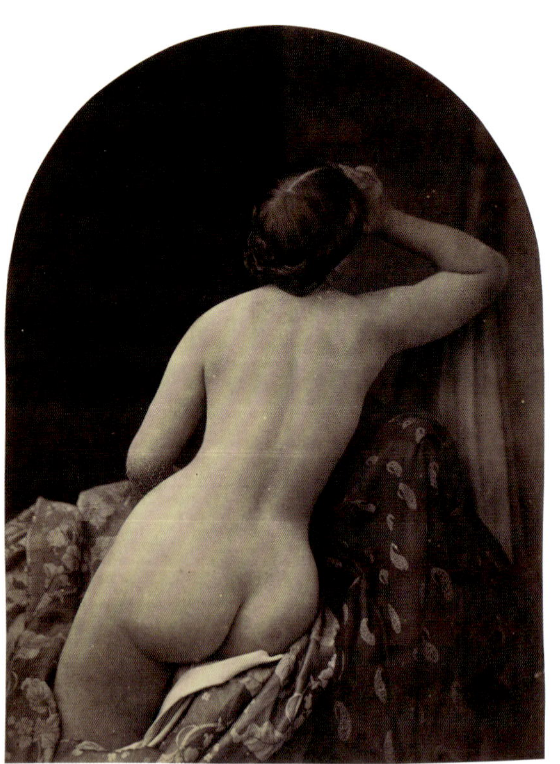

fig. 1: Oscar Gustave Rejlander, *Ariadne*, 1857, albumen print, National Gallery of Art, Washington, Paul Mellon Fund

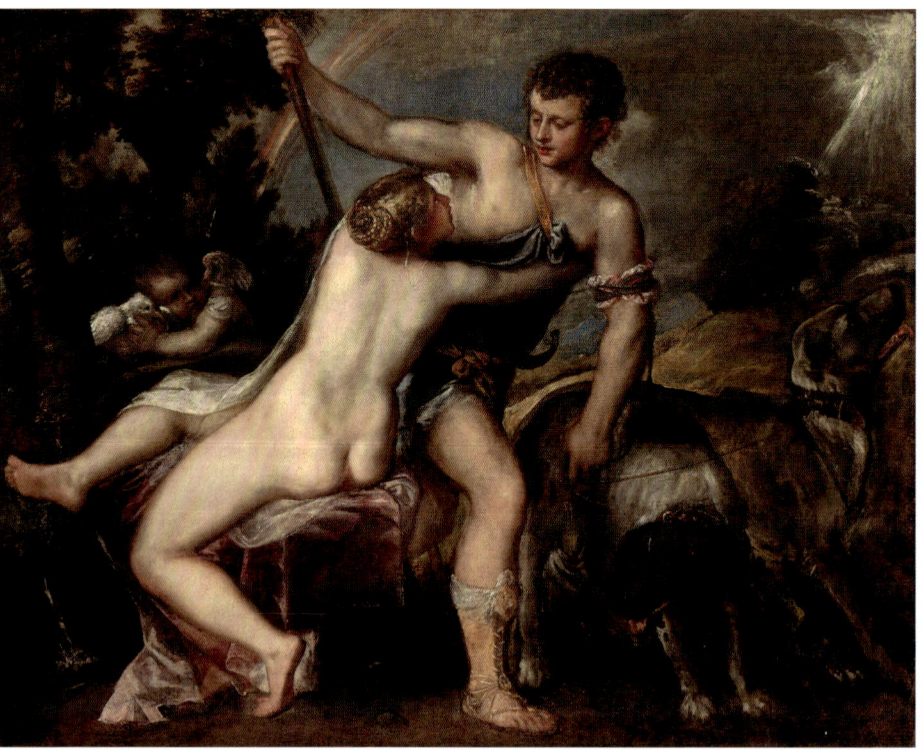

fig. 2: Titian, *Venus and Adonis*, c. 1560, oil on canvas, National Gallery of Art, Washington, Widener Collection

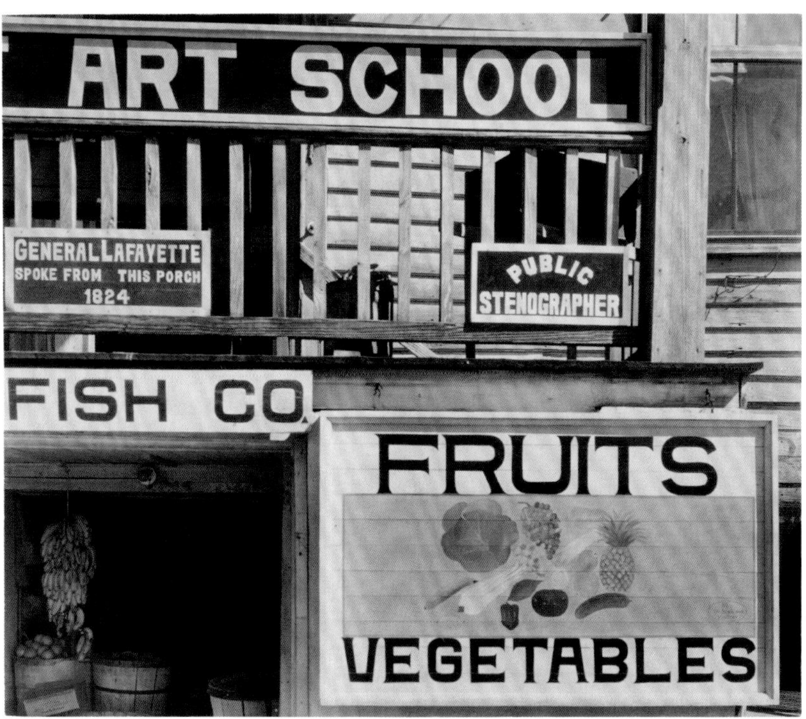

fig. 3: Walker Evans, *Signs, Beaufort, South Carolina*, March 1936, gelatin silver print, National Gallery of Art, Washington, Horace W. Goldsmith Foundation through Robert and Joyce Menschel

titled *Ariadne* (1857, fig. 1) on Titian's *Venus and Adonis* (c. 1560, fig. 2) to show how the painter had strayed from correct anatomical depiction and prove that photography could render facts more accurately. Nor were Sherman or any of the Pictures Generation artists the first photographers to draw on vernacular culture. Walker Evans, the Bechers, and numerous other earlier twentieth-century photographers had turned to the artifacts of everyday life, understanding them as important cultural evidence (fig. 3). Unlike Evans or the Bechers, though, Sherman and the other Pictures Generation artists saw the vernacular not as a subject matter to be prized, studied, and elevated, but merely as a means to make pictures. Sherman made this clear by purposefully and playfully emphasizing the artificiality of her pictures: she made deliberately rough prints, reminiscent of poor press photographs; she repeatedly posed herself as all the different characters, often with crude makeup or props; and, on occasion, she even included the shutter release cord. Far from documents, Sherman's photographs are pictures that openly acknowledge themselves as such.

Thirteen years later, when Thomas Struth made *Alte Pinakothek, Self-Portrait, Munich 2000* (pl. 5), the dialogue between photography as document and photography as art had changed and the lines between the two had become fascinatingly blurred. As one of the Bechers' first students, Struth had adopted many of their methodological and stylistic approaches. Seeking to address the culture of his age and the character of individual metropolitan environments, his initial black-and-white photographs from the late 1970s and 1980s depict empty urban vistas and are recorded frontally from a slightly elevated vantage point while standing in the middle of a street (fig. 4). Austere and dispassionate, they strive to be neutral records of fact. But *Alte Pinakothek, Self-Portrait, Munich 2000* is a different kind of picture altogether. Showing Struth standing near the German Renaissance artist Albrecht Dürer's highly celebrated *Self-Portrait* (1500), this is clearly a carefully constructed photograph about art and its importance to our history and culture. Like a Russian nesting doll, it is also a picture within a picture—in this case, a double self-portrait—that becomes more complex and intriguing as we unpack it.

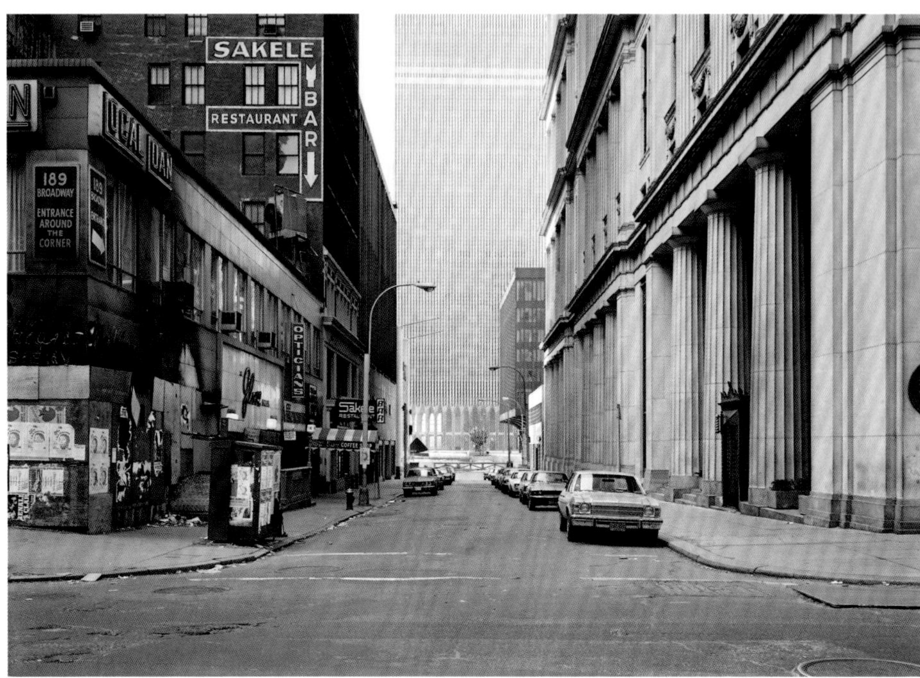


fig. 4: Thomas Struth, *Dey Street, Financial District, New York*, 1978, gelatin silver print, Courtesy Atelier Thomas Struth

The Dürer *Self-Portrait* is often hailed as a daringly original work, one of the first frontal self-portraits ever made, and a pose previously reserved for religious depictions, especially of Christ. Through his portrayal of himself as an inspired creator and humanist intellectual, Dürer signaled the rising centrality of the individual and the arts in the Renaissance. In the years since, Dürer's bold articulation of himself served as an important touchstone, especially for those artists who, like Struth, came of age after World War II and struggled with what it meant to be a German artist in the wake of the Holocaust. By incorporating Dürer's self-portrait into his own self-portrait, Struth constructed a dialogue with his artistic past, as if to imply that the two artists were conversing across the centuries.

As its title unobtrusively suggests, *Alte Pinakothek, Self-Portrait, Munich 2000* is also a picture about the relationship between photography and the other arts. Like the other Meyerhoff-Becker artists, Struth matured during a time when the study of the history of photography proliferated in colleges, universities, and art schools, and when museums increasingly exhibited photographs alongside the other arts. This growing exposure to the history of the medium, coupled with the ability to see photographs displayed in new settings, once again raised questions for many about the different ways in which photographers express their ideas from those working in other media.[7] Reflecting on these differences, Struth depicted himself in this picture, which he considers his only self-portrait to date, in a very dissimilar way to Dürer.[8] Standing to the side and seen from the back, he shows only a portion of his torso and jaw—no face or head, no thick mane of curly hair. Even his hand is hidden in his pocket, unlike Dürer's elegant rendering of his fingers that has sparked much discussion about his intention.[9] Partial, out of focus, and seemingly fleeting, ephemeral, and contingent, Struth's appearance contrasts markedly to how he presented the Dürer painting, head-on and in exquisitely sharp detail. By utilizing key attributes of photographic vision—detail, focus, blur, crop, and what Wall calls the "accidental quality" of a snapshot—Struth expanded the dialogue he set up in this picture beyond that of past to present and artist to artist, to one about the relationship of photography to the other arts.[10]

Yet *Alte Pinakothek, Self-Portrait, Munich 2000* is more than just a picture of a picture or one about the relationship between photography and painting. Measuring more than 62 × 73 inches, it, like many of the other photographs in the Meyerhoff-Becker Collection, is big — so big, in fact, that Struth reproduced the Dürer painting almost exactly the same size as the original, while his own figure is much larger than life-size. The scale of the photograph clearly signals that it, like Dürer's painting, was made to be seen on the walls of a museum, not reproduced in a magazine or book (which had been the goal of so many earlier twentieth-century photographers). Its size also forces us to approach the photograph not as a personal object we might hold in our hands, but as a public declaration, like a painting with all of that medium's concomitant authority, seriousness of intent, and presence.[11]

In addition, *Alte Pinakothek, Self-Portrait, Munich 2000* is in color and face-mounted to a sheet of plexiglass, making the colors appear saturated, vibrant, and glowing. Throughout much of the twentieth century, most photographers who sought to create works of art made black-and-white, not color, prints; high gloss was seen as a sign that a photographic print was a snapshot or made for reproduction, not to be contemplated as an aesthetic object. By the 1970s and 1980s, as technological improvements enabled the production of both more stable color prints and much larger ones, numerous fine-art photographers began to make big color pictures. Color by itself conveys a striking and beguiling immediacy, as it so closely approximates how we see and experience the world. With face-mounted prints that sense of propinquity is intensified, as the colors seductively vibrate with luminosity. More important, large color face-mounted prints like Struth's self-portrait not only seem more lifelike, they also create an odd spatial relationship for viewers. Because *Alte Pinakothek, Self-Portrait, Munich 2000* depicts objects at their original size or larger, it plays on the confusion in photography between document and art, between what is depicted (in this case, a painting and a person) and the reality of what the photograph actually is (a two-dimensional picture) while simultaneously seeming to tempt us to enter into the picture itself. Both inviting and disconcerting, this strangely destabilizing experience prompts an almost visceral response in viewers, of a different kind and magnitude than we usually have when looking at paintings.

*Alte Pinakothek, Self-Portrait, Munich 2000* thus becomes what Jean-François Chevrier has perceptively described as a "tableau," a picture that is "designed and produced for the wall, summoning a confrontational experience on the part of the spectator."[12] That "confrontational experience" is not new in photography: the desire to transform the act of looking at pictures into a dizzying new experience was the impetus for Louis-Jacques-Mandé Daguerre, one of the medium's two primary inventors, to discover photography. Daguerre's diorama, which he invented in the early 1820s, was a theater that displayed giant, 45 × 71 foot translucent paintings that seemed to come to life through varying color and lighting effects, dazzling the audience. Daguerre never succeeded in making photographs as large and as spatially disorienting as the paintings presented in his diorama, but twentieth-century commercial photographers did — in giant billboards and other photographic advertisements, such as the Colorama, an 18 × 60 foot backlit transparency installed in the main arrival and departure hall in Grand Central Station, New York, from 1950 to 1990. But as Chevrier notes, that confrontational experience did not appear in fine-art photography and on museum walls until the late 1970s, first in the three-dimensional light boxes of Wall that assume a sculptural presence and alter the relationship that visitors have to viewing photographs. No longer small or unassuming, no longer intended for reproduction, Wall's light boxes, and, later in the 1980s and 1990s, the supersized prints of Ruff and Gursky (often measuring from 7 × 5 to 6 × 11 feet), fundamentally changed the dynamics of how and where photographs were viewed and altered the discourse in the debate about them as documents or works of art. This new tableau photograph could, as Chevrier asserted, either spring from a documentary impulse, as in Struth's *Alte Pinakothek, Self-Portrait, Munich 2000* or Ruff's *Portrait (P. Stadtbäumer)* (pl. 15), or from a more purely artistic one; it may be unmanipulated and "straight," as Edward Weston would have demanded, or it may be staged and manipulated. What matters, Chevrier insists, is that the tableau asserts its presence not through its subject matter but as an object unto itself: designed specifically for exhibition, it "affirms its status as an autonomous image" and it "presents more than it represents."[13]

Höfer's *Musée du Louvre Paris VIII* (2005, pl. 10) functions in this way. One of the first of the Becher students to consistently use color, she is known for her rigorously centered photographs of empty museums and libraries. Fascinated by the way the art and culture of the past is made visible in the present in these edifices, she draws on the rich history of architectural photographs. Architecture was a favorite subject for nineteenth-century photographers: it did not move during long exposures and it enabled them to demonstrate the ability of the new medium to record, preserve, and celebrate important historic monuments. The nineteenth-century French photographer Charles Marville did just that when he photographed galleries at the Louvre in 1851 (fig. 5). In addition, by positioning his camera off-center at eye level and using its ability to abruptly crop forms, he imparted a sense of life and immediacy to his picture, presenting the scene as viewers themselves might have experienced it as they walked through the galleries.

Höfer did something quite different in *Musée du Louvre Paris VIII*. She placed her 4 × 5 inch view camera at a slightly elevated vantage point in the middle of a gallery displaying Greek and Roman sculpture. Like Marville, she used mainly natural, not artificial, light, yet few shadows animate her composition, nor do any people populate the scene. Instead, the soft, even light, the insistently perspectival point of view, and even the absence of people all seductively pull us into the composition. As our eye wanders through the surprisingly empty scene we are drawn to a distant window,

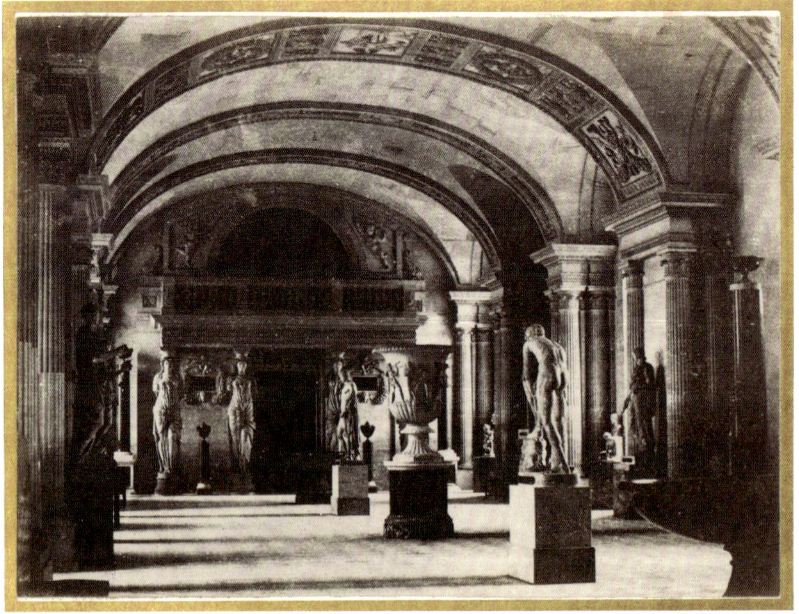

fig. 5: Charles Marville, *Salle des Cariatides, au Musée du Louvre*, c. 1851, salted paper print, National Gallery of Art, Washington, Patrons' Permanent Fund

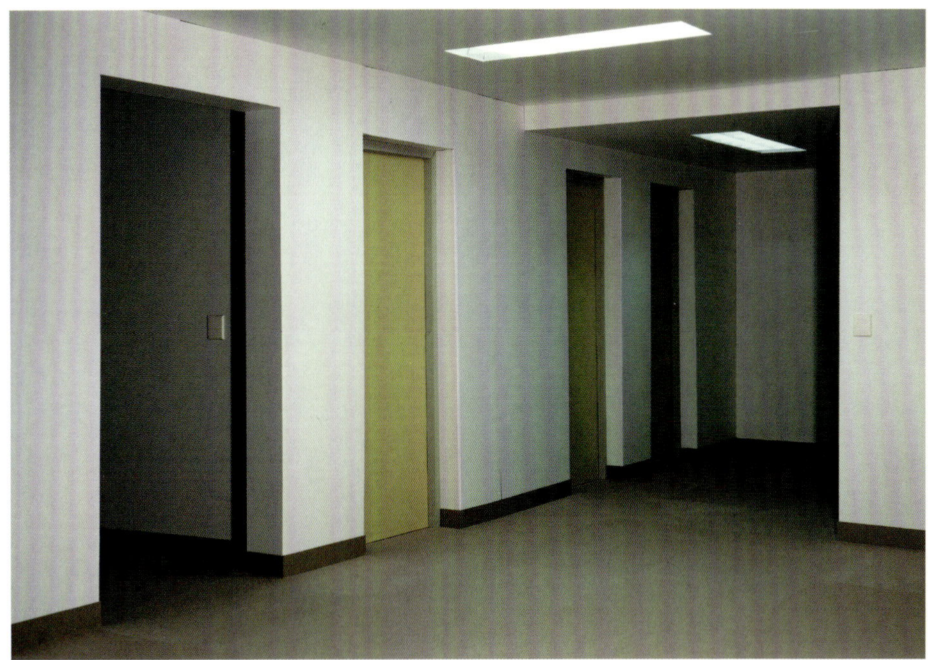

fig. 6: Thomas Demand, *Corridor*, 1995, chromogenic print, Courtesy Matthew Marks Gallery

surrounded by a radiant arch, in the exact center of the composition. Yet oddly, because the window and the luminous path of light leading to it are the brightest elements of the composition, they do not recede in space but come forward to the front of the picture frame. Although Höfer is fascinated with the ways in which art is displayed in museums, she also seeks to heighten the tension that exists in viewing works of art within her own art — "the presentation of presentation," as she notes. She intensifies these actions of both sucking us into the illusion of three-dimensional space and shoving us back to its flat surface by creating large, exceptionally detailed pictures that invite a "slow and careful reading of details distributed over space," as she asserts, and entice people "to fully expose themselves to the temptations of a three-dimensional perception of what is but a printed image." [14] Whereas the imprecision in Marville's photograph (a result of the softness of his paper negative and salted-paper print) infuses the scene with a suggestive ambience and human presence, Höfer's almost unnaturally detailed prints convey both a sense of abundance and absence, dazzling us with their lavishness but always pushing us back to their surface. Even the one lone shadow of the head and torso of a sculpture on a plinth in the lower left remains firmly on the foreground. In the process, she transforms the architectural space into an impenetrable abstraction: a picture, not a document. [15]

Demand's *Clearing* (2003, pl. 28) explores this same idea but from a different perspective. Although he attended the Kunstakademie Düsseldorf when Bernd Becher taught there, Demand did not study with him but instead focused on sculpture, making small paper architectural models. Recognizing their inherent fragility, he learned how to photograph in the late 1980s in order to document them, but in 1993 he changed course and made his photographs his finished works of art. Striving to explore shared cultural memories, he appropriates images from news archives, magazines, films, and television programs — often of highly charged scenes, as in *Corridor* (1995, fig. 6), a picture of the hallway in the apartment building where the serial killer Jeffrey Dahmer lived and murdered his victims. Demand then makes painstaking, full-size replicas of these pictures using paper and cardboard that he photographs, later destroying his models. Walking a thin line between the credibly real and the oddly artificial, he uses

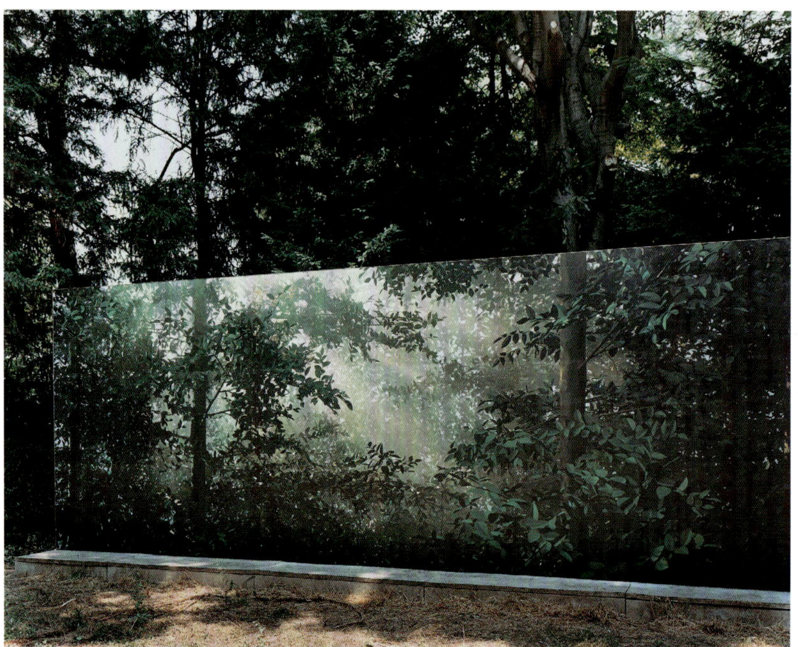

fig. 7: Thomas Demand, *Clearing*, 2003, installation view, offset print on affiche papier, Courtesy Matthew Marks Gallery

the enhanced resolution and verisimilitude of a large-format camera to simultaneously reveal the strikingly precise details of his constructions (the light switches in *Corridor*, for example) and their artifice (there are no knobs on any of the doors in *Corridor*). By playing with detail and omission, specificity and ambiguity, Demand explores key characteristics of both analogue and digital photography. Our faith in the veracity of analogue photography resides largely in its seeming fidelity to reality, while our apprehension about the deceitful nature of digital lies in its ability to so easily alter facts. Thus in these potent pictures Demand raises questions about the relationship between photography, truth, and image-making while also commenting on the unstable relationship — the "truthiness," as the satirist Stephen Colbert terms it — between fact and fiction in the twenty-first century.[16]

When *Clearing* was made, it was somewhat of an anomaly in Demand's work. One of only two landscapes and the largest photograph Demand had made to date, it was conceived for his participation in the 2003 Venice Biennale. Unlike much of his other earlier work, though, it is not based on an emotionally fraught historical occurrence but a scene in one of Venice's public parks, the Giardini della Biennale, where the art fair is held. Using 270,000 paper leaves that were die-cut into eighty different shapes, he constructed a handmade forest in a steel frame that measured approximately 18 × 50 × 32 feet. He illuminated his model to replicate the light in the original scene (a feat in itself, as the intense lights threatened to ignite the paper) and photographed it. He then made a huge print slightly larger than 6 × 16 feet, exactly the same size as the original scene. His previous photographs were triply removed from reality: they were photographs of constructions based on photographs of a scene.[17] In *Clearing*, he took his practice one step further: he shipped his print from his studio in Berlin to Venice and installed it in front of the very forest it depicted, thus completing a circle from reality to two-dimensional photograph to three-dimensional construction to a two-dimensional print and back to the thing itself (fig. 7). Even when *Clearing* is separated from its installation in Venice and seen on the walls of a museum, its monumental size and quietly insistent artificiality force us to contemplate it not merely as a straightforward depiction of a real space but as a work of art in itself.

Jeff Wall is another artist in the Meyerhoff-Becker Collection who walks the line between art and document, verisimilitude and reality. Although he began his career as a painter, he was drawn to photography as a young student, especially as it was used by conceptual artists such as Ruscha, Graham, and Robert Smithson. He largely stopped making art between 1971 and 1977 and concentrated instead on art history, first studying at the Courtauld Institute of Art in London and later teaching. His first backlit color transparency, *The Destroyed Room* (fig. 8), was made and exhibited in 1978 and was inspired both by illuminated advertisements and commercial window displays of clothing and furniture. In this picture, which is a staged scene of an aggressively ransacked bedroom, filled with premonitions of violence and death, Wall "passed his ideas…of the punk phenomenon, which was quickly filtering through the whole cultural environment," as he said a few years later, "through the historical prism" of another work — Eugène Delacroix's *The Death of Sardanapalus* (fig. 9).[18] Replicating things he had seen but not necessarily photographed, Wall describes this aspect of his work as "cinematographic" to suggest both his process of collaborating with others to make the pictures and also the influence of cinema itself, particularly the work of Luis Buñuel, Jean-Luc Godard, and Rainer Werner Fassbinder, who moved seamlessly between documentary-style films and elaborately staged ones. Cinematographic pictures give Wall, as he has said, "a certain freedom to then re-create or reshape what I saw."[19] Freezing a seemingly precise moment in time, some of his cinematographic pictures have a snapshotlike quality but on closer inspection, the action sometimes (but not always) seems too bizarre to be true. Often meticulously constructed, using actors, artificial lighting, and carefully selected props, his strangely resonant pictures suggest a narrative that is never fully explicated and leave viewers wondering what happened in the moments before and after his exposure. As with so many of the photographs in the Meyerhoff-Becker Collection, scale matters profoundly in Wall's work. If his pictures were small, they might seem to have parallels to other staged pictures from the nineteenth or early twentieth century, where photographers like Rejlander conceived and deliberately posed each element in their pictures. The strikingly large size of his images (over 8 × 10 feet), their glowing luminosity as backlit transparencies, and the physical presence of the aluminum light boxes themselves, coupled with the scenes they depict, transform them into an entirely different experience. But they are not big merely to be big or to imitate the other arts. "A sense of scale," Wall has written, "is one of the most precious gifts given to us by Western painting." And that scale, he believes, must be tuned to the human body: "The size and scale proper to pictorial art," he writes, "is the scale of the body, the making of pictures in which objects and figures are limned so that they appear to be on about the same scale as the people looking at the picture."[20]

Although Wall categorizes many of his pictures as cinematographic, he describes others made from the mid-1980s onward as documentary, using the term as any other traditional photographer, such as Walker Evans or Paul Strand, would have done: these are pictures where he selects the time and place but does not intervene in the site or scene in any way. *Hotels, Carrall St., Vancouver, summer 2005,* is one of those documentary photographs (pl. 32). Showing a sunlit street in Vancouver, the picture depicts a row of buildings, some of which are under renovation. At first glance, the photograph seems oddly simple, a casual snapshot made perhaps from a moving car to note the progress of construction. Yet as we look more closely we see that if it is indeed a snapshot, someone with a discerning eye must have made it. The picture is filled with rectangles and triangles, punctuated by lines, stripes, and cylinders of richly saturated colors — yellow, orange, red, green, and even white (if we may count that as a color) — set against a lush red background that ranges from Bordeaux to burgundy. Stretching

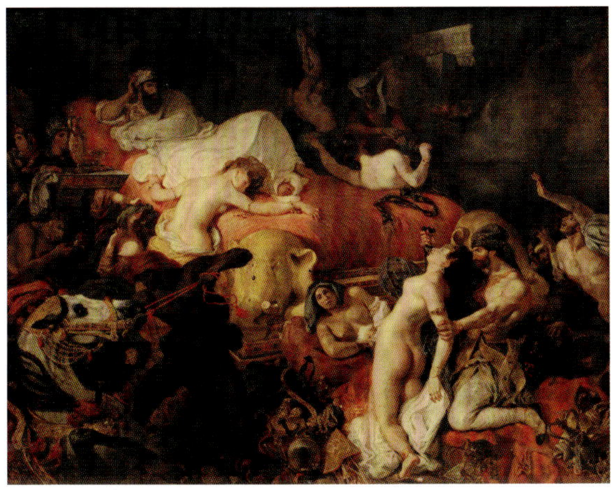

fig. 8: Jeff Wall, *The Destroyed Room*, 1978, transparency in light box, Courtesy of the artist

fig. 9: Eugène Delacroix, *The Death of Sardanapalus*, 1827, oil on canvas, Musée du Louvre, Paris, Acquired on the arrears of the bequest of Maurice Audéoud, 1921

from left to right and top to bottom, the colors and forms make the picture read more like an abstract painting than a photograph; indeed, Wall himself likened it to Robert and Jane Meyerhoff's *Autumn Gold* (1957) by Hans Hofmann (fig. 10).[21] When it is back-lit and illuminated in a light box, *Hotels, Carrall St., Vancouver, summer 2005* displays the sort of vibrant interaction between color and form that Hofmann, in reference to his own paintings, described as "push and pull," energizing the space and "helping with the transference of three-dimensional experience to two dimensions."[22]

But as with any documentary photograph, this is also a picture of specific objects made at a specific time and place. Wall makes this clear in his title: it is a picture of hotels on Carrall Street in Vancouver, Canada, in the summer of 2005. Although Carrall Street is one of the shortest streets in Vancouver, for much of the city's history it was a commercial hub and connection between several other major points in the city. By the early 2000s, it was a tough area, home to some of Vancouver's trendiest bars and restaurants but also "a stone's throw from…junkies and crackheads huddled around doorways like extras from *Night of the Living Dead*," as a reporter in the *Vancouver Sun* noted.[23] When Wall made his photograph, a project was under way to revitalize the area and transform Carrall Street into a "Greenway," as the banners in his photograph proclaim. Other pictures painted on the plywood covering the construction site depict a pond surrounded by mountains and trees, perhaps showing how the area once looked when it was inhabited by First Nations people before the intrusion of others. Above the mural, a sign for "Darwin Construction," the company no doubt responsible for the renovation, suggests that Carrall Street, like everyplace else, is subject to the laws of evolution.

In an essay published in his 2005 catalogue raisonné, Wall reflected on the evolution of his ideas about photography. For a long time, he noted, he thought it necessary "to contest the classical aesthetic of photography as too absolutely rooted in the idea of fact," too closely linked to a documentary tradition. At this earlier stage,

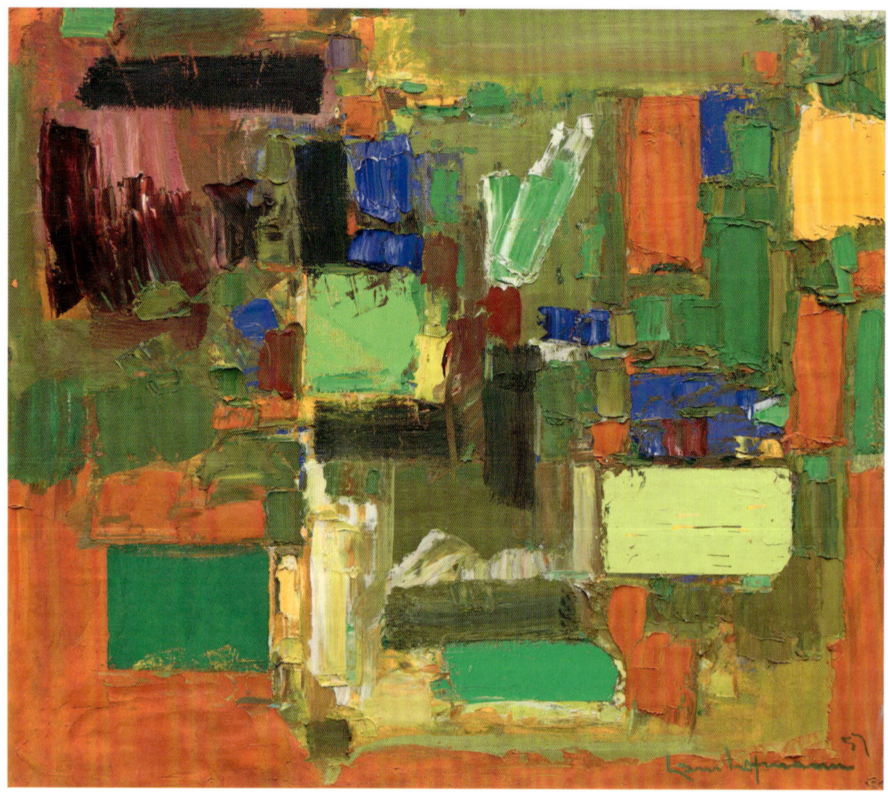

fig. 10: Hans Hofmann, *Autumn Gold*, 1957, oil on canvas, National Gallery of Art, Washington, Robert and Jane Meyerhoff Collection

he believed that the way to do so was to make photographs "that put the factual in suspension, while still creating an involvement with factuality for the viewer." Dancing on the line between fact and fiction, this approach emphasized photography's relationship with "other picture-making arts, mainly painting and the cinema, in which the factual claim has always been played with in a subtle, learned and sophisticated way." Initially conceiving of this method as an imitation of the other arts, he came to realize that this "mimesis was of course taking place on the foundation provided by photography itself." Merging art and document, trace and picture, he eventually saw that "it was possible to turn photography toward itself, as an equal player in the mimetic game. Now I see the possibility of developing a mimesis of photography, as photography."[24] Skillfully navigating this line between documentary representation and art, Wall and the other photographers in the Meyerhoff-Becker Collection, through their new conceptualization of the medium, their dynamic and innovative exploration of color and scale, and their choice of powerful and provocative subjects, have helped to repurpose, redefine, and reimagine photography for the twenty-first century.


1. Rheda Becker to Sarah Greenough, March 1, 2016.

2. Jeff Wall, http://www.artic.edu/aic/exhibitions/jeff_wall/themes.html.

3. See Harry Cooper, "I Think I See . . . ," in *The Robert and Jane Meyerhoff Collection: Selected Works* (National Gallery of Art, Washington, 2009), 3–5.

4. David Shapiro, "Jeff Wall: Interview by David Shapiro," *Museo Magazine*, 1999, http://www.museomagazine.com/jeff-wall.

5. Douglas Crimp, *Pictures* (Artists Space, 1977), 1. Crimp expanded this essay in a later one, also titled "Pictures," *October* 8 (Spring 1978): 75–88.

6. For further discussion, see Douglas Eklund, *The Pictures Generation, 1974–1984* (Metropolitan Museum of Art, New York, 2009).

7. The study of the history of photography as a discipline emerged in the 1930s with the first histories published just before World War II. Although some museums exhibited photographs starting in the first decades of the twentieth century, most did not embrace the medium until the 1970s.

8. Francis Outred, "In Conversation with Thomas Struth," *Christie's Daily*, June 24, 2015, http://www.christies.com/features/reflections-on-the-self-portrait-thomas-struth-6290-1.aspx.

9. Joseph Leo Koerner, *The Moment of Self-Portraiture in German Renaissance Art* (Chicago, 1993), 171–176.

10. Jeff Wall, "Marks of Indifference: Aspects of Photography in, or as Conceptual Art," reprinted in *The Last Picture Show: Artists Using Photography, 1960–1982*, ed. Douglas Fogle (Walker Art Gallery, Minneapolis, 2003), 39–44.

11. For further discussion, see Michael Fried, *Why Photography Matters as Art as Never Before* (New Haven, 2008).

12. Jean-François Chevrier, "The Adventures of the Picture Form in the History of Photography," in *The Last Picture Show: Artists Using Photography, 1960–1982*, 116.

13. Jean-François Chevrier, "The Tableau and the Document of Experience," in *Click Doubleclick: The Documentary Factor,* ed. Thomas Weski (Haus der Kunst, Cologne, 2006). See also Olivier Lugon, "Before the Tableau Form," *Études Photographiques* 25 (May 2010): 2.

14. Carolyn Yerkes, "Candida Höfer: Interview by Carolyn Yerkes," *Museo Magazine*, 2010, http://www.museomagazine.com/candida-hofer.

15. For further discussion, see Mary-Kay Lombino, "Inner Order," in *Candida Höfer: Architecture of Absence,* ed. Constance W. Glenn (New York, 2004), 24–25.

16. Elizabeth Armstrong, "On the Border of the Real," in *More Real: Art in the Age of Truthiness,* ed. Elizabeth Armstrong (Minneapolis Institute of Arts), 48–49.

17. Roxana Marcoci, "Paper Moon," in *Thomas Demand,* ed. Roxana Marcoci (Museum of Modern Art, New York, 2005), 10.

18. Jeff Wall, 1985, as quoted in "Jeff Wall: In His Own Words," http://www.moma.org/interactives/exhibitions/2007/jeffwall/.

19. Sean O'Hagan, "Jeff Wall: I'm Haunted by the Idea That My Photography Was All a Big Mistake," *The Guardian*, November 3, 2015, http://www.theguardian.com/artanddesign/2015/nov/03/jeff-wall-photography-marian-goodman-gallery-show.

20. Jeff Wall, "Frames of Reference," 2003, reprinted in *Jeff Wall: Catalogue Raisonné*, ed. Theodora Vischer and Heidi Nael (Göttingen, 2005), 444–445.

21. Wall in conversation with Rheda Becker and Robert Meyerhoff. I am grateful to Rheda Becker for sharing this information with me.

22. Hofmann as quoted by Kerry Rose, "Hans Hofmann," in *Modernism from the National Gallery of Art: The Robert and Jane Meyerhoff Collection*, ed. Harry Cooper (National Gallery of Art, Washington, 2014), 80.

23. John Mackie, "Carrall Street: Home to Some of Vancouver's Coolest Bars, a Stone's Throw Away from Crackheads," *Vancouver Sun*, October 18, 2008.

24. Jeff Wall, "Three Thoughts on Photography 1999," in *Jeff Wall: Catalogue Raisonné*, 441.

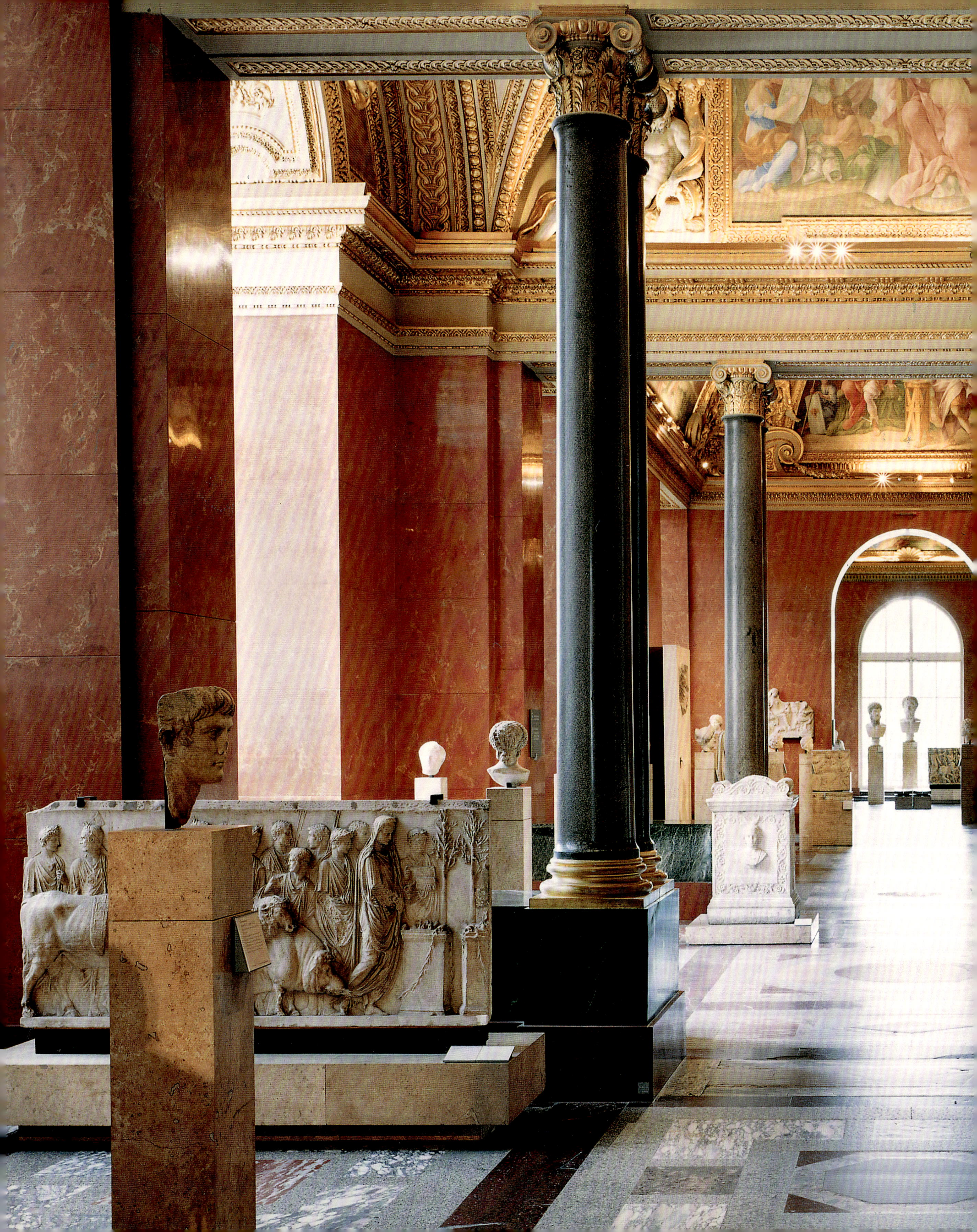

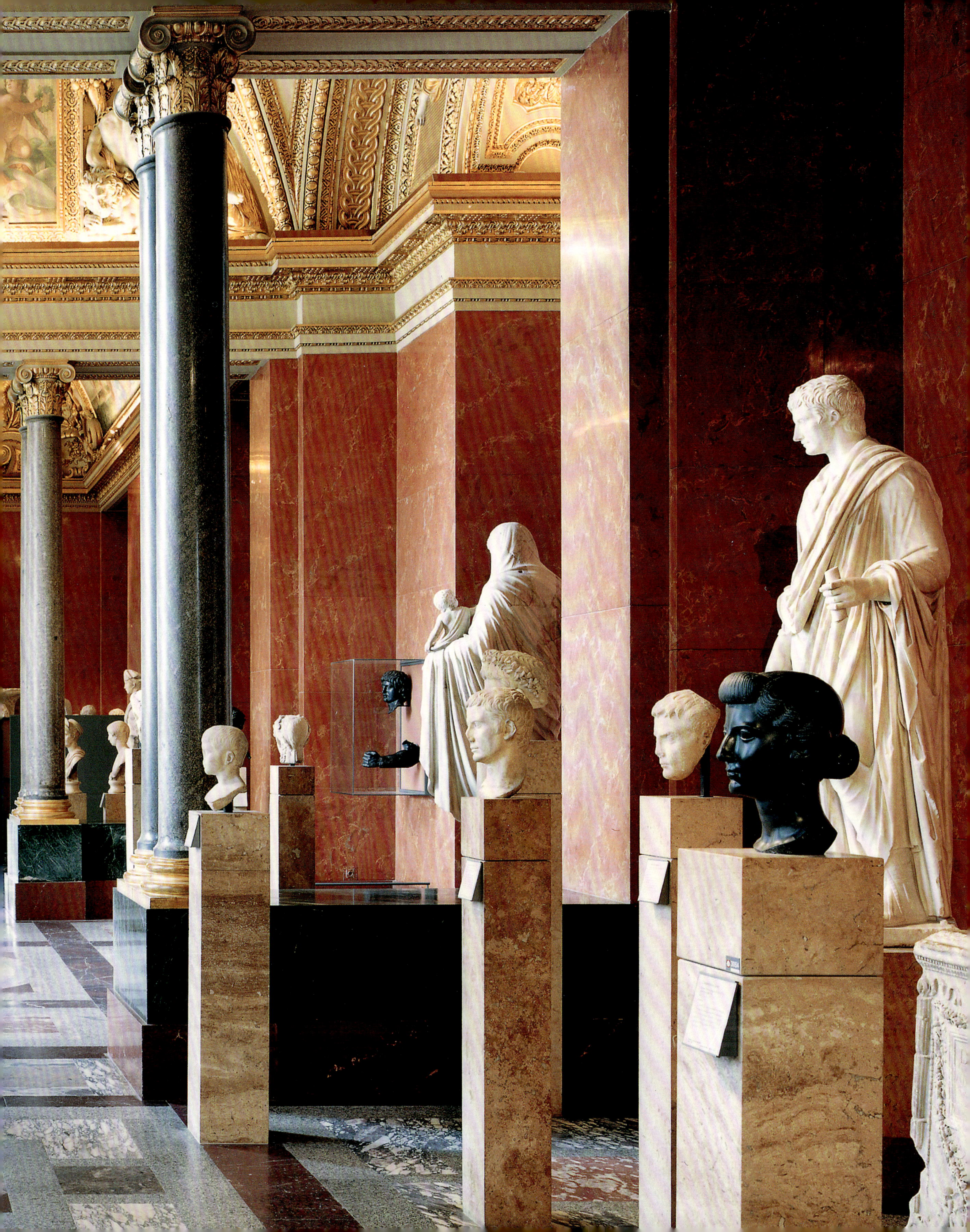

# Bernd and Hilla Becher

German, 1931–2007; 1934–2015

---

1

*Water Towers*, 1972–2009
nine gelatin silver prints
each: 56.2 × 46.36 cm (22⅛ × 18¼ in.)
Promised Gift from the
Collection of Robert E.
Meyerhoff and Rheda Becker

---

FEW ARTISTS HAVE EXERTED as strong an influence on contemporary photography as Bernd and Hilla Becher, and fewer still have captured the spirit of the late industrial era as succinctly and profoundly. When they first began to work together in the late 1950s, it was "good etiquette," they noted, "to ignore history and pay no attention to immediate reality." Rebelling against this conventional belief and the highly personal and experimental style of subjective photography, they sought instead to return to the "true sources of photography"—its seemingly objective, documentary nature.[1] They recorded the mundane, overlooked industrial landscape of Europe and the United States, making cool, unsentimental pictures of factories, blast furnaces, winding towers, and other rapidly disappearing structures. Yet it was not just their subject matter or nonconformist stance that was so revolutionary; it was also the conceptual rigor of their carefully elucidated methodology. They limited themselves to prescribed subjects, approaches, compositions, and formats, and usually organized their photographs by type, which they installed as grids of six, nine, or fifteen pictures. Their influential typologies, situated between traditional notions of documentary photography and art, allowed reflection on an ideal form while inviting comparisons between structures that were influenced by different cultural, geographic, and historical factors.

Bernd Becher was born in Siegen, one of Germany's oldest industrialized regions, to a family who had worked in steel mills and mines, but when he came to maturity, many of those industries were closing and their structures slated for demolition. As Germany turned its back on the industrial strength that had helped precipitate two world wars, no government agency documented this architecture that had so powerfully defined the life and character of the country. In 1957, when Becher met Hilla Wobeser, a commercially trained photographer enrolled in the Kunstakademie Düsseldorf, the two came to believe that "just as the medieval thought is manifest in a Gothic cathedral, our age reveals itself in the technological buildings and devices." Determining "to record the plants threatened with demolition before they disappeared once and for all," they drew inspiration from earlier German photographers such as Karl Blossfeldt, August Sander, and Albert Renger-Patzsch, along with the Frenchman Eugène Atget and the American Walker Evans, all of whom constructed massive archival examinations of nature, culture, and humankind.[2] The Bechers worked first in the Siegerland and the Ruhr valley, then soon expanded the scope of their project beyond Germany, making trips to industrialized areas in the Netherlands, Belgium, France, Luxembourg, and later Great Britain and the United States. In order to reinforce the objectivity of their work, they also quickly established a strict methodology that they applied to all their pictures. At each site, they photographed the overall landscape of the plant to show how the structures related to one another, then made individual photographs of the buildings. Rigorously avoiding depictions of people, who would distract attention from the edifices themselves, the Bechers centered the buildings frontally within their compositions, usually photographing them from a slightly elevated point of view so they stood out but were not isolated from their surroundings. Working in the spring and fall, when the trees and bushes had the fewest leaves, they photographed only early in the morning on overcast days when the soft, diffuse light did not cast harsh shadows or distort the forms. To facilitate comparisons between similar structures, they endeavored to place the horizon at the same point in their compositions, usually a quarter or a third of the way up from the bottom. And, to obtain maximum detail and a high degree of precision, they used a large-format, 13 × 18 cm camera and fine-grained, black-and-white film.

In 1967, they began to select the most telling examples of particular edifices—cooling towers, gasometers, coal bunkers, lime kilns, or grain silos, for example—and arranged them into grids for exhibition. In 1969, they began to refer to their work as

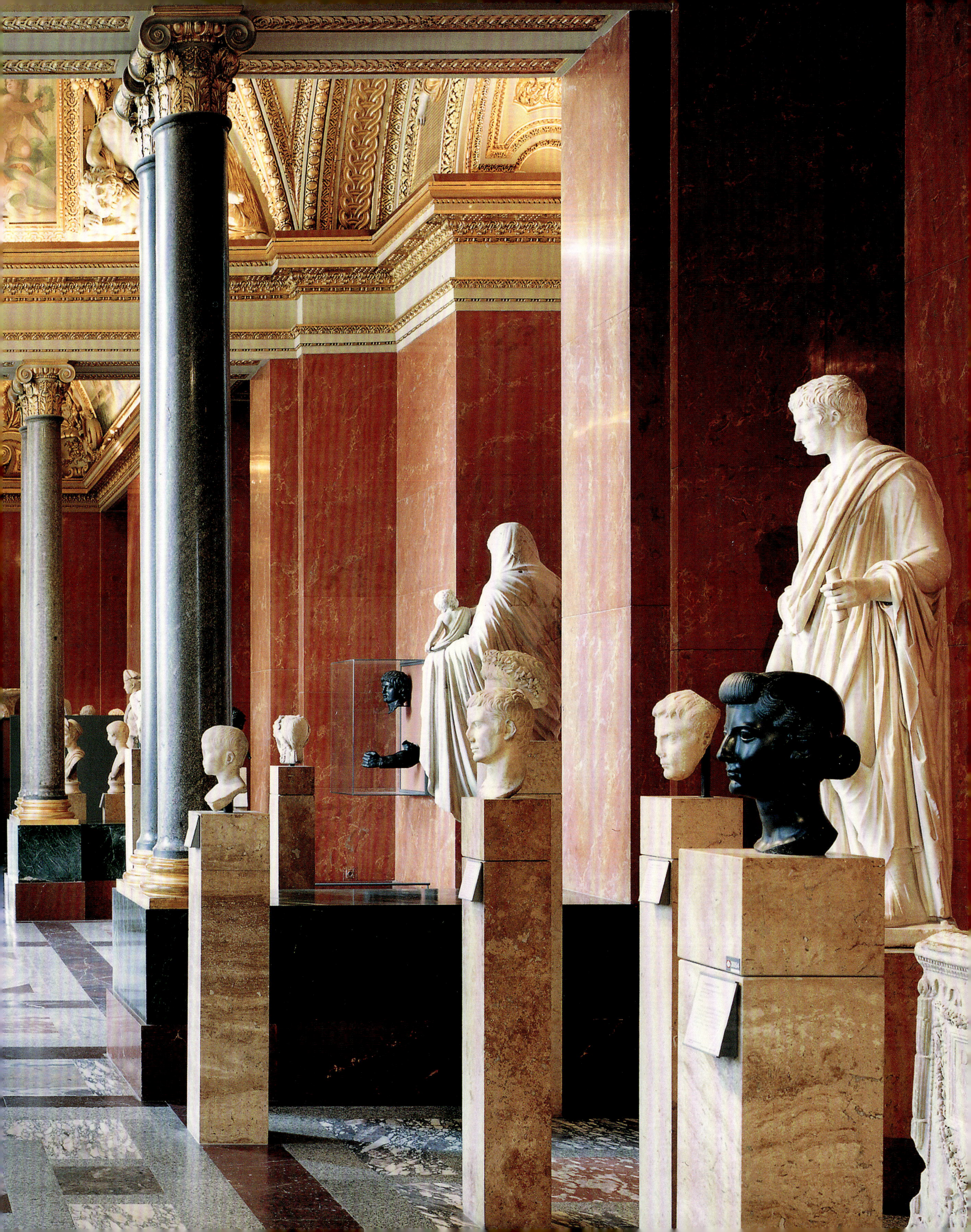

# Bernd and Hilla Becher

German, 1931 – 2007; 1934 – 2015

---

1

*Water Towers,* 1972 – 2009
nine gelatin silver prints
each: 56.2 × 46.36 cm (22⅛ × 18¼ in.)
Promised Gift from the
Collection of Robert E.
Meyerhoff and Rheda Becker

---

FEW ARTISTS HAVE EXERTED as strong an influence on contemporary photography as Bernd and Hilla Becher, and fewer still have captured the spirit of the late industrial era as succinctly and profoundly. When they first began to work together in the late 1950s, it was "good etiquette," they noted, "to ignore history and pay no attention to immediate reality." Rebelling against this conventional belief and the highly personal and experimental style of subjective photography, they sought instead to return to the "true sources of photography" — its seemingly objective, documentary nature.[1] They recorded the mundane, overlooked industrial landscape of Europe and the United States, making cool, unsentimental pictures of factories, blast furnaces, winding towers, and other rapidly disappearing structures. Yet it was not just their subject matter or nonconformist stance that was so revolutionary; it was also the conceptual rigor of their carefully elucidated methodology. They limited themselves to prescribed subjects, approaches, compositions, and formats, and usually organized their photographs by type, which they installed as grids of six, nine, or fifteen pictures. Their influential typologies, situated between traditional notions of documentary photography and art, allowed reflection on an ideal form while inviting comparisons between structures that were influenced by different cultural, geographic, and historical factors.

Bernd Becher was born in Siegen, one of Germany's oldest industrialized regions, to a family who had worked in steel mills and mines, but when he came to maturity, many of those industries were closing and their structures slated for demolition. As Germany turned its back on the industrial strength that had helped precipitate two world wars, no government agency documented this architecture that had so powerfully defined the life and character of the country. In 1957, when Becher met Hilla Wobeser, a commercially trained photographer enrolled in the Kunstakademie Düsseldorf, the two came to believe that "just as the medieval thought is manifest in a Gothic cathedral, our age reveals itself in the technological buildings and devices." Determining "to record the plants threatened with demolition before they disappeared once and for all," they drew inspiration from earlier German photographers such as Karl Blossfeldt, August Sander, and Albert Renger-Patzsch, along with the Frenchman Eugène Atget and the American Walker Evans, all of whom constructed massive archival examinations of nature, culture, and humankind.[2] The Bechers worked first in the Siegerland and the Ruhr valley, then soon expanded the scope of their project beyond Germany, making trips to industrialized areas in the Netherlands, Belgium, France, Luxembourg, and later Great Britain and the United States. In order to reinforce the objectivity of their work, they also quickly established a strict methodology that they applied to all their pictures. At each site, they photographed the overall landscape of the plant to show how the structures related to one another, then made individual photographs of the buildings. Rigorously avoiding depictions of people, who would distract attention from the edifices themselves, the Bechers centered the buildings frontally within their compositions, usually photographing them from a slightly elevated point of view so they stood out but were not isolated from their surroundings. Working in the spring and fall, when the trees and bushes had the fewest leaves, they photographed only early in the morning on overcast days when the soft, diffuse light did not cast harsh shadows or distort the forms. To facilitate comparisons between similar structures, they endeavored to place the horizon at the same point in their compositions, usually a quarter or a third of the way up from the bottom. And, to obtain maximum detail and a high degree of precision, they used a large-format, 13 × 18 cm camera and fine-grained, black-and-white film.

In 1967, they began to select the most telling examples of particular edifices — cooling towers, gasometers, coal bunkers, lime kilns, or grain silos, for example — and arranged them into grids for exhibition. In 1969, they began to refer to their work as

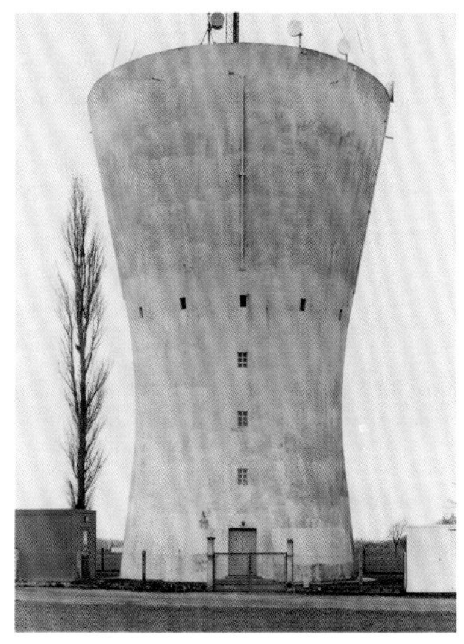
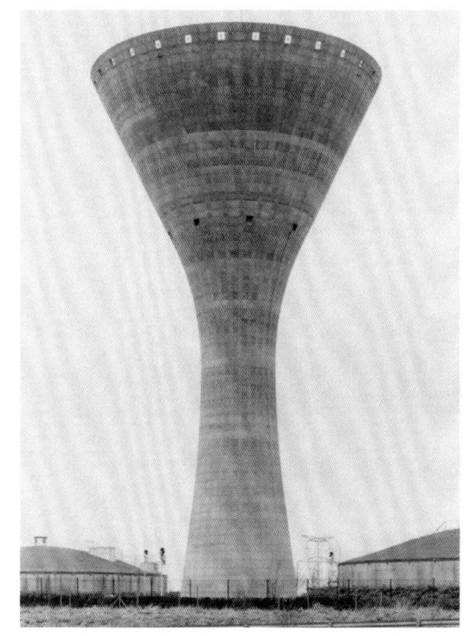
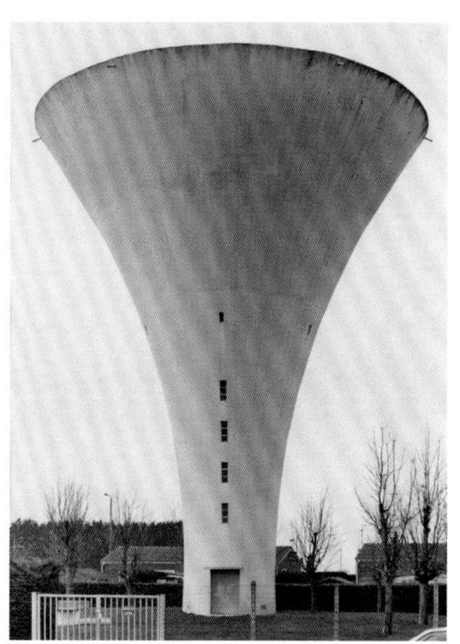
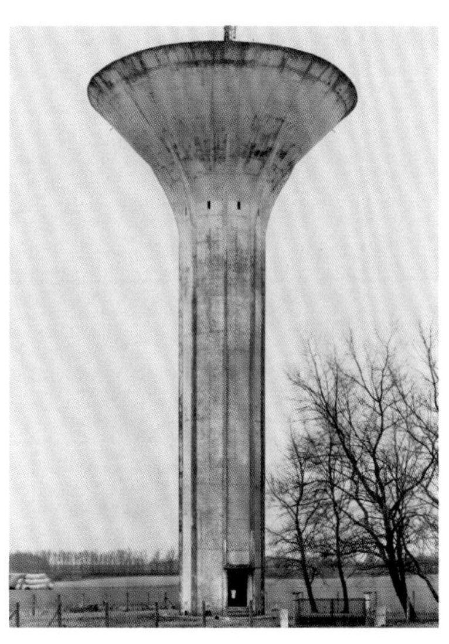
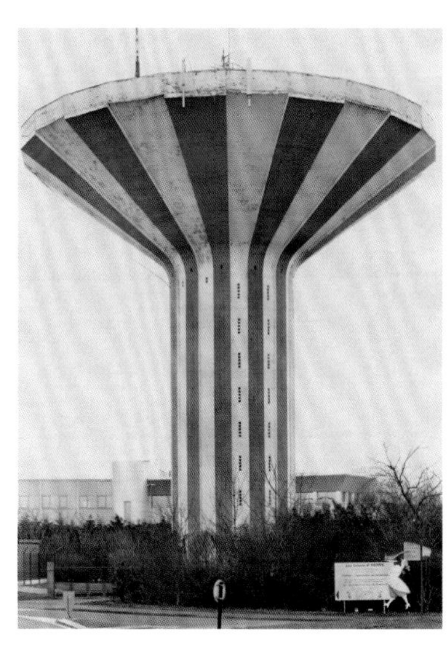
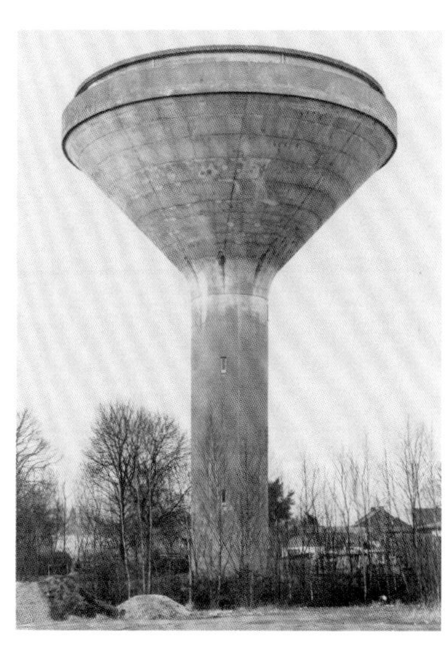
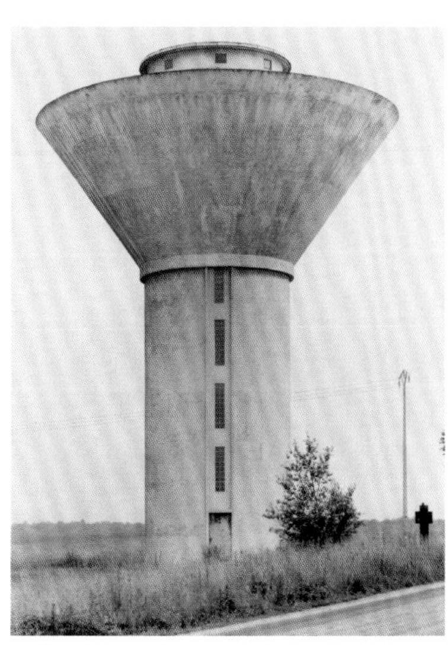
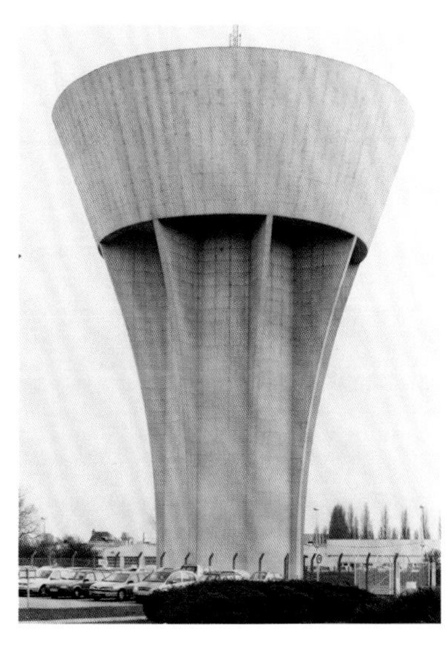
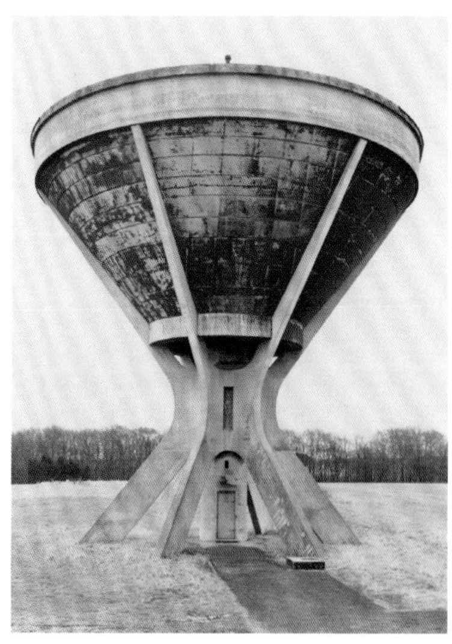

1. Bernd and Hilla Becher in conversation with Michel Guerrin in *Le Monde*, May 23, 2001, as quoted by Armin Zweite, *Typologies: Bernd and Hilla Becher* (Cambridge, MA, 2004), 7.

2. Susanne Lange, *Bernd and Hilla Becher: Life and Work* (Cambridge, MA, 2007), 10.

3. Lange, *Bernd and Hilla Becher,* 9, 64–66.

4. Carl Andre, "A Note on Bernhard and Hilla Becher," *Artforum*, December 1972, 59.

5. Bernd and Hilla Becher, *Water Towers* (Cambridge, MA, 1988).

6. Bernd and Hilla Becher, as quoted by Lange, *Bernd and Hilla Becher,* 62.

7. Reyner Banham, "The Becher Vision," in *Water Towers*, 1988, 8.


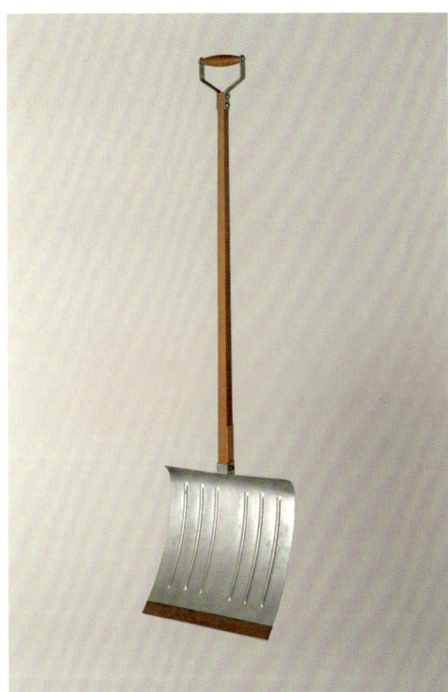

fig. 1: Marcel Duchamp, *In Advance of the Broken Arm*, August 1964 (fourth version, after lost original of November 1915), readymade, wood and galvanized metal snow shovel, The Museum of Modern Art, New York, Gift of The Jerry and Emily Spiegel Family

"Anonymous Sculpture," alluding to Marcel Duchamp's readymades (fig. 1) and signaling their artistic stance; by the early 1970s, they began to call these groupings "typologies."[3] Although their structuralist approach and typological sets distanced them from more traditional photography of the time, their pictures were exhibited in the late 1960s and early 1970s alongside work by such conceptual and minimal artists as Carl Andre, Douglas Huebler, Sol LeWitt, and Mel Bochner. In 1972, Andre, who became a close friend of the couple, was the first to highlight the Bechers' juxtapositions of formally related buildings in an article in *Artforum*, thus launching the discussion of both their work and contemporary photography more generally in the larger international artistic community.[4] Bernd's appointment as a professor at the Kunstakademie Düsseldorf in 1976 further solidified their growing influence. Although the Kunstakademie's policy prohibited Hilla's simultaneous appointment, she was an equal partner with Bernd and also inspired many students. Together they trained a generation of photographers, including Andreas Gursky (pls. 13, 14), Candida Höfer (pls. 10–12), Thomas Ruff (pls. 15, 16), and Thomas Struth (pls. 2–9), who embraced their objective use of photography and their comparative technique. Others beyond Germany were also influenced by their work, including those associated with the "New Topographics" movement, such as Robert Adams, Lewis Baltz, and Stephen Shore. Like the Bechers, they looked at the neglected, banal built environment in the United States and employed the same rigorous uninflected approach and comparative technique.

First published as a book in 1988, the Bechers' photographs of water towers have elicited considerable attention, in large part because their typologies revealed the exceptional structural and material diversity of these simple objects.[5] Although elevated water-storage systems have been used since ancient times, water towers proliferated in the Industrial Revolution as steam pumping became more prevalent and trains needed water for their engines. As the Bechers themselves noted, "there is hardly a construction style that has not functioned at some point as the model for the embellishments on water towers." Some of these "historical costumes," as they referred to them, include "Arab mosques, Greek temples, the Colosseum, Gothic and Romanesque churches, Baroque castles, and, repeatedly, city gates and fortified towers of all sorts." By contrast, they note that ones such as those depicted in *Water Towers*, which "feature no ornamentation," actually "kindle associations with current or future models: balloons, flying saucers, space capsules."[6] In their seemingly limitless number and variety, water towers are evidence of the importance of water to industry and life, but they also allude to both the nature of industrial production itself—unending, relentless, inhuman—and the profound implication it has on the environment. Monolithic, intractable, elevated high above the surrounding landscape like altars to the gods, water towers are, as the architectural critic Reyner Banham insisted, "memorials to one of the most drastically rapid rearrangements of the Earth's crust and its resources since the beginning of geological time."[7] GREENOUGH

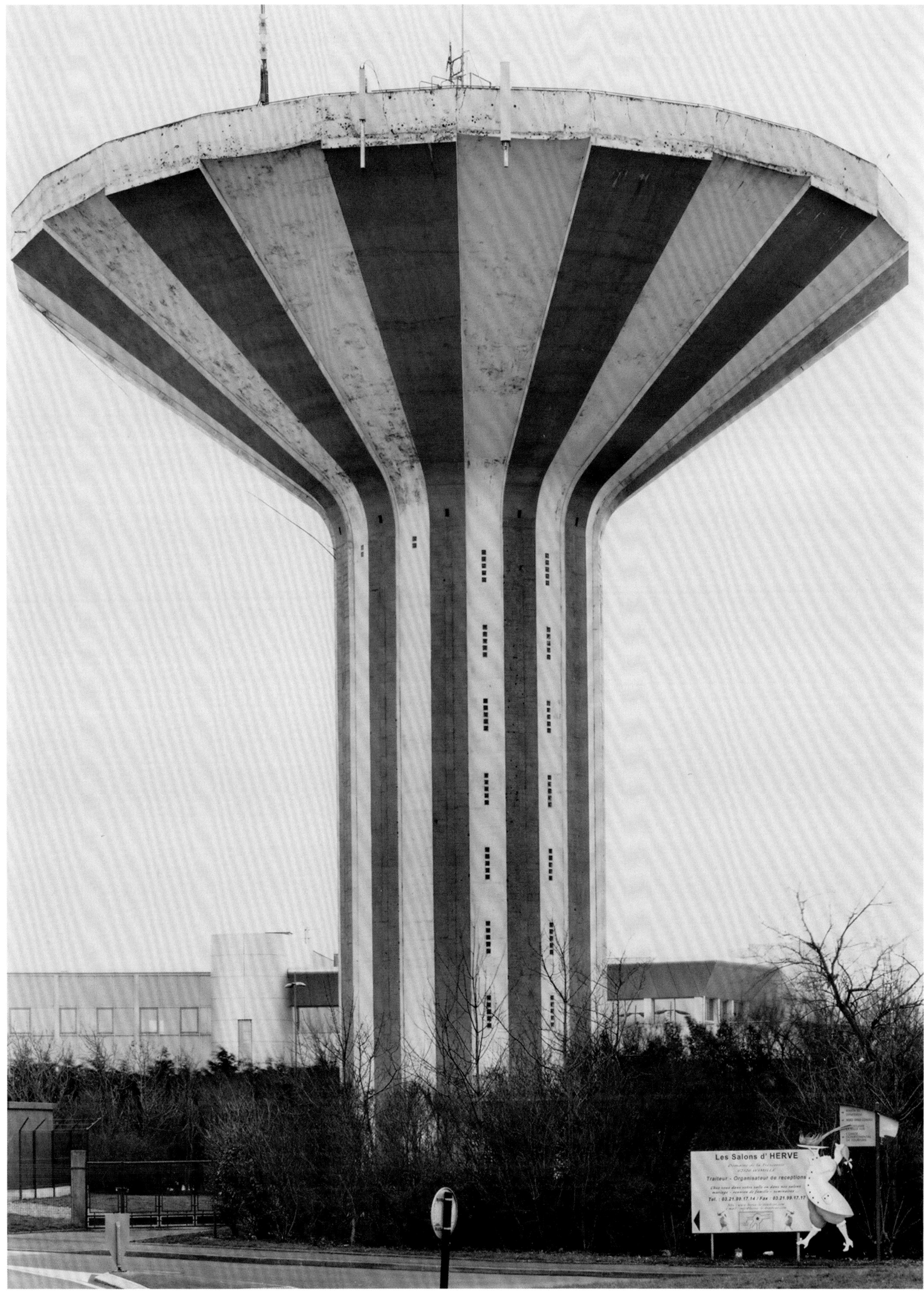
Les Salons d' HERVE
Traiteur - Organisateur de receptions

# Thomas Struth

German, born 1954

---

2

*Restorers at San Lorenzo
Maggiore, Naples 1988*, 1988
chromogenic print
118.75 × 159.39 cm (46¾ × 62¾ in.)
Collection of Rheda Becker

---

3

*Pergamon Museum 6,
Berlin 1996*, 1996
chromogenic print
176.21 × 247.02 cm (69⅜ × 97¼ in.)
Promised Gift from the
Collection of Robert E.
Meyerhoff and Rheda Becker

---

4

*Museo del Prado 7, Madrid
2005*, 2005
chromogenic print
182.25 × 223.52 cm (71¾ × 88 in.)
Promised Gift from the
Collection of Robert E.
Meyerhoff and Rheda Becker

---

5

*Alte Pinakothek, Self-Portrait,
Munich 2000*, 2000
chromogenic print
161.93 × 189.87 cm (63¾ × 74¾ in.)
Promised Gift from the
Collection of Robert E.
Meyerhoff and Rheda Becker,
in Honor of the 25th Anniversary
of Photography at the National
Gallery of Art

---

6

*National Gallery 2, London
2001*, 2001
chromogenic print
153.04 × 175.26 cm (60¼ × 69 in.)
Promised Gift from the
Collection of Robert E.
Meyerhoff and Rheda Becker

---

7

*Notre Dame, Paris 2000*, 2000
chromogenic print
186.06 × 229.55 cm (73¼ × 90⅜ in.)
Promised Gift from the
Collection of Robert E.
Meyerhoff and Rheda Becker

---

8

*Tokamak Asdex Upgrade
Interior 2, Max Planck IPP,
Garching 2009*, 2009
chromogenic print
146.05 × 180.34 cm (57½ × 71 in.)
Promised Gift from the
Collection of Robert E.
Meyerhoff and Rheda Becker

---

9

*Queen Elizabeth II and The Duke of
Edinburgh, Windsor Castle 2011*, 2011
chromogenic print
175.58 × 218.44 cm (69⅛ × 86 in.)
Promised Gift from the
Collection of Robert E.
Meyerhoff and Rheda Becker

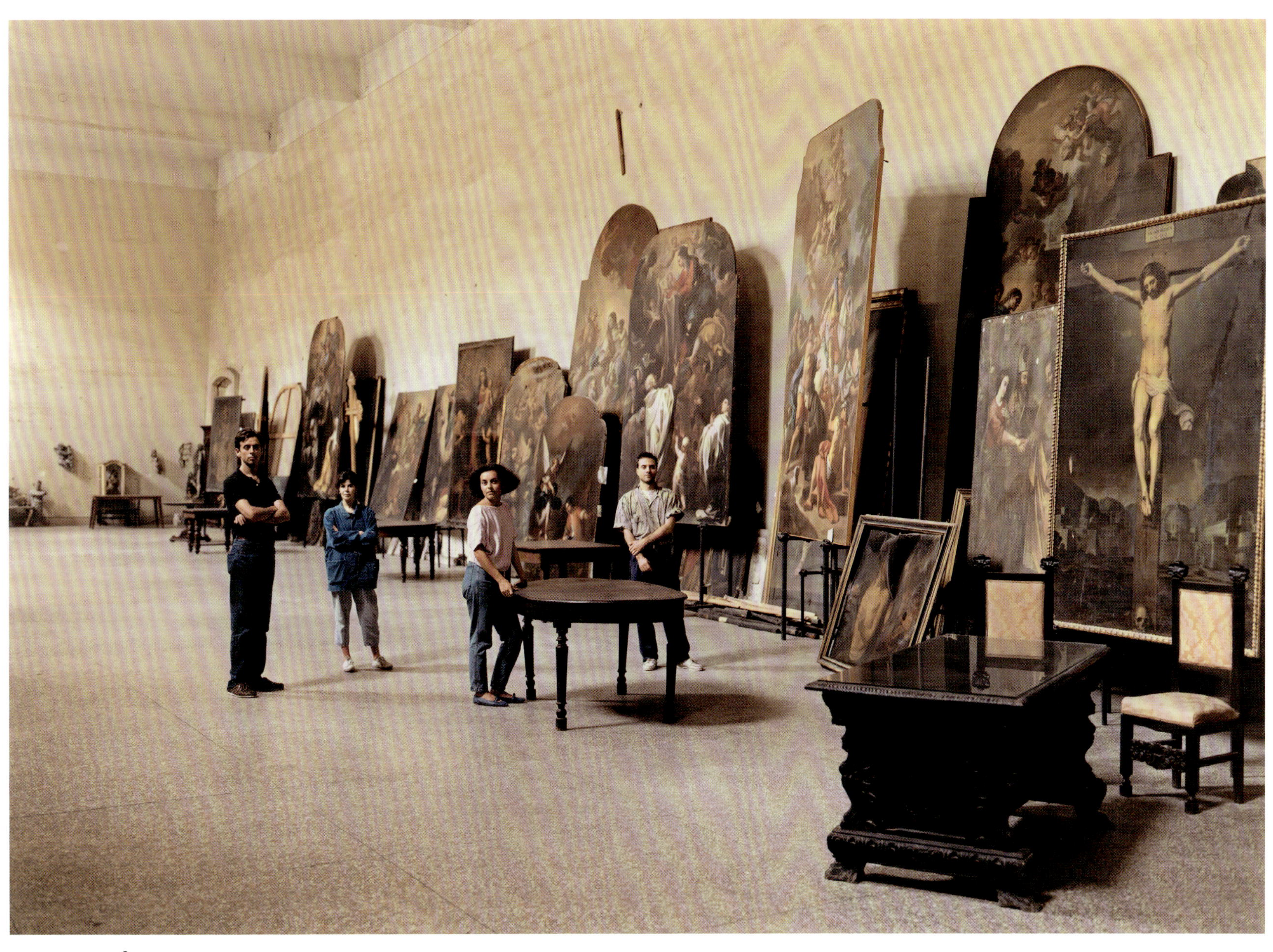

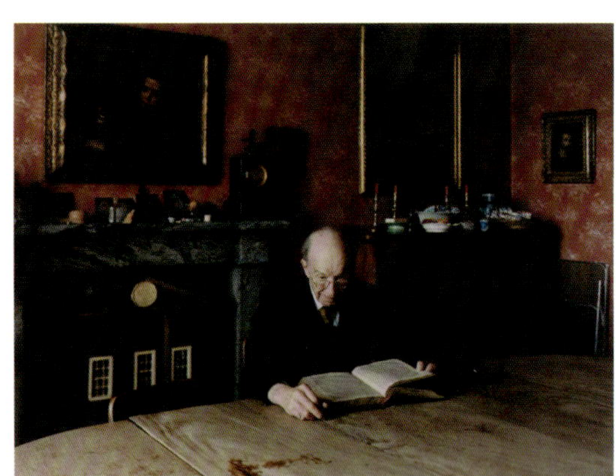

fig. 1: Thomas Struth, *Giles Robertson, Edinburgh 1987*, 1987, chromogenic print, Courtesy Atelier Thomas Struth

IN 1988, after more than a decade photographing around the world, Thomas Struth spent three months in Rome and Naples. In his mid-thirties, Struth, who first studied painting with Gerhard Richter at the Kunstakademie Düsseldorf and then became one of Bernd and Hilla Becher's earliest and most important students, had begun to establish an international reputation. Like so many others of his generation, he was born into "the culture of guilt" and had grappled with the fundamental question of postwar Germany: "How do you live," as he said, "with history?" His initial answer was to seek to understand how "history is embedded in the architecture of a city" and "how a community represent[s] itself in its architecture, truthfully or otherwise."[1] Working in Düsseldorf, New York, Paris, Shanghai, Tokyo, and elsewhere in the late 1970s and 1980s, he had made austere, direct, dispassionate black-and-white photographs of empty, almost stagelike urban environments, striving to capture the structures that summarize the character of a culture.

Yet in the late 1980s his work began to change. A few years earlier he had started to explore portraiture, making a handful of pictures, some in color, of family and friends he had stayed with during his travels. Although he initially conceived of these works as a remembrance, the results intrigued him with their ability to show, in his words, "personality, character, and culture through the environment," as well as the family dynamic.[2] His work changed even more in Naples in 1988. He found the city immensely "thought-provoking."[3] Its chaotic jumble of old and new, sacred and secular architecture fascinated him, prompting him to abandon the central perspective, inherited from the Bechers' work, which had characterized his earlier photographs. Giulia Zorzetti, a painting conservator with whom he stayed, also inspired him. Struth later said that she rekindled his interest "with the medium I had given up a decade earlier," but she did far more than that. When she took him to see some of the paintings she and her colleagues were restoring in a church, he was struck, as he noted, by the "intimate proximity" they had with the art and, even more, by the close connection painting had with religion in the past.[4] He photographed Zorzetti and her colleagues in color in the cavernous former refectory where they worked (pl. 2). Standing before a line of damaged religious paintings stacked up against a wall, they gaze directly at the camera, each posed slightly differently as if they were artists' models, their arms and clothes quietly echoing the gestures and drapery of the painted figures beside them. The conservators and the paintings themselves appear as part of the same tableau: bathed with a soft, glowing light, they seem to share a silent communication across the centuries, the people and the art energizing and reaffirming one another. Struth also printed this image almost twice as big as his previous pictures, introducing a new scale to his work that allowed his viewers to have the same sense of intimate proximity with the art and the people in his photographs that the conservators had with the paintings.

This photograph, plus one he made in 1987 of the art historian Giles Robertson seated in front of several paintings while looking down at a book (fig. 1), propelled him to embark on a series of pictures titled *Museum Photographs*. Made in some of the world's most celebrated museums, including the Louvre, the National Gallery, London, and the Prado, Struth's large color photographs of crowds of people explore the different functions that art fulfills in our modern, secularized world and the ways in which people experience paintings today. With his understanding of art and architecture as emblematic of cultural ideals and beliefs, and his growing interest in the social dynamics of group portraits, he wanted, as he asserted, to "bring together the time of the picture and the time of the viewer."[5] Acknowledging the museum as a pilgrimage site, Struth, who was raised Catholic, infused the *Museum Photographs* with a sense of worship. Like a patient penitent, he most often set up his camera in front of or to the side

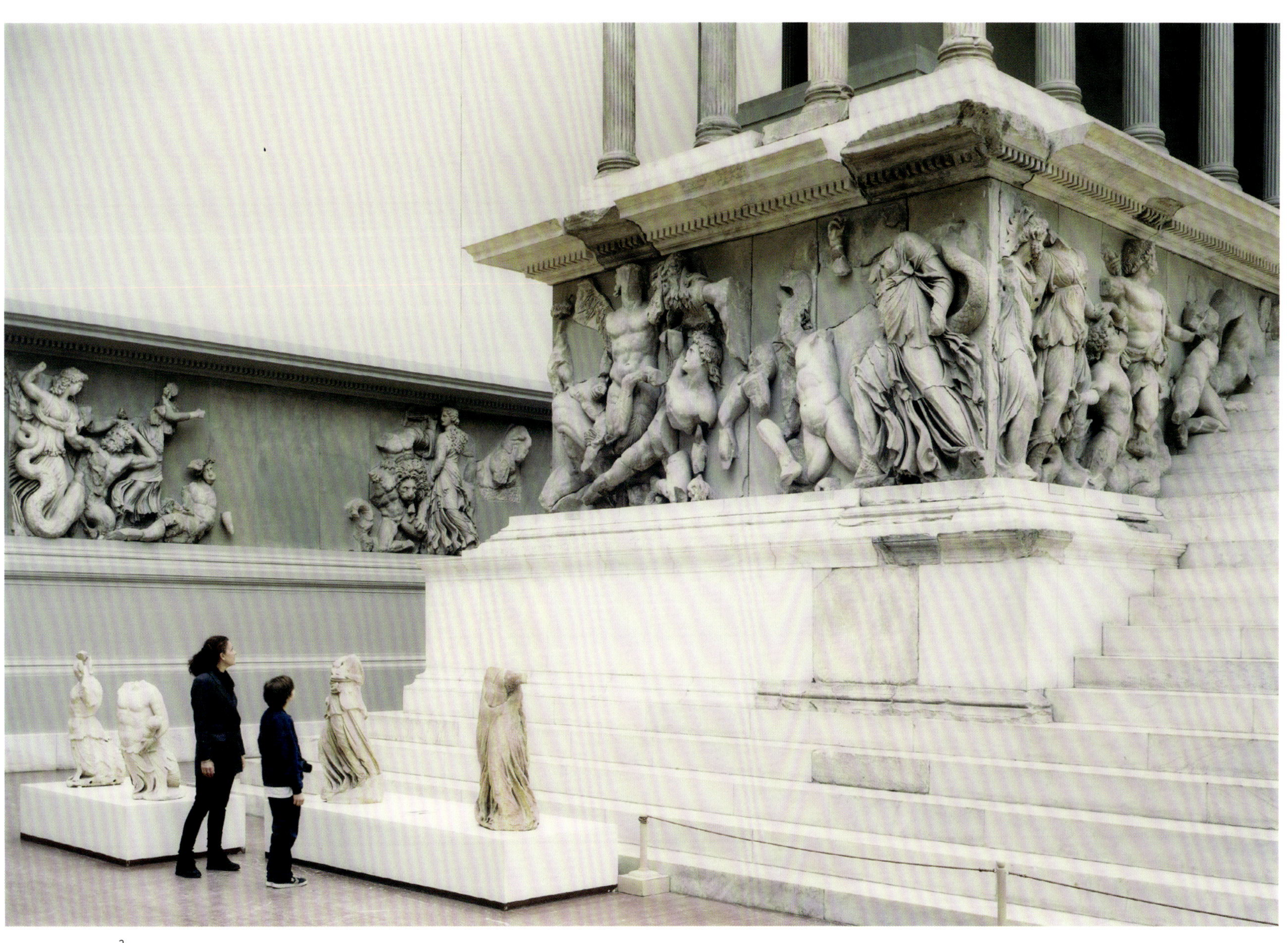

of the work of art he wanted to photograph and waited until the visitors formed themselves into a compelling composition. Occasionally though, as in *Pergamon Museum 6, Berlin 1996* (1996, pl. 3), serendipity did not favor him and he was forced to pose people. Some visitors pay devout homage to the art, venerating the paintings as their ancestors (or perhaps even they themselves) might have revered the religious beliefs the paintings often encapsulate. Others are more engrossed in their guides or in one another's company, suggesting that the social ritual of seeing renowned art in venerated museums is more important than the objects themselves. Often the age, gender, gestures, and stances of the visitors complement the subjects depicted. In *Pergamon Museum 6,* for example, a woman and child standing at the foot of the Great Altar of Pergamon form a quiet chorus reflecting on the battle between the giants and the Olympian gods above them, their expressions and poses as fixed and permanent as the marble ones. In *Museo del Prado 7, Madrid 2005* (2005, pl. 4) a group of schoolgirls, with one slightly in front of the others, stands before Diego Velázquez's *Las Meninas,* mimicking the entourage surrounding the young Infanta in the painting. Off to the right a boy, pad and pen in hand, surveys the scene in much the same way that Velázquez does in the painting, standing behind his easel with paintbrush in hand. We as viewers are also implicated in this picture for we, like Struth, stand in the back, off to the side and slightly above the crowd, observing the scene—much like the queen's chamberlain in the background of Velázquez's painting, who seems, like us, to have happened upon this chance encounter. As we become enmeshed in this hall of mirrors—where people observe paintings while the figures in the paintings appear to observe them and we observe them all— these photographs make us aware of the paramount importance of the very *act* of looking and the knowledge, insight, and responsibility that it gives to us. Struth is not simply creating pictures within pictures; he is also layering the past onto the present, showing how sustained, careful looking can endow time with a different quality, distilling it into discrete moments while simultaneously seeming to stretch it.[6]

Two pictures stand apart from the other *Museum Photographs*: *Alte Pinakothek, Self-Portrait, Munich 2000* (2000, pl. 5) and *National Gallery 2, London 2001* (2001, pl. 6). Devoid of the large crowds that usually cluster before such masterpieces, both are more intimate views, privileged encounters that establish a dialogue between painting and photography to speak about both Struth's relationship with history and our own. As he had done in his portrait of Giles Robertson, whom he depicted with paintings and a book to suggest his relationship to history and culture, so too in his own self-portrait did Struth place himself in front of Albrecht Dürer's *Self-Portrait* painted exactly five hundred years earlier. Coming to terms with his own German heritage, he hoped to construct a "conversation," as he described it, "not only with myself, but with the world of art and with an artist who, like me, is German [and comes] from the same cultural foundation."[7] While Struth understands self-portraiture as an act of "reaffirmation"— a process "of asking yourself about your own identity"—a double self-portrait, as he deftly acknowledges in this picture, is about validating not only oneself but also another.[8] He does so in *Alte Pinakothek, Self-Portrait* by printing his picture so that the reproduction of Dürer's *Self-Portrait* in his photograph is almost the size of the original painting. He also positioned himself off to the side and slightly out of focus, as if he had just walked into the scene to address the Dürer painting. Thus he allows Dürer, who depicted himself with striking directness and in a pose previously used only for depictions of Christ, to stare directly into the camera and speak to us across the centuries.

*National Gallery 2,* on the other hand, is the only picture from Struth's *Museum Photographs* that does not draw out subtle relationships between the paintings and their viewers but focuses exclusively on light and installation. It shows Johannes

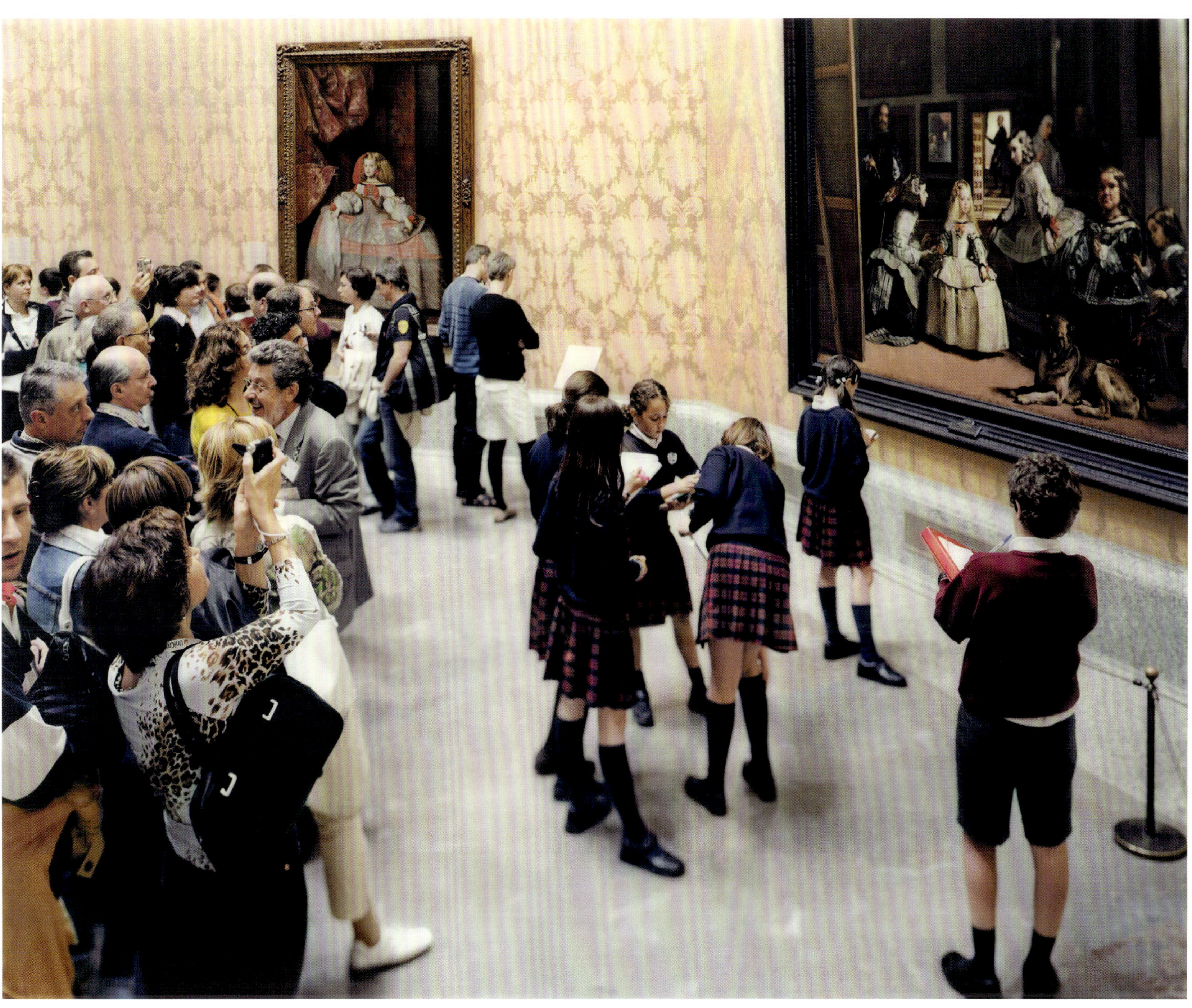

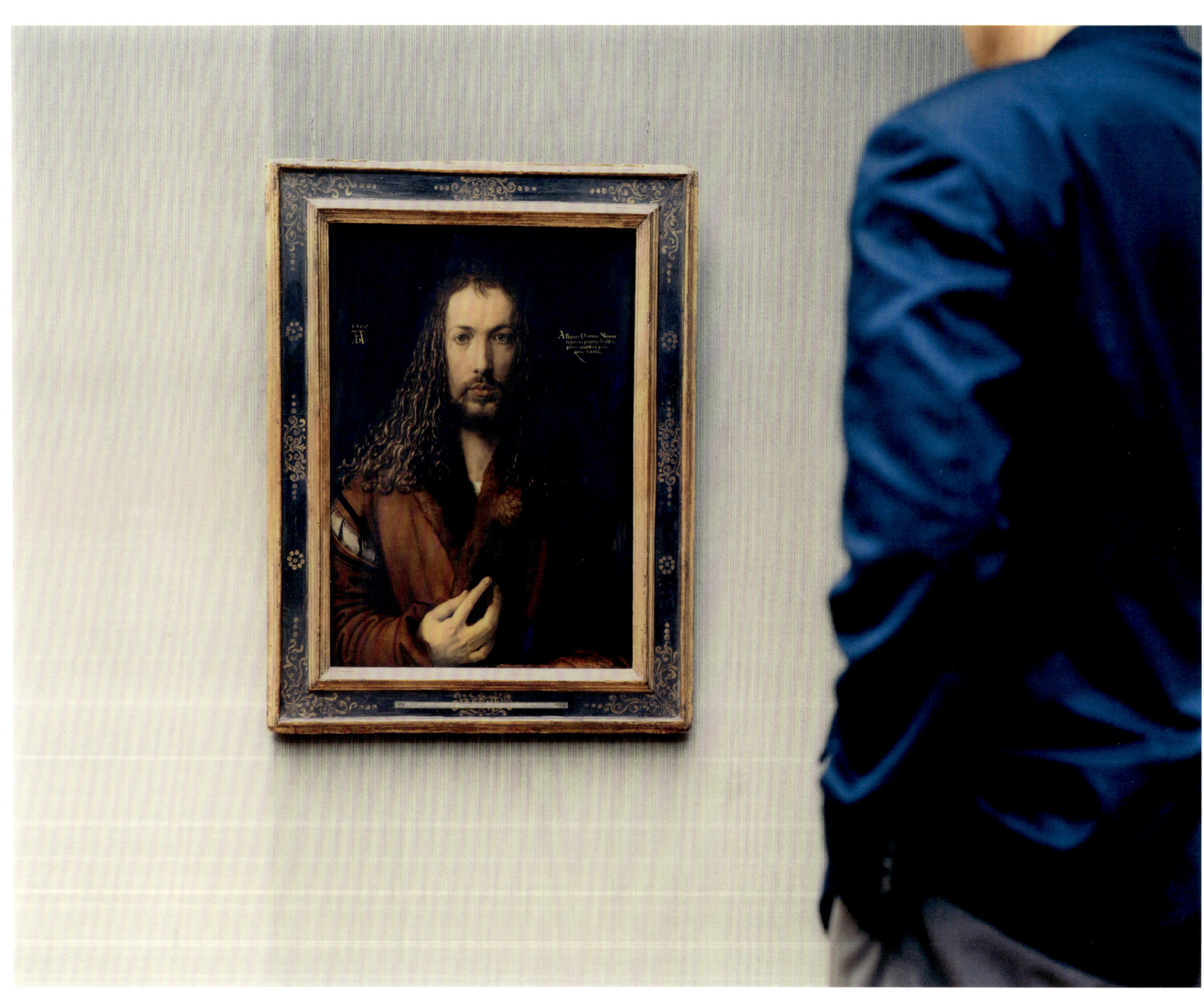

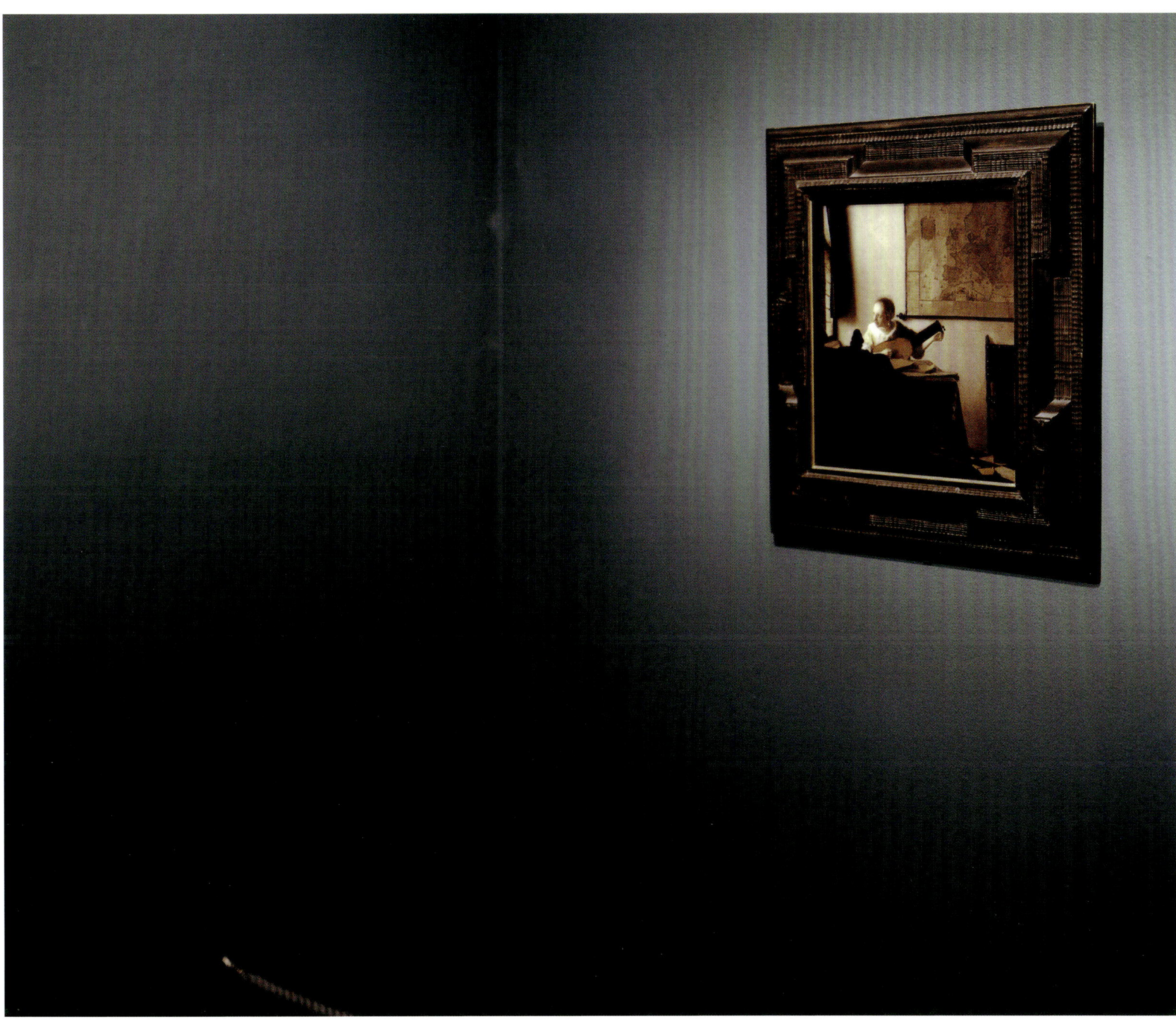

Vermeer's painting *Woman with a Lute* (c. 1662–1663), part of the collection of the Metropolitan Museum of Art, on view at the National Gallery, London. Struth heightened the quiet, contemplative quality of the painting by isolating it from the others in the installation and noting its position tucked into a corner. He also paid particular attention to the way the museum light bathes the picture, mimicking the light in the painting as it illuminates the woman seated at the table. Yet one wonders: Why, of all the paintings available to Struth, did he select this picture by Vermeer for such special treatment? Vermeer was, after all, a Dutch painter—not German like Dürer—and thus Struth was not setting up a dialogue with someone from "the same cultural foundation." He was, though, conversing with an artist who utilized the same kind of allusions to social and political culture that fascinate him: in *Woman with a Lute*, the map on the wall, the musical instruments, even the woman's fur-trimmed, yellow morning jacket all speak of the life, learning, and status of this upper-middle-class woman in mid-seventeenth-century Delft. Vermeer is also known to have been enthralled with light, contrasts in tone, and changes in focus—all fundamental elements of photography—and more specifically, with the camera obscura, an optical device and the earliest known camera. As if silently applauding the work of an earlier artist equally interested in the act of looking and in the ways in which the camera could aid in the knowledge of the natural world, Struth acknowledges these aspects of Vermeer's practice by emphasizing in his photograph the strong contrasts between light and dark, the haloing of light around the painting, and even changes in focus, all of which are characteristics of a camera obscura.

As his interest in the idea of worship and pilgrimage expanded, in 1995 Struth launched a series titled *Places of Worship*. While working on *Museum Photographs* he had become fascinated with both true believers and cultural tourists who look at paintings in their original settings—and thus, within the belief systems for which they had been made, not taken out of context and isolated in museums. Seeking places that offer, as he said, "monumental emotional packages of overwhelming experience," he initially photographed Christian sites but soon expanded the project to include Buddhist temples and even places of powerful secular significance, such as El Capitan in Yosemite National Park.[9] He also made a number of pictures of imposing architecture facades, such as *Notre Dame, Paris 2000* (pl. 7). Harking back to the rigorous architectural studies of the Bechers, he followed his mentors' precedent and selected a central, elevated perspective (albeit much higher than the Bechers would have used) to allow the building to rise up from its surroundings, creating an imposing picture of the magisterial west front of Notre Dame cathedral. Although Struth separates himself and his viewers from the people on the street, these diminutive figures are rendered with no less fidelity or care than the building itself; indeed, Struth once again equated their forms with the sculptures on the cathedral, depicting the people as one with the object of their veneration.

In 2007, Struth embraced a new subject. Perhaps in homage to Bernd Becher, who died that year, he began to investigate massive technological structures such as industrial complexes, research laboratories, and NASA, places that are "at the crossroads of technology and ambition, where the limits of what is possible are continually being tested."[10] However, whereas the Bechers always remained on the outside and found visual logic in diverse architectural structures, Struth dove into the inner workings of almost inconceivably complex facilities. And while he himself had once explored art and architecture to find meaning in history, now he looked at these "machines that manufacture the future," as he described them, to strive to comprehend the technological and political forces that created them."[11] Among his largest pictures to date (some measure 109 × 137 inches), they are dense, cluttered, and sometimes indecipherable— "landscapes of the modern brain," he calls them—expressing both his wonder and

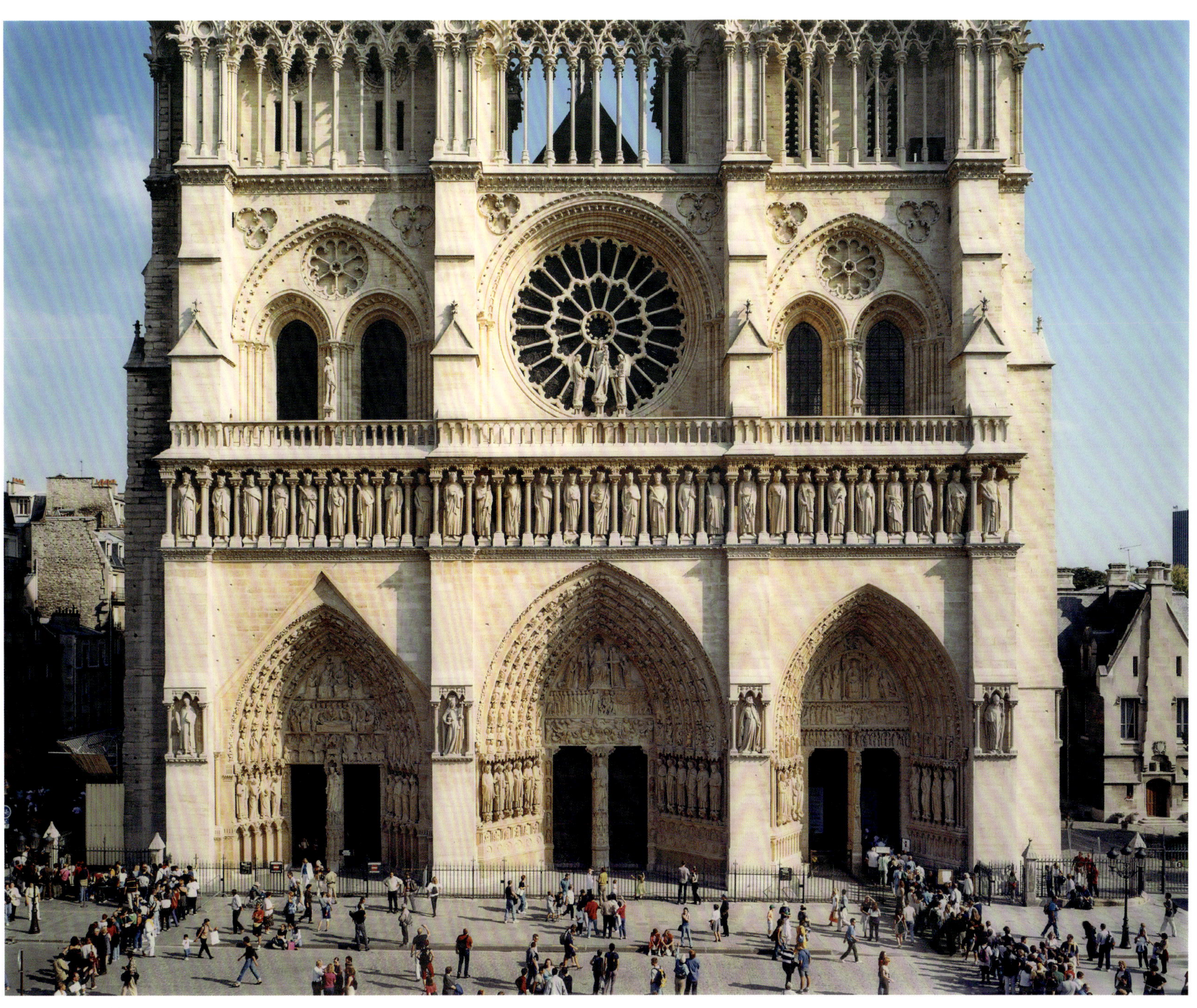

1. Thomas Struth, as quoted by Janet Malcolm, "Depth of Field," *The New Yorker*, September 26, 2011; and Thomas Struth, as quoted Sean O'Hagen, "Thomas Struth: Photos So Complex 'You Could Look at Them Forever,'" *The Guardian*, July 2, 2011, http://www.theguardian.com/artanddesign/2011/jul/03/thomas-struth-interview-photography-whitechapel.

2. Thomas Struth, as quoted by Francis Outred, "In Conversation with Thomas Struth," *Christie's Daily*, June 24, 2015, http://www.christies.com/features/reflections-on-the-self-portrait-thomas-struth-6290-1.aspx.

3. Struth quoted in Anette Kruszynski, Tobia Bezzola, and James Lingwood, *Thomas Struth, Photographs, 1978–2010* (Kunsthaus Zürich, 2010), 196.

4. Struth, *Thomas Struth, Photographs, 1978–2010*, 196.

5. Struth, *Thomas Struth, Photographs, 1978–2010*, 198.

6. James Lingwood, "Composure [or On Being Still]," in *Still* by Guy Tosatto, Hripsimé Visser, Régis Durand, and James Lingwood (New York, 2001), 122.

7. Struth, as quoted by Outred, "In Conversation with Thomas Struth."

8. Struth, as quoted by Outred, "In Conversation with Thomas Struth."

9. Struth, as quoted by Outred, "In Conversation with Thomas Struth."

10. Struth, as quoted by Sabina Griffith, "An Almost Religious Entanglement," *Iter Newsline*, https://www.iter.org/newsline/singleprint/-/659; and Struth, *Thomas Struth, Photographs, 1978–2010*, 222.

11. Struth, as quoted by Griffith, "An Almost Religious Entanglement," *Iter Newsline*.

12. Thomas Struth, "Thomas Struth: Photos So Complex 'You Could Look at Them Forever.'"

13. Max Planck Institute for Plasma Physics (Greifswald), http://www.mpg.de/155019/ipp_greifswald.

14. Thomas Struth, "Thomas Struth: Photos So Complex 'You Could Look at Them Forever.'"

15. Struth, as quoted by Malcolm, "Depth of Field," *The New Yorker*.

concern about humankind's abilities, priorities, and hubris.[12] *Tokamak Asdex Upgrade Interior 2, Max Planck IPP, Garching 2009* (pl. 8) depicts a device that uses magnetic fields to produce controlled fusion reactions in hot plasma at the Max Planck Institute for Plasma Physics in Germany, a facility that seeks, it says, "to fetch the Sun's fire to earth."[13] Devoid of people and a sense of scale and orientation, this deliberately "exhausting" picture, as Struth notes, reveals his concern that there is "a one-sided investment in technology and science as the promised better future." Like the rest of Struth's work, this picture clearly and objectively describes the scene in front of his camera, but in doing so it gives us no greater knowledge of what it depicts or what it portends: it is aesthetically glorious but intellectually incomprehensible. This incomprehensibility—this "dwindling of political thought and engagement as our thinking has become problematically entangled in these kinds of self-focused, endlessly repeating desires"—is precisely what concerns Struth.[14]

In 2011, Struth accepted an unusual commission to photograph Queen Elizabeth II and the Duke of Edinburgh to commemorate the Diamond Jubilee of her reign (pl. 9). Although he had been making *Family Portraits* since late 1980s, most of the people he photographed were friends, rarely celebrities. However, after reading a biography of Elizabeth and realizing she and the duke were the same age as his parents, he accepted the commission. Striving to make them appear as "real people," not "comic impersonators of their function," he prepared extensively. He analyzed acclaimed portraits of royalty by Titian, Giovanni Bellini, Andy Warhol, and Lucian Freud; he looked at old photographs of the couple to learn from the mistakes of those pictures; he carefully determined the location, noting that the queen often looked overwhelmed by her surroundings; and he met with the queen's dresser to select the most flattering attire for her.[15] When he arrived at the shoot, he selected a settee so that the pair would sit together but also slightly apart, and he positioned it at an angle so the queen, who is actually smaller than the duke, would appear larger and more prominent. He also allowed the natural light to fall more directly on her so that the duke receded behind her. Through these preparations and his acute observation of details, Struth constructed a portrait that, despite its grand setting, seems genuine and even somewhat humble. Like all his *Family Portraits*, it is infused with a sense of the forces that inform his subjects' lives: we intuit the political and social structures that rule and constrain the outward nature of their existence; we note the simultaneous closeness and distance between the couple; we see that she has the hands of a grandmother and blood vessels on her legs that reveal the strain of time, while he has alert but tired eyes. As he has done throughout his career, Struth exploits the gap between what was planned and what actually transpired—something that is so fundamental to the art of photography—to create a portrait of the queen and the duke not as royalty but as human beings who regard us with soft but unyielding gazes. GREENOUGH

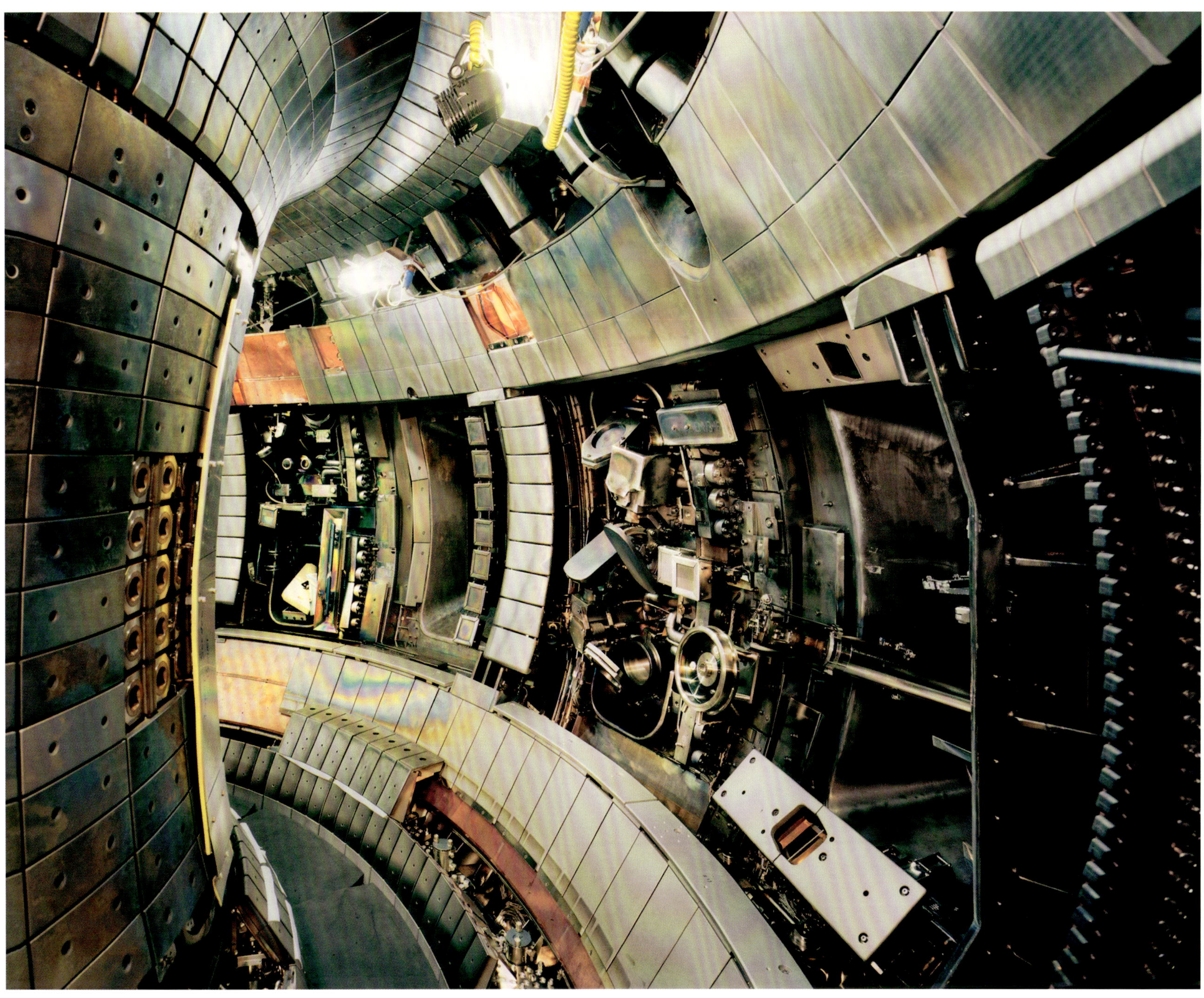

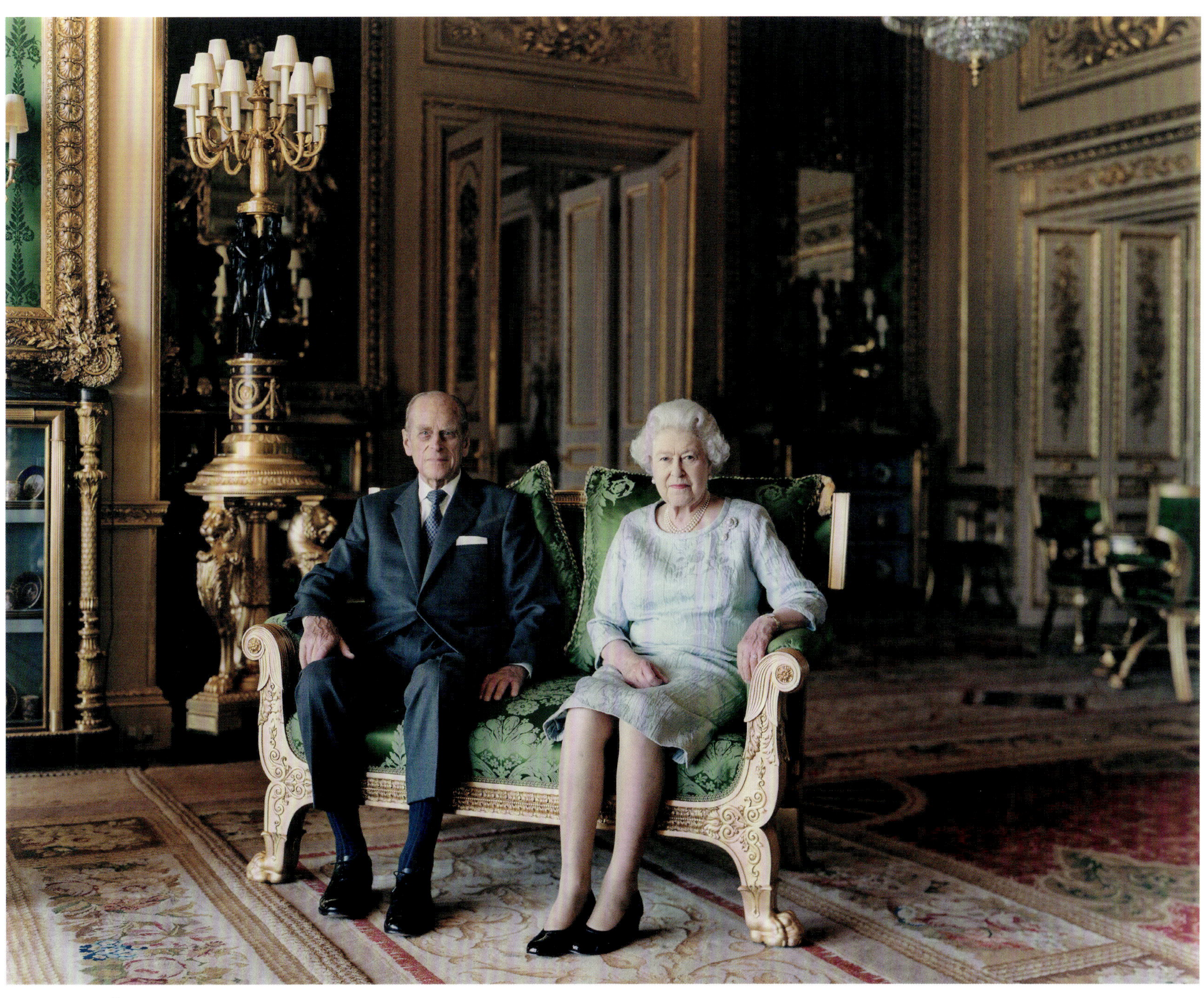

# Candida Höfer

German, born 1944

---

**10**

*Musée du Louvre Paris VIII*, 2005
chromogenic print
204.79 × 276.23 cm (80⅝ × 108¾ in.)
Promised Gift from the
Collection of Robert E.
Meyerhoff and Rheda Becker

---

**11**

*George Peabody Library*
*Baltimore*, 2010
chromogenic print
184.15 × 196.53 cm (72½ × 77⅜ in.)
Promised Gift from the
Collection of Robert E.
Meyerhoff and Rheda Becker

---

**12**

*The Walters Art Museum*
*Baltimore I*, 2010
chromogenic print
184.15 × 227.33 cm (72½ × 89½ in.)
Promised Gift from the
Collection of Robert E.
Meyerhoff and Rheda Becker

---

IN STRIKING VIEWS of architectural interiors, Candida Höfer seeks to capture the physical and psychological experience of space. Her photographs feature not the facades of monumental buildings but rather their internal rooms, allowing her to focus on the ways in which space is socially articulated. Höfer has been photographing in this manner for over thirty years, explaining, "I am interested in the presentation of culturally made objects in spaces and the spaces themselves as such objects, the presentation of presentation."[1] Much of her work is concerned with major public institutions such as art museums and libraries. As buildings designed for the accumulation and preservation of objects—artworks, artifacts, and books—these spaces are archival in nature. Although they house and attempt to categorize an encyclopedic range of knowledge important to the construction of history and cultural memory, they are also spaces for aesthetic pleasure and contemplation, for leisure and learning.[2] Thus Höfer is less interested in depicting an iconic view of a particular structure than with creating photographs that explore the different kinds of activities that take place inside a public building over time.[3]

Höfer belongs to a group of prominent German photographers, including Thomas Struth, Andreas Gursky, and Thomas Ruff, among others, who have reassessed the subject of architecture within the field of contemporary art. Often called the Düsseldorf school because they were taught by the influential photographers Bernd and Hilla Becher at the Kunstakademie Düsseldorf, these photographers have challenged several commonplace notions of architectural photography—a commercial genre where prints often appear as either slick or functional documents made by a photographer working in the service of an architect.[4] Already a trained photographer who had apprenticed in the studio of Werner Bokelberg, Höfer entered the Kunstakademie Düsseldorf in 1973 to study film, but later transferred to the photography course in 1976 when Bernd Becher was appointed as a professor. One of the first Becher students to work with color photography, Höfer brought to the program a project called "Interior Rooms," which became the cornerstone of her career, following her instructors' precedent and advice to find her own path and stick to it.[5]

A rigorous formalism shapes Höfer's oeuvre. Harkening back to seventeenth-century depictions of interior spaces, from topographic prints to paintings, her photographs possess sweeping perspectival views and exhaustive detail.[6] A case in point is *Musée du Louvre Paris VIII* (2005, pl. 10), an intriguing example from her series on the illustrious museum. Focusing on the gallery as a space constructed to display art, Höfer took the photograph from an elevated vantage point using only existing light conditions. Her reliance on natural light makes the space appear more tangible and physically present. In addition to her steadfast attention to perspective, symmetry, and light, Höfer studies the relationship of different historical time periods within the spaces she photographs. Her ability to reveal "the past *within* the present" creates a space layered with history for the viewer to experience.[7] A royal residence until Louis XIV moved his court to Versailles in 1682, the Louvre opened to the public in 1793 with only two departments—paintings and antiquities. *Musée du Louvre Paris VIII* features the ground-floor galleries that now house the Greek, Roman, and Etruscan art collection but were once the summer apartments of Anne of Austria, queen consort and mother to Louis XIV. Partially visible in the photograph, the original ceiling decorations by sculptor Michel Anguier and painter Giovanni Francesco Romanelli still frame the space, provocatively revealing the rich historical associations at play.[8]

While Höfer's works may seem objective in appearance—she does not rearrange any of the objects within the spaces she photographs and limits the amount of digital manipulation she uses during the printing process—it is important to understand that they are not archival documents that simply mirror the space before her

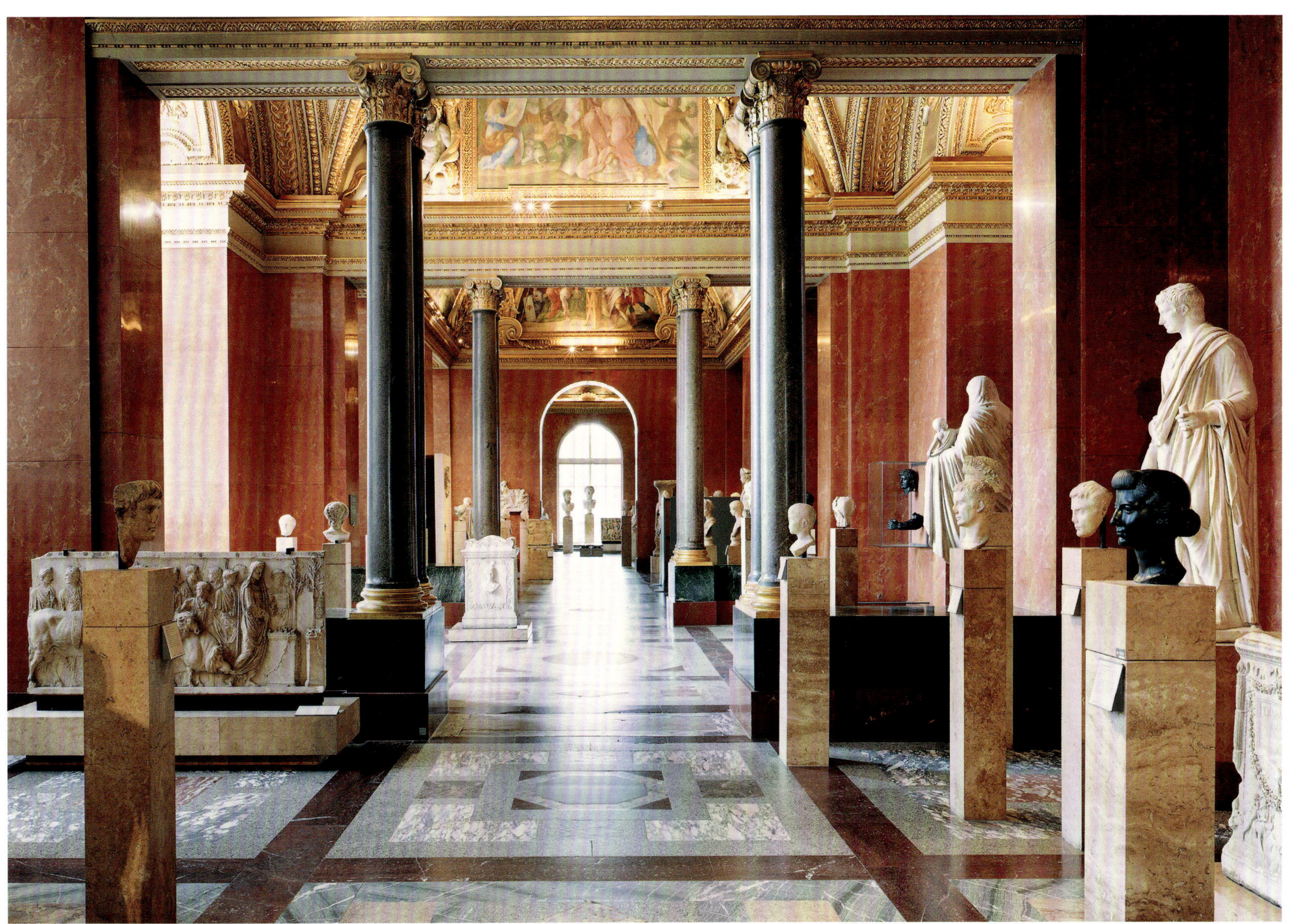

1. Carolyn Yerkes, "Candida Höfer: Interview by Carolyn Yerkes," *Museo Magazine*, 2010, http://www.museo-magazine.com/candida-hofer.

2. Marie-Laure Bernadac, "Candida Höfer," in *Candida Höfer Louvre* (Munich, 2006), 14.

3. Virginia Heckert, "Candida Höfer's Balancing Act," in *Candida Höfer: Architecture of Absence,* ed. Constance W. Glenn (New York, 2004), 31.

4. Jae Emerling, "A Becoming Image: Candida Höfer's Architecture of Absence," in *Contemporary Art about Architecture: A Strange Utility,* ed. Isabelle Loring Wallace and Nora Wendl (Farnham, Surrey, 2013), 69.

5. Constance W. Glenn, "Candida Höfer: Absence in Context," in *Candida Höfer: Architecture of Absence,* ed. Constance W. Glenn (New York, 2004), 16.

6. Yerkes, "Candida Höfer: Interview."

7. Emerling, "A Becoming Image," 70.

8. Designed by Louis Le Vau in 1655 under the order of King Louis XIV.

9. Yerkes, "Candida Höfer: Interview."

10. Emerling, "A Becoming Image," 72–73.

11. Rheda Becker to Sarah Greenough, March 1, 2016. Becker sent a picture of the George Peabody Library to Höfer's representative at Sonnabend Gallery asking if he thought she would be interested in photographing it. As the library was already on Höfer's wish list of buildings to photograph, she responded enthusiastically, inquiring about other buildings in the area that might be of interest. Becker suggested the Walters Art Museum and then made the arrangements for Höfer to access the spaces.

12. "The George Peabody Library: History," http://peabody events.library.jhu.edu/history/. Now a division of the Johns Hopkins University, the library holds some 300,000 volumes dating from the eighteenth to the early twentieth century and remains a noncirculating collection open to the general public.

13. Yerkes, "Candida Höfer: Interview." A notable distinction from her fellow Düsseldorf school colleagues, Höfer did not turn to using a large-format camera and producing oversize prints until 1997.

14. Mary Carole McCauley, "BMA's 'Interior Worlds' Highlights Baltimore Buildings," *The Baltimore Sun,* November 19, 2011, http://articles.baltimoresun. com/2011-11-19/entertainment/bs-ae-hofer-photos-20111119_1_kristen-hileman-baltimore-museum-walters-art-museum.

camera. Höfer shares the Bechers' interest in analyzing a specific cultural type or structure, yet her goal is not to make a full inventory of the artworks in the Louvre or a typological study of every art museum in Paris, for that matter; instead, she is trying to reconstruct her memory of visiting the Louvre. Thus, her initial response to the space, and the impact it had on her both mentally and physically, is critical as a guide, a balance that helps her to create, in her words, "an image that renders justice to the space."[9] Rather than attempting to convey this awareness through multiple images arranged in a grid, like her mentors the Bechers, Höfer instead creates a sense of multiplicity in each of her photographs. As Jae Emerling has insightfully noted, each print embodies "a distinct experience of the 'interplay' between her and the place: her memory and the camera's vision, the photograph as art-object and the viewer, the theme and the variation."[10]

To make her photographs, Höfer needs access to spaces when they are normally closed to the public; therefore, she often depends upon special invitations and extensive communications with others. In 2010, philanthropists and art collectors Robert E. Meyerhoff and Rheda Becker initiated Höfer's trip to Baltimore, Maryland, to photograph at the George Peabody Library and the Walters Art Museum.[11] The visit culminated with the exhibition *Candida Höfer: Interior Worlds* at the Baltimore Museum of Art. One of the four photographs included in the exhibition that features the city's architecture is the stunning *George Peabody Library Baltimore* (2010, pl. 11). Showcasing the central reading room designed by architect Edmund G. Lind that was completed in 1878, Höfer's photograph draws viewers in through a pronounced recession into space. The intricate recording of the magnificent cast-iron columns and ornamental railings as they wrap around six floors of dense shelving creates a stimulating and breathtaking view.[12]

More austere in design, *The Walters Art Museum Baltimore I* (2010, pl. 12) depicts the museum's elegant Italian Renaissance–style court built in the early twentieth century. A little larger than 6 × 7 feet, this print powerfully conveys the formal presence of the space and, in Höfer's own words, "invites a slow and careful reading of details."[13] Sometimes seen as blemishes, objects such as the utility plate on the floor and the lamps on top of the column pediments reveal the contemporary life of the building. These details are all the more noticeable because the courtyard is devoid of visitors. Höfer's photographs, animated by light, patterns, and forms, make reference to humans—but their absence is palpable and uncanny. For instance, a subtle shadow cast from the classical statue of Marcellus as Hermes in the lower lefthand corner of *Musée du Louvre Paris VIII* appears as a specter, underscoring the human absence and eerie stillness of the scene while exposing the area that expands beyond the photograph's frame. Such intense feelings of absence focus attention exactly on the meaning of human presence in these spaces; as Höfer explains, "spaces become more outspoken about what they do for people, about what they do to people and what people have done to them. Just like an absent guest captures the conversation of those present."[14]

Candida Höfer has built a successful career out of a sustained examination of space. Her oversize, luminous color photographs appear at first to be straightforward views of interior rooms, but through exaggerated perspective, sharp focus, and repetition of forms they reveal themselves as directed scenes. Höfer's works are imbued with tension; they are closed-off, static images of spaces that paradoxically trigger imaginary journeys through space and time, making viewers more conscious of the intricacies involved in the act of observation. NELSON

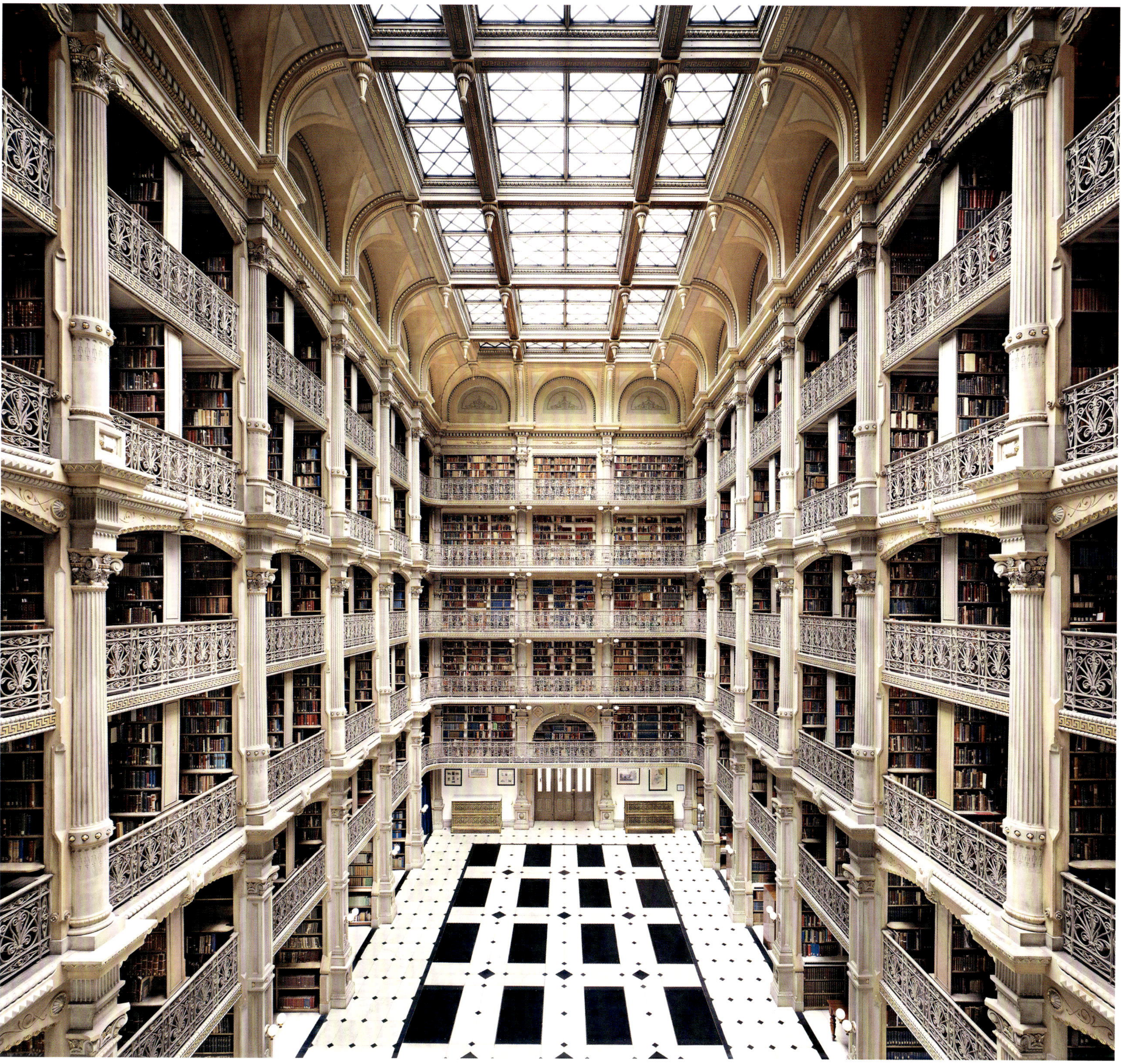

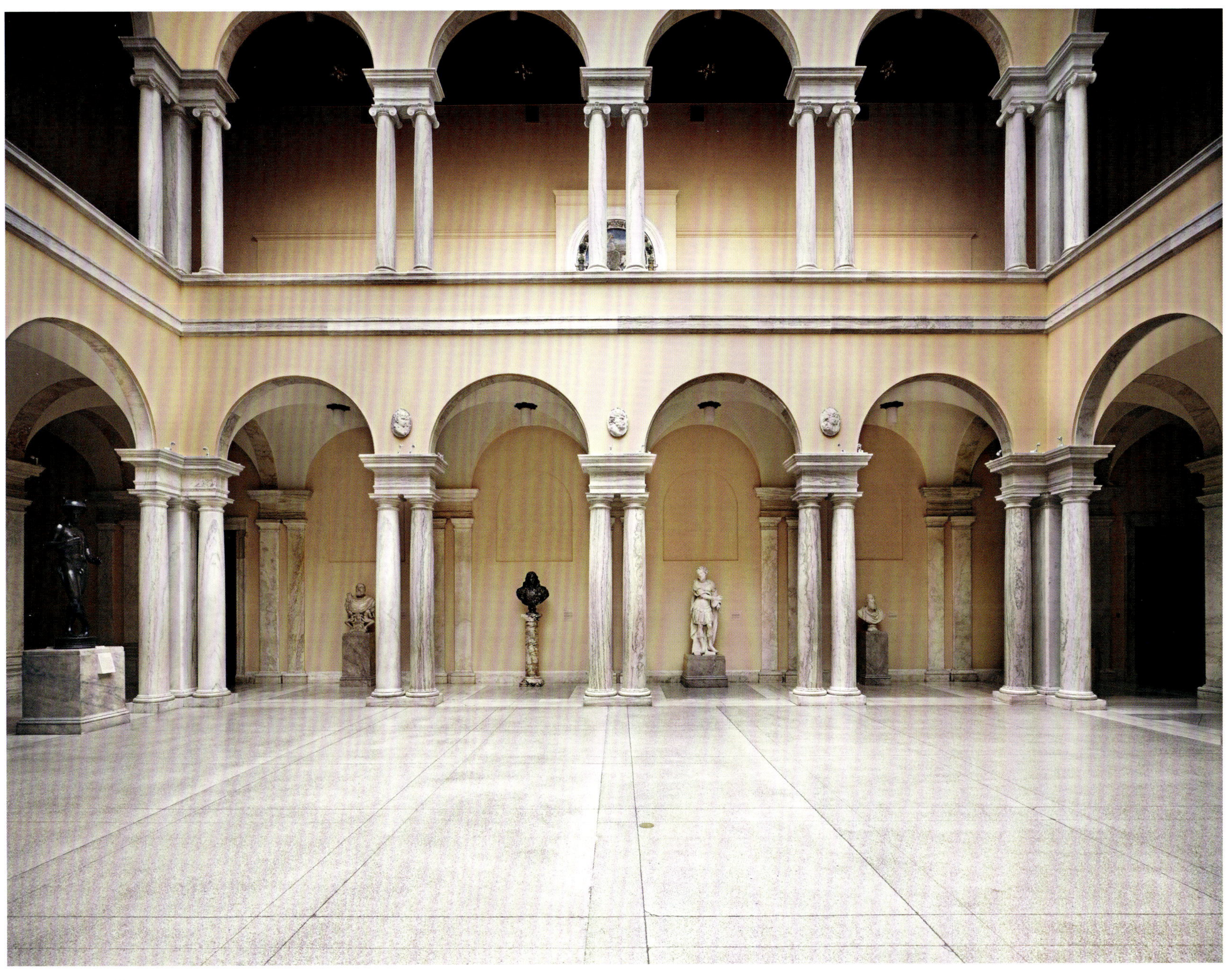

# Andreas Gursky

German, born 1955

---

**13**

*Rimini,* 2003
silver dye bleach print
298.13 × 207.01 cm (117⅜ × 81½ in.)
Promised Gift from the
Collection of Robert E.
Meyerhoff and Rheda Becker

---

**14**

*Bahrain II,* 2007
chromogenic print
307 × 213.1 cm (120⅞ × 83⅞ in.)
Promised Gift from the
Collection of Robert E.
Meyerhoff and Rheda Becker

---

FOR MORE THAN THIRTY YEARS, the German photographer Andreas Gursky has created intense, awe-inspiring photographs that visualize the uneasy experience of living in a postmodern, globalized world. With subjects that are simultaneously spectacular and bland, Gursky's images of popular tourist sites, crowded entertainment venues, sprawling industrial factories, and chaotic stock exchanges reveal the paradoxical nature of globalization with its expansive, borderless networks of technology and business set within a disconnected, fractured existence.

Gursky is well known for digitally altering his photographs, a practice he started in the early 1990s. Conveying the "most contemporary possible view," his works depict scenes both recognizable and imagined, leaving us to question, somewhat apprehensively, what has been changed with the aid of a computer.[1] His hybrid process establishes a new type of perspective that often substitutes a horizon line for an "all-over" sense of fluidity. This is achieved with software that flattens the depth of field, creates repetitions, and heightens color.[2] By rendering reality both familiar and strange, Gursky uses extreme clarity and detail not for documentary purposes but to challenge the viewer's understanding of the nature of photographic recording. His works also evoke the aesthetic of the sublime and have significantly changed the discussion concerning both photographic truthfulness and photography as a fine art. Gursky's monumentally sized photographs captivate with their saturated color and cinematic hyperrealism yet they are also deeply engaged with issues of perception and the representation of space. His subjects often present fascinating contrasts from spaces of exclusive luxury to mass public events and his structured, formal approach depicts these scenes of contemporary life as vast, unending loops, traps of our own making.

Hailing from a family tradition of photography (both his father and grandfather were professional photographers), Gursky was familiar with the intimate workings of the medium at an early age. Born ten years after the end of World War II, he grew up amid West Germany's miraculous economic recovery, but in the aftermath of the upheavals and protests of the late 1960s and 1970s he renounced his father's successful commercial practice as too closely associated with the country's obsessive materialism.[3] Despite this, after eighteen months as a health-care assistant—the alternative given to him after he refused compulsory military service—Gursky decided to pursue a career in photography. He studied visual communication with the celebrated photographer Otto Steinert at the Folkwang Hochschule in Essen, an important training ground for all types of professional photography but especially photojournalism following the model of Magnum photo agency cofounder Henri Cartier-Bresson. After Gursky's first attempts to work as a professional photojournalist failed, he followed the suggestion of his friend Thomas Struth and applied to the Kunstakademie Düsseldorf. With instructors such as Joseph Beuys, Sigmar Polke, and Gerhard Richter, the Kunstakademie had become a center of postwar avant-garde and conceptual art, and under the direction of Bernd Becher, the photography program was cultivating a practice that was separate from journalism and commerce. This was taking place during a time when new art galleries were opening that specialized in photography, and fellowships, grants, and university programs were providing support for artists working with the camera.[4]

By the end of his studies in 1987, Gursky was already publicly exhibiting his photographs, forging his own path away from the supportive yet competitive sphere of the Kunstakademie. Rather than developing a systematic typology or working with an established series like his mentors and fellow students, Gursky explored the "slow impact of history," the consequences of ever-changing human intervention on the surrounding environment.[5] This concern is still very much evident in the midcareer photograph *Rimini* (2003, pl. 13), which features the shoreline of the popular seaside

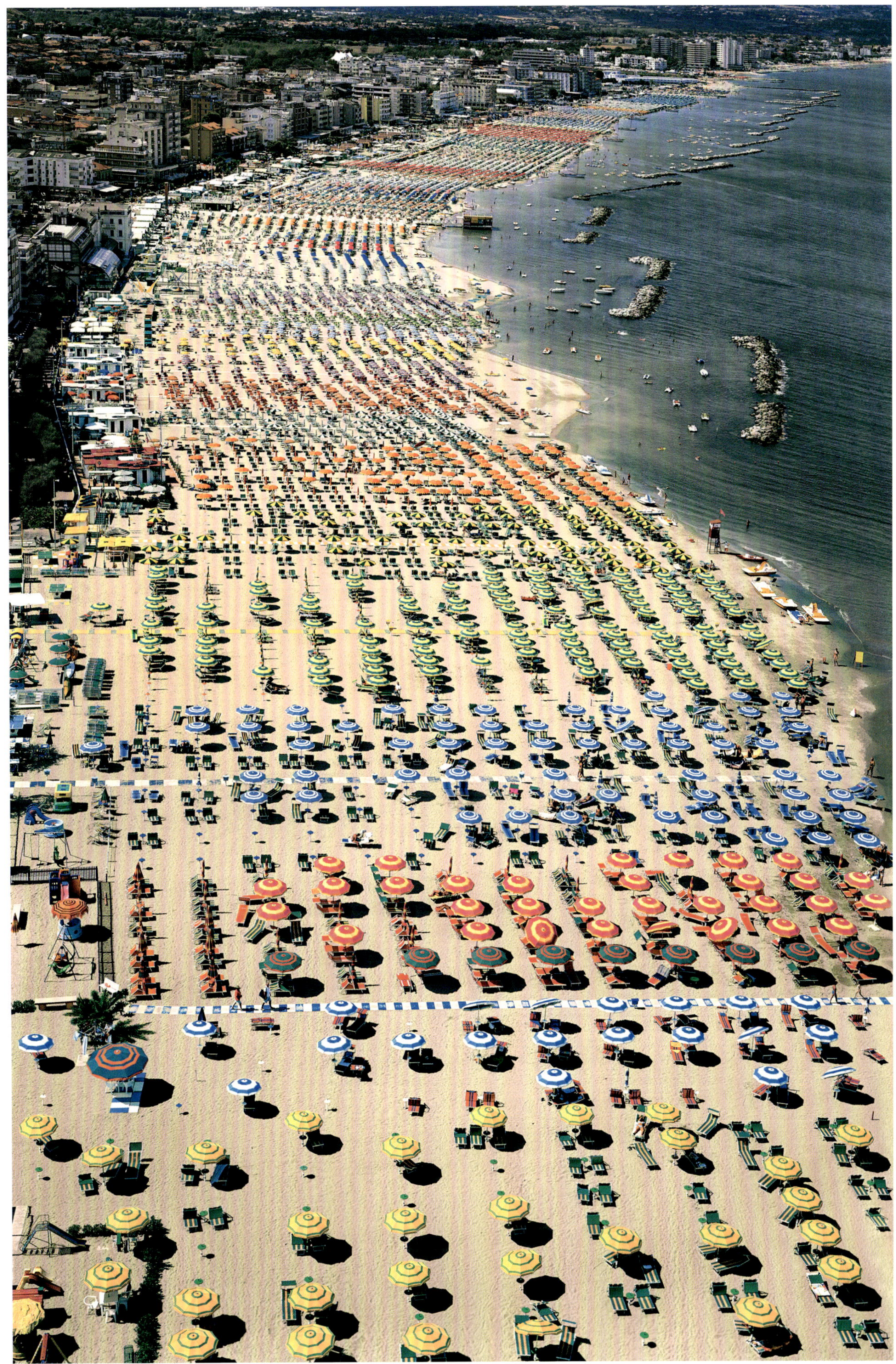

1. Zanny Begg, "Recasting Subjectivity: Globalisation and the Photography of Andreas Gursky and Allan Sekula," *Third Text* 19, no. 6 (November 2005): 633.

2. Begg, "Recasting Subjectivity: Globalisation and the Photography of Andreas Gursky and Allan Sekula," 634.

3. Peter Galassi, *Gursky's World* (Museum of Modern Art, New York, 2001), 12.

4. Galassi, *Gursky's World*, 12.

5. Greg Hilty, "The Occurrence of Space," *Andreas Gursky Images* (Tate Gallery Liverpool, 1995), 22.

6. Andreas Gursky as quoted in Stefan Gronert, "Reality Is Not Totally Real: The Dubiousness of Reality in Contemporary Photography," in *Thomas Demand, Andreas Gursky, Edward Ruscha* (Kunstmuseum Bonn, 1999), 16.

7. Matthew Biro, "From Analogue to Digital Photography: Bernd and Hilla Becher and Andreas Gursky," *History of Photography* 36, no. 3 (2012): 358.


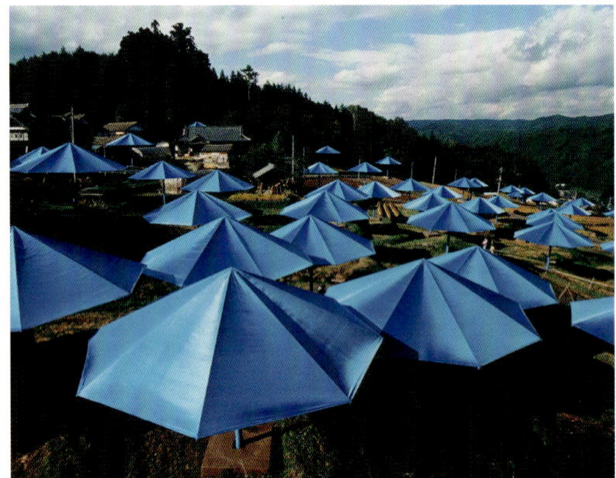

fig. 1: Christo and Jeanne-Claude, *The Umbrellas, Japan-USA, 1984–1991*, 1991, chromogenic print by Wolfgang Volz, National Gallery of Art, Washington, Dorothy and Herbert Vogel Collection

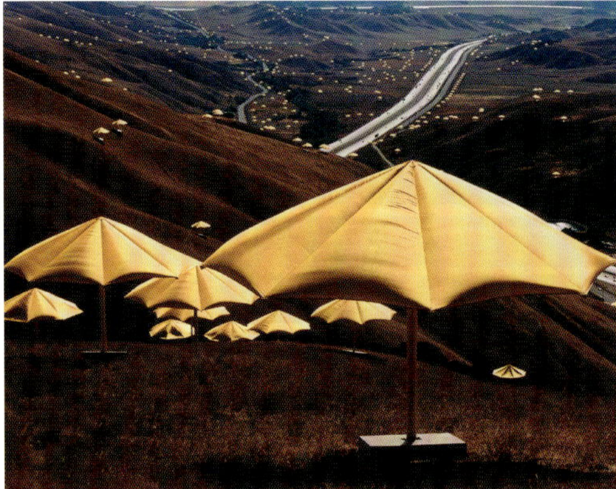

fig. 2: Christo and Jeanne-Claude, *The Umbrellas, Japan-USA, 1984–1991*, 1991, chromogenic print by Wolfgang Volz, National Gallery of Art, Washington, Dorothy and Herbert Vogel Collection

resort town in Italy. Taken from a high vantage point, the sweeping vista is dotted with painstakingly aligned, color-coded umbrellas and lounge chairs. The perfected repetition creates a harmonic composition that does not match up to the more messy reality of being on a crowded beach. With highly saturated color and an obsessive sense of organization, Gursky creates a dazzling pattern of objects and people that overwhelms the terrain. This cool and detached look at leisure time is tinged with a sense of alienation. Maintaining a tension between the micro and macro with a rigid formal structure that is both attractive and unsettling, the photograph emits a sense of falseness that we instinctively mistrust. The colorful scene also evokes Christo and Jeanne-Claude's *Umbrellas* project of 1984–1991, where 3,100 umbrellas were installed (1,760 yellow ones in the Tejon Pass, just north of Los Angeles, and 1,340 blue ones in Ibaraki, Japan) to prompt a deeper understanding of the social customs and the environment of both countries (figs. 1, 2). While two vastly different projects, they both utilize spectacle in order to engage in a conversation about human interaction with the land, cross-cultural relations, leisure, and labor.

Gursky's ability to manipulate his images, coupled with the elaborately detailed and grand scale of his prints, draws striking similarities to the craft and artifice of painting. Gursky courts this analogy as his photographs often make reference to the work of other artists—from the German romantic painter Caspar David Friedrich to the American minimalist sculptor Dan Flavin—yet he has responded to such remarks by saying, "I think it is more the fact that a general vocabulary of pictures exists and has always existed, which is why good subjects taken up by painting are simply there and will always be taken up again and again."[6] In either case, whether he is directly corresponding with the history of art or exploring long-standing representation strategies, his photographs open up critical discussions on the theory of perception as well as present a compelling way to examine popular culture and bland commercial environments.

Resembling a color field painting, *Bahrain II* (2007, pl. 14) was created while Gursky was working on a larger series concerned with motor racing, *F1 Pit Stop*. An image of a Formula 1 racetrack built in the Bahrain desert in 2004, *Bahrain II* is based on aerial photographs Gursky took from a helicopter. Here, he has integrated three different sections of the curving, snakelike track, which appears at first glance to be a gestural black line amidst a beige background. A striking example of how a seemingly mundane image can be transformed into a provocative work of art, Gursky's manipulation compresses time and space, giving his photograph an aura of timelessness. Yet small signs, such as a cellular phone company logo, ground the work in reality, as does the premise for the construction of the track in the first place: this motorsport venue, a national objective for Bahrain, hosted the first Grand Prix in the Middle East in 2004.

Gursky's altered photographs are fitting commentary on the contemporary social condition. By creating a sense of order out of the multiplicities of everyday experience, his photographs reveal not only the complex structures of cultural and economic interaction, but also the profound impact of the built environment on daily life. An important figure who continues to shape the definition of photographic practice as it has shifted to the digital, Gursky also makes it clear in his works that one should not simply pit analogue against digital.[7] Photographers have always selected how they frame the world before the lens, establishing a medium with a rich history of experimentation and manipulation as a means to construct images. Gursky, not one to make light of historical precedent, astutely uses the wealth of past knowledge to produce stunning, insightful, and sublime photographs: in effect, today's history paintings. NELSON

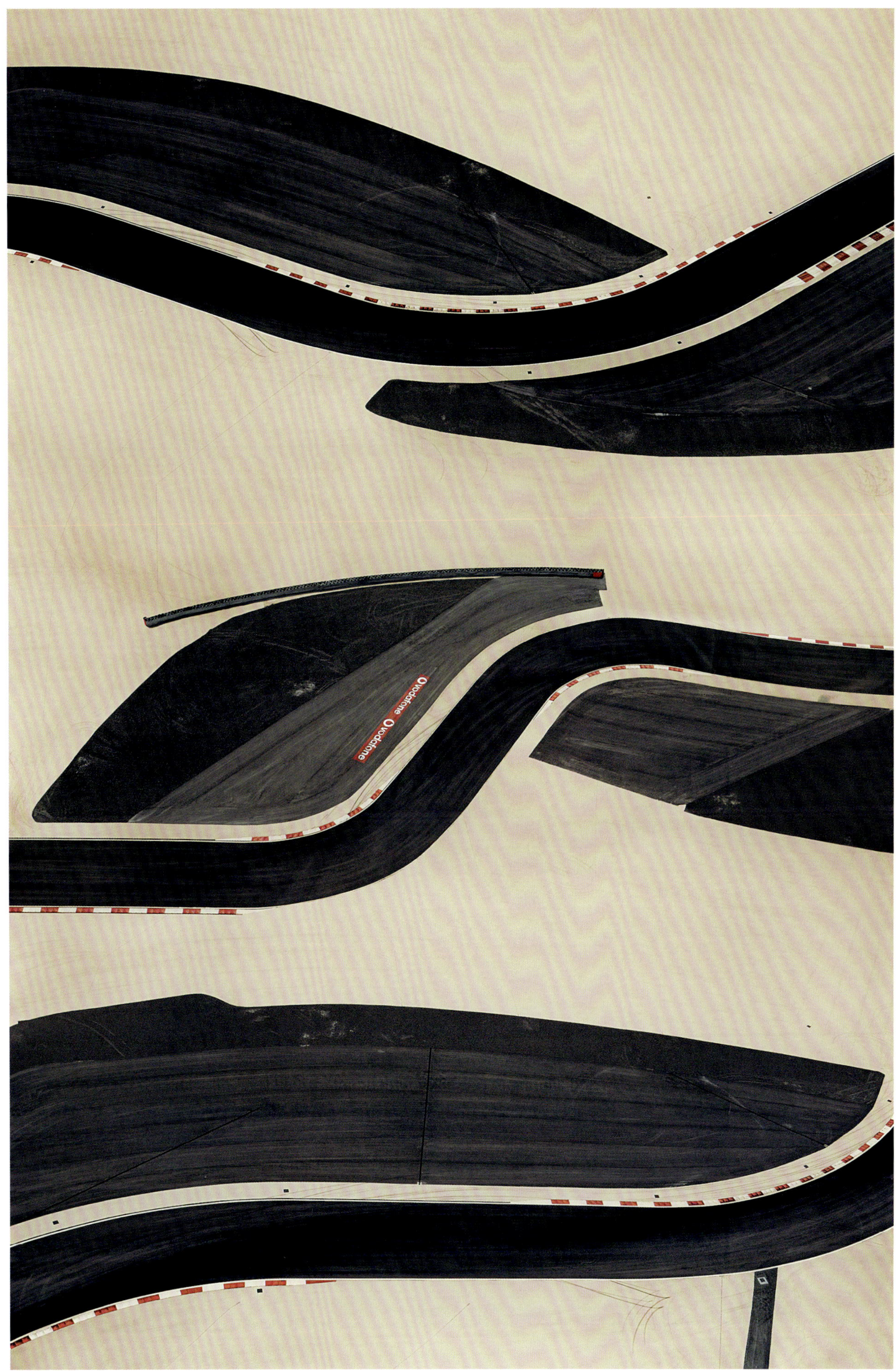

# Thomas Ruff

German, born 1958

---

### 15

*Portrait (P. Stadtbäumer)*, 1990
chromogenic print
210.19 × 165.42 cm (82¾ × 65⅛ in.)
Promised Gift from the
Collection of Robert E.
Meyerhoff and Rheda Becker

---

### 16

*Portrait (T. Ruff)*, 1991
chromogenic print
185.74 × 180.66 cm (73⅛ × 71⅛ in.)
Promised Gift from the
Collection of Robert E.
Meyerhoff and Rheda Becker,
in Honor of the 25th Anniversary
of Photography at the National
Gallery of Art

---

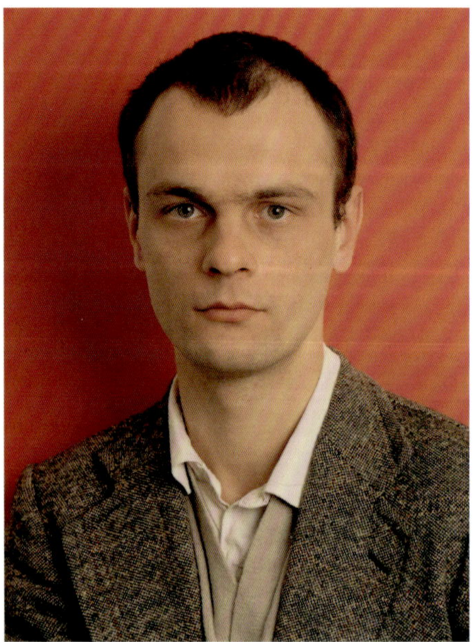

fig. 1: Thomas Ruff, *Portrait (B. Jünger)*, 1981, chromogenic print, Courtesy David Zwirner, New York/London

IN 1981, when Thomas Ruff began making portraits of his fellow students at the Kunstakademie Düsseldorf, conversation in the studio often turned to George Orwell's book *1984*. At the time, West Germany was still reeling from the events surrounding the Red Army Faction—not only the group's terrorist acts, but also their capture and suspicious deaths while incarcerated by the state. Coupled with living in an already intense era of Cold War surveillance, the students wondered about the future as daily life felt more and more constrained.[1] While the Kunstakademie had become a center for postwar avant-garde and conceptual art practice, Ruff chose to work in the unpopular genre of studio portraiture in order to create what he called an official portrait of his generation. Inspired by postcards and passport and press photographs—collective uses of photography to advertise, identify, and record—Ruff's portraits reveal very little about the character of his sitters who confidently stare, but not smile, at the viewer.[2] Instead they depict a generation attuned to the complexities of visual imagery, including the ease with which photographs can be manipulated to suit different purposes.

As one of the youngest students of the distinguished photographers Bernd and Hilla Becher, Ruff came to the Kunstakademie Düsseldorf in 1977 a mostly self-taught amateur. Looking back, he recalls that he "wanted to travel around the world taking beautiful photographs of beautiful landscapes and people."[3] Shocked at first and then taken by the type of documentary photography being produced by his instructors, Ruff soon found a uniform structure to guide his practice. Creating highly detailed photographs using an even light and a minimal background, he refined a visually objective, even deadpan approach that can be seen as a directly influenced by the Bechers. In fact, of all the Bechers' students, Ruff has been the one most engaged in "a radical pursuit of photographic objectivity" by exploring a wide variety of subjects and photographic processes.[4] He is concerned overall with the concept of perception and the mechanics of photography, explaining, "I don't think my portraits can present actual personalities. I'm not interested in making a copy of my own interpretation of a person. It's more my personal idea of photography that is accentuated in my portraits. I believe that photography can only reproduce the surface of things."[5]

Working with color film, Ruff's first series from 1981 to 1985 featured portraits that were relatively small in size at 24 × 18 cm (9⁷⁄₁₆ × 7¹⁄₁₆ in.) (fig. 1). This allowed him to construct "a gallery of images," some one hundred prints that he displayed in a horizontal row.[6] When his sitters came to his studio dressed in their everyday clothes, he asked them to pick which colored photographic cardboard they wanted for their simple backdrop. He then took bust-length portraits capturing his subjects from various points of view. Between 1984 and 1986, Ruff started to experiment with the size of his portraits. After earning enough money to print a select few on the largest sheets of photographic paper available at the time, approximately 210 × 165 cm (82¹¹⁄₁₆ × 64¹⁵⁄₁₆ in.), he experienced a breakthrough. This monumental size produced a completely new photograph, as seen in *Portrait (P. Stadtbäumer)* (1990, pl. 15). More commanding and alluring in presence, with an intensified level of detail and lush color, these oversize prints were also more clearly experienced as a constructed image, akin to a poster or billboard rather than an authentic likeness. For his second series of portraits from 1986 to 1991, Ruff dropped the colored backdrops in favor of neutral ones that would not overwhelm the sitter and photographed more strictly from a frontal viewpoint, producing both small and oversize prints.

In many ways, Ruff's photographic portraits are antithetical to the common understanding of the genre as a means to reveal hidden truths or encapsulate the essence of a subject's being. He has said, "The portraits are about each individual and at the same time about all individuals. An individual portrait is especially suited to

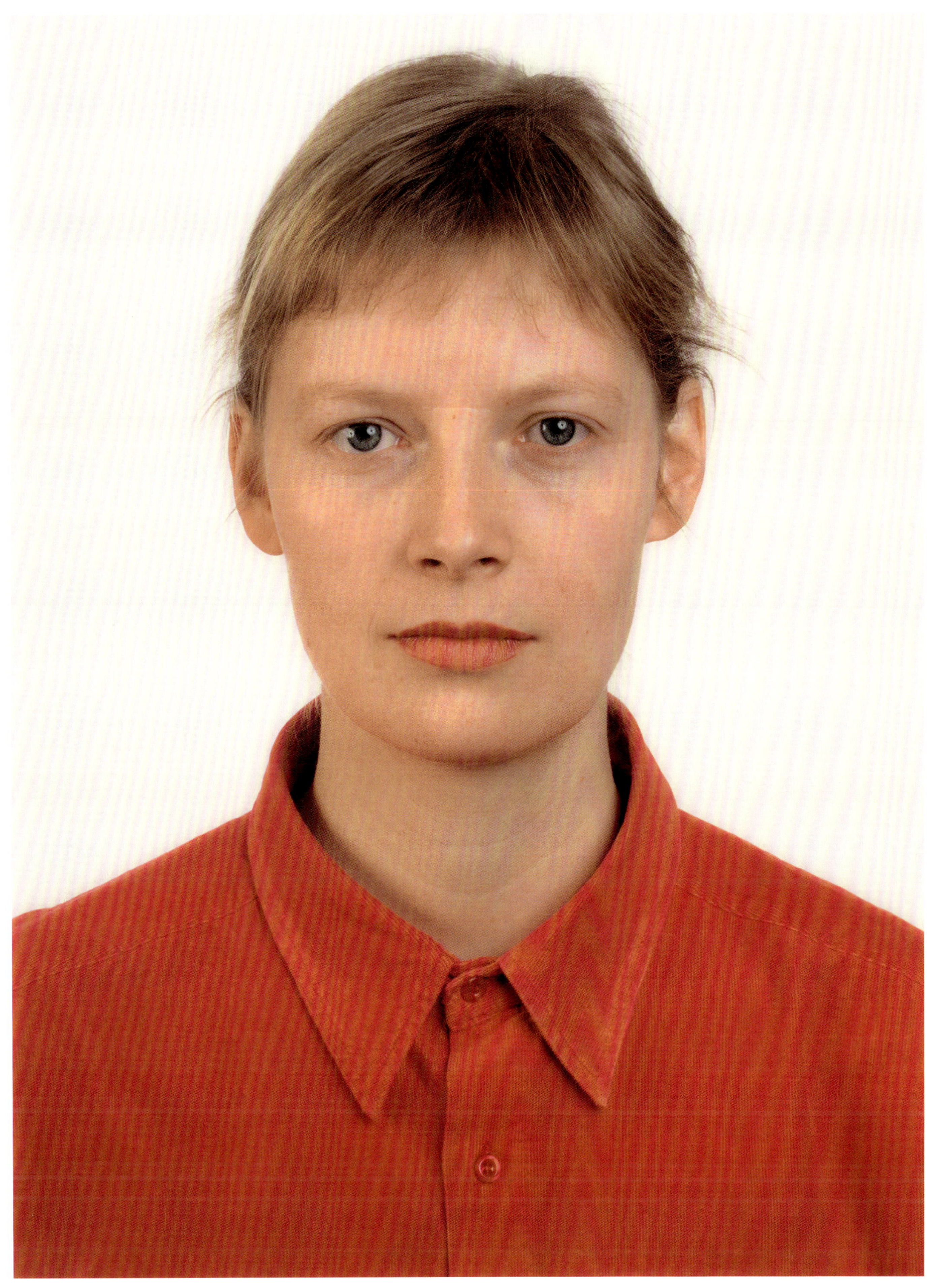

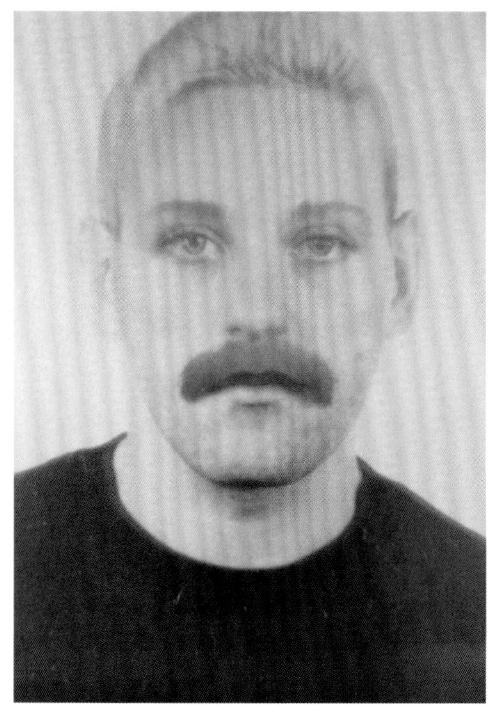

fig. 2: Thomas Ruff, *Other Portrait Nr. 122/138*, 1994/1995, silkscreen print, Courtesy David Zwirner, New York/London

1. Gil Blank, "Gil Blank and Thomas Ruff in Conversation," *Influence* 2 (2004): 51.

2. Blank, "Gil Blank and Thomas Ruff in Conversation," 51.

3. "Thomas Ruff with Vicki Goldberg," *The Brooklyn Rail*, June 1, 2005, http://brooklynrail.org/2005/06/art/thomas-ruff.

4. According to Gerhard Mack, as noted in Matthias Winzen's "A Credible Invention of Reality," in *Thomas Ruff: 1979 to the Present*, ed. Matthias Winzen (New York, 2003), 135.

5. Winzen, "A Credible Invention of Reality," 138.

6. Winzen, "A Credible Invention of Reality," 166.

7. Winzen, "A Credible Invention of Reality," 142.

8. Winzen, "A Credible Invention of Reality," 139.

9. Rodchenko then put this theory into practice with his compelling portrait series of the poet Vladimir Mayakovsky.

10. Winzen, "A Credible Invention of Reality," 142.

showing that a photographed face can have something very general, very anonymous about it."[7] In fact, we can deduce very little about P. Stadtbäumer from her portrait, except for cursory notions based on appearance. Her hairstyle and clothing, for example, appear more conservative than trendy, yet the bold red of her shirt and matching lipstick might suggest otherwise. There exists in Ruff's works a quiet tension between form and content: where the richness of detail should lend specificity and insight into the sitter's character, viewers are instead confronted by an impenetrable, flat photographic representation.[8] In style and ambition, his series draw many parallels to August Sander's encyclopedic project *People of the 20th Century*, a sociological study of German society that occupied Sander for over fifty years but remained unfinished. Producing his portraits as representative types, Sander grouped and titled them by the profession or social class of the sitter, including farmers, politicians, artists, and soldiers. Unlike Sander, however, Ruff does not provide any contextualizing information other than the sitter's name. Informed by this rich history of German photography, Ruff is also working in a very different historical moment, one that questions such classification schemes based on visual codes. His project thus deconstructs both Sander's atlas of the German people and other, more contemporary approaches by photographers such as Diane Arbus and Richard Avedon predicated on the revelatory power of portraiture.

Ruff continues to question the integrity of portraiture in *Portrait (T. Ruff)* (1991, pl. 16). The artist's self-portrait is a longstanding trope in art history, but here he presents an unsettling, doubled version. With two different iterations of himself in one print, he counters the idea that a single photographic image can adequately provide a comprehensive sense of identity. Aleksandr Rodchenko took up a similar discussion more than sixty years earlier in his 1928 essay "Against the Synthetic Portrait, For the Snapshot." Here Rodchenko advocates for a new type of portraiture that consists of a series of snapshots that reveal the sitter in different situations and different moments of time.[9] Rather than creating a series of self-portraits, Ruff's intriguing print seems to have opened a door to a deeper investigation into montage and composite imagery. His next series, titled *Other Portraits*, comprises unsettling composite pictures he produced using a Minolta Montage Unit that he borrowed from the Police History Collection in Berlin (fig. 2). The machine was used in the 1970s by law enforcement agencies in Germany to create identikit images of criminals. Ruff used the machine to superimpose photographs selected from his earlier *Portraits* series. He then took the composites and enlarged them, printing the final versions as black-and-white silkscreen prints that resemble photographs found in newspapers.[10] With this project, Ruff engages once again with fundamental questions of the nature of photography. Recalling the work of both Alphonse Bertillon (1853–1914), the inventor of the mugshot, and Andy Warhol's *Thirteen Most Wanted Men*, a massive grid of silkscreened panels of New York Police Department mugshots created for the city's World's Fair in 1964, his *Other Portraits* are, however, highly distorted images that undermine recognizability—the intended goal of the police images. Ruff reveals that just as identity cannot be fixed, neither can the meaning of a photographic representation.

After achieving international recognition for his *Portraits* series, Ruff embraced a variety of experimental themes and techniques. He has photographed architecture, used archival scientific negatives as source material, rephotographed newspaper photographs, appropriated imagery from the Internet, and made night-vision photographs as well as computer-generated photograms. Guided by an unrelenting desire to question the kind of information embedded in a photograph, Ruff continues to make work that explores the ways in which photography constructs images and, therefore, has a powerful effect on how we perceive the world. **NELSON**

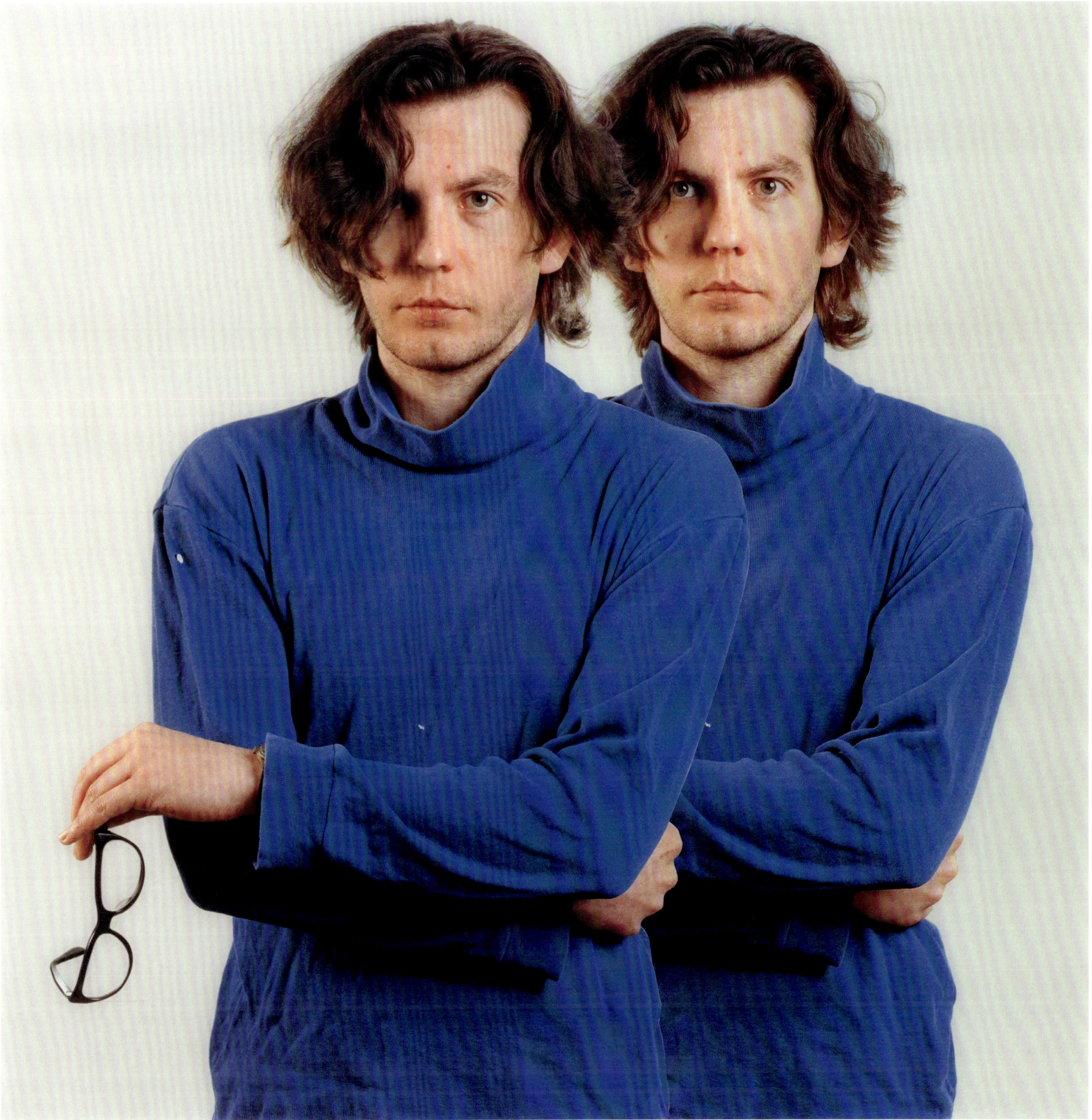

# Cindy Sherman

American, born 1954

---

**17**

*Untitled Film Still #4*, 1977
gelatin silver print
92.08 × 108.59 cm (36 ¼ × 42 ¾ in.)
Promised Gift from the
Collection of Robert E.
Meyerhoff and Rheda Becker,
in Honor of the 25th Anniversary
of Photography at the National
Gallery of Art

---

**18**

*Untitled #211*, 1989
chromogenic print
117.79 × 102.24 cm (46 ⅜ × 40 ¼ in.)
Promised Gift from the
Collection of Robert E.
Meyerhoff and Rheda Becker

---

SINCE CHILDHOOD, Cindy Sherman has transformed herself into countless different characters and, in the process, produced works that have influenced generations of artists working with portraiture and photography. What started as a game has informed Sherman's approach to her work, for which she has donned an array of costumes, from the clothing of victims and vixens to the furs and silks of historical figures. Initially a painting student at Buffalo State College, Sherman soon adopted photography as her chosen medium. Well versed in conceptual and performance art practices of the 1960s and 1970s, Sherman, like other artists of her time, experimented with appropriating existing imagery for her works. *Untitled Film Stills* (1977 – 1980), a series first exhibited at alternative art spaces such as Hallwalls in Buffalo and Artists Space in New York City, brought Sherman to the attention of the art world and placed her squarely in the center of the milieu that defined much of American art in the late 1970s and 1980s.

Although Sherman had already dressed up for the camera for other projects, including *Bus Riders* (1976) and *A Play of Selves* (1976), between 1977 and 1980 she turned to guises that recalled movie characters played by Brigitte Bardot, Jeanne Moreau, and Monica Vitti, in film noir and neorealist movies of the 1940s, 1950s, and 1960s.[1] For the seventy staged photographs of *Untitled Film Stills* she posed, usually alone, in her apartment or in public spaces, and produced images that allude to promotional materials often made on movie sets. In *Untitled Film Still #4* (1977, pl. 17), Sherman wears a skirt suit and oversized coat. With her eyes closed, she appears to be eavesdropping as she leans against a door, perhaps hoping that someone will let her in. The character Sherman created seems unaware of any implied viewer — of someone standing in the hallway, sitting in a movie theater watching the story unfold on screen, or looking at the photograph in an exhibition.[2]

*Untitled Film Still #4* does not have a clear narrative yet the imagery may seem familiar and is therefore unsettling.[3] The *Untitled Film Stills* are what the art historian Rosalind Krauss calls "a copy *without* an original"; each is reminiscent of earlier films, but never a copy of a particular one.[4] The analogy also extends to Sherman's approach to the "types" of women she depicts in each of the photographs, whether bombshells, career girls, or ingénues. As Krauss and other feminist scholars have discussed, Sherman has constructed pictures that question the depiction of women in popular culture. While she draws on and feeds viewers' assumptions about "types" of women in works that hinge on the interplay of memory, nostalgia, and stereotypes, many of her figures do not seem quite right.[5] With their wigs slightly askew, ill-fitting clothes, and contrived facial expressions, they are off-putting, disconcerting. And while Sherman's characters disrupt standardized depictions of women, they do not offer a straightforward message that can be easily mapped onto feminist politics.

Throughout her career, Sherman has often disquieted viewers' expectations. She continued to do so in her series *History Portraits* (1989 – 1990), which developed as she worked on a project for the artist-designed tableware firm Artes Magnus. Working with the French porcelain company Limoges, Sherman designed a tea and dinner set modeled on molds created for Madame de Pompadour.[6] In 1989, she made photographs based on the French Revolutionary period and further developed the series during a two-month sojourn in Rome and later in New York.[7] She worked from reproductions of old master works, rather than from the paintings themselves.[8] Carefully planning the photographs, she selected the backgrounds and rummaged through thrift stores for props and costumes. Using prosthetics and heavy makeup, she transformed herself into the men and women, both mythical characters and historical figures, depicted in the paintings. The referent works remain vaguely recognizable. Battista Sforza's high forehead, for instance, still appears in *Untitled #211* (1989, pl. 18),

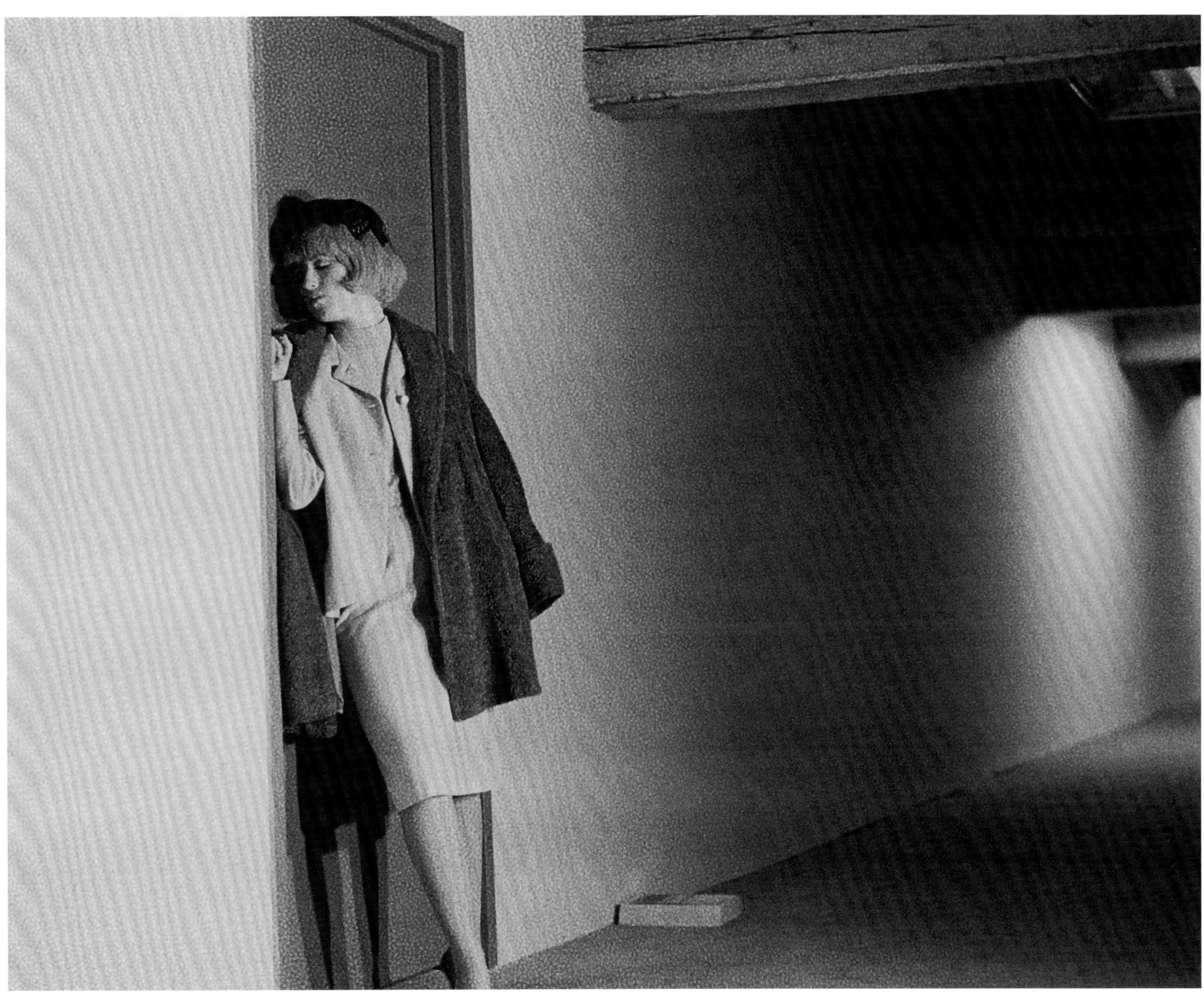

1. Cindy Sherman, "The Making of *Untitled*," in *Cindy Sherman: The Complete* Untitled Film Stills, ed. David Frankel (Museum of Modern Art, New York, 2003), 5.

2. Feminist scholars, in particular, have discussed the *Untitled Film Stills* through the study of the "male gaze," as described by Laura Mulvey, "Visual Pleasure and Narrative Cinema," in *Screen* 16, no. 3 (Autumn 1975): 6–18.

3. Sherman, "The Making of *Untitled*," 6.

4. Rosalind Krauss, "Cindy Sherman: Untitled," in *Cindy Sherman: 1975–1993* (New York, 1993), 17.

5. Judith Williamson, "A Piece of the Action: Images of 'Woman' in the Photography of Cindy Sherman," reprinted in *October Files #6: Cindy Sherman*, ed. Johanna Burton (Cambridge, MA, 2006), 39.

6. Eva Respini, "Will the Real Cindy Sherman Please Stand Up?" in *Cindy Sherman* (Museum of Modern Art, New York, 2012), 40–41.

7. Cindy Sherman in Michael Kimmelman, "At the Met with: Cindy Sherman; Portraitist in the Halls of Her Artistic Ancestors," *New York Times*, May 19, 1995.

8. *Cindy Sherman: Retrospective* (Museum of Contemporary Art, Chicago, and The Museum of Contemporary Art, Los Angeles, 1997), 151–152.

9. Arthur C. Danto, "Past Masters and Post Moderns: Cindy Sherman's *History Portraits*," in *Cindy Sherman: History Portraits* (New York, 1990), 9–13.

10. Sherman in Karsten Löckemann, "A Conversation with Cindy Sherman," in *Cindy Sherman*, ed. Ingvild Goetz and Karsten Löckemann (Sammlung Goetz, Munich, 2015), 91.

11. Abigail Solomon-Godeau, "Photography after Art Photography," in *Photography at the Dock: Essays on Photographic History, Institutions, and Practices* (Minneapolis, 1991), 113–114.

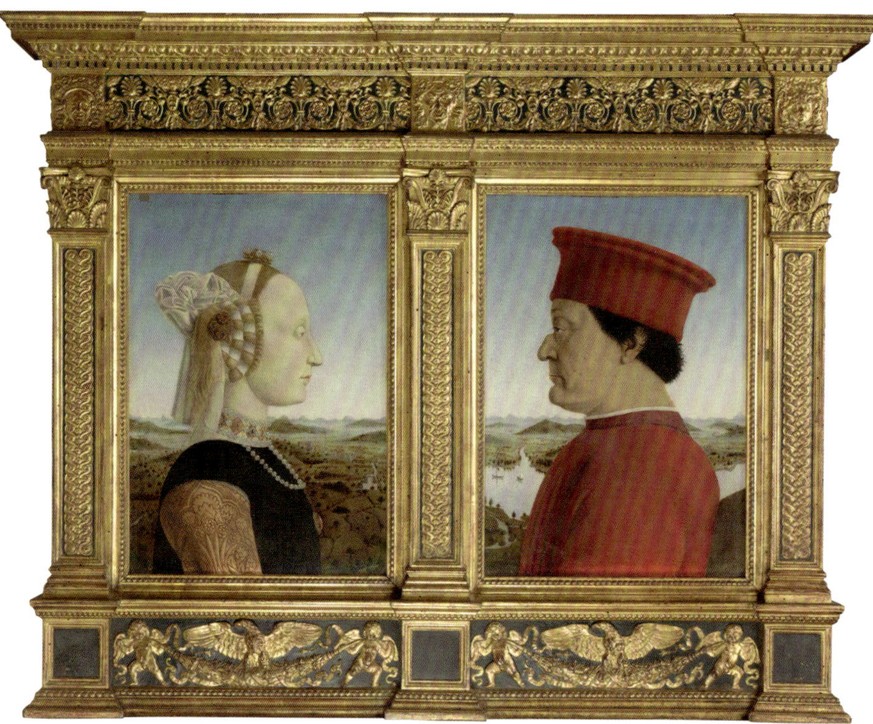

**fig. 1:** Piero della Francesca, *Portraits of the Duke and Duchess of Urbino*, 1465–1472, tempera on panel, Galleria degli Uffizi, Florence

but Sherman does not produce an exact replica of Piero della Francesca's portrait of the Duchess of Urbino at the Galleria degli Uffizi (1465–1472, fig. 1). Instead, she over-emphasizes her nose and her hair appears loose, while the original duchess's is neatly tucked under her ornate headdress. Sherman wears pearls around her neck that are similar but not identical to the sitter's intricate pearl-and-jewel-encrusted choker. Sherman's dark vest is roomy, while Sforza wears a snug bodice. A blue curtain stands in for Piero's landscape background, and rather than being part of a rectangular double portrait, the female figure now appears alone and not facing her husband, Federico da Montefeltro, the Duke of Urbino.

Sherman draws inspiration from the art-historical canon, and our ability to recognize works that are a part of it, while she simultaneously breaks it down.[9] When the *History Portraits* were first exhibited in New York in 1990, visitors were perplexed at not being able to identify a specific source. As the critic Arthur C. Danto noted, those with a broad knowledge of art history were especially flummoxed by their inability to identify the original pictures. After all, Sherman was merely alluding to "the style of some profiles where the models don't look so attractive" rather than directly quoting a particular work of art.[10]

In drawing from preexisting imagery Sherman emphasizes the constructed nature of her work, and has thus helped redefine photography's role in artistic practice.[11] Dressing up for the camera had been done before, even as early as the mid-1860s when the British photographer Julia Margaret Cameron staged photos of her housemaid and children costumed as the Madonna and child. However, with works such as *Untitled #211* and the deliberately grainy *Untitled Film Still #4*, Sherman highlights photography's performative and contrived aspects. UREÑA

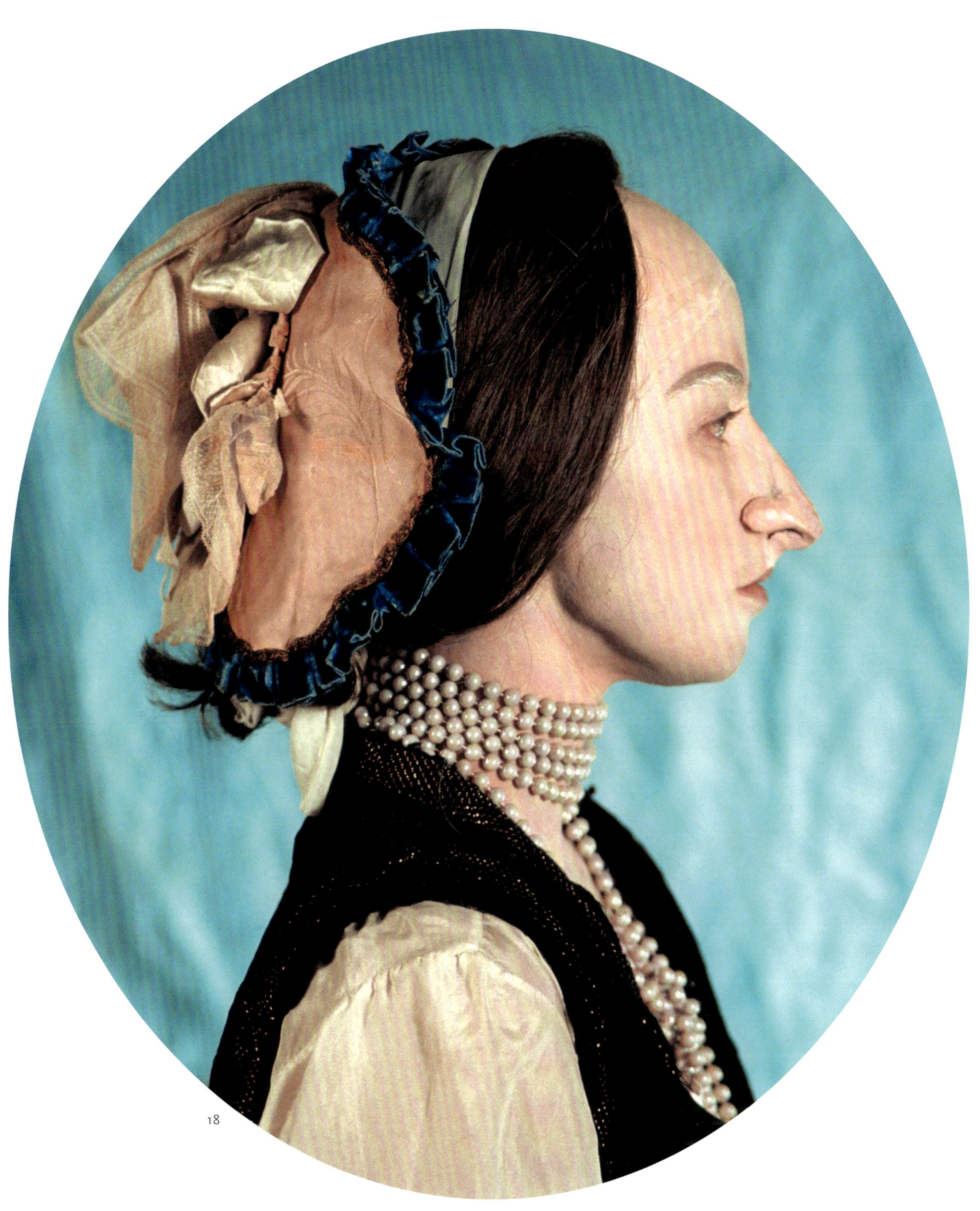

18

# John Baldessari

American, born 1931

19

*Conductor/Pianist/Orchestra
(Red/Yellow/Blue)*, 1995/2007
inkjet print with acrylic paint,
printed 2007
181.29 × 251.14 cm (71⅜ × 98⅞ in.)
Promised Gift from
the Collection of Robert E.
Meyerhoff and Rheda Becker

DURING THE MID- TO LATE 1960S, when conceptual art was brewing and many other artists were engaged with the consumer-themed irony of pop art, Californian John Baldessari made a startling series of paintings that combined large, blown-up snapshots silkscreened on canvas, with short texts hand-lettered below by a sign painter. Carefully drawn under one ill-composed depiction of a nondescript Southern California parking lot are the words "An artist is not merely the slavish announcer of a series of facts, which in this case the camera has had to accept and mechanically record" (fig. 1). Both a formal and a linguistic strategy, Baldessari's text captions the picture and serves as unassuming instruction about the artist's relationship to what is seen. His deadpan declaration that photography—with all its machine-driven, fact-collecting limitations—could be understood as both art and its antithesis established his ongoing relationship to mediated photomechanical images.

Through much of his career, Baldessari has redrawn the traditional boundaries between photography and art. Abandoning painting on canvas by 1970, he began to use photographs in new conceptual contexts by combining, resequencing, and modifying both staged and found images, all the while questioning the veracity of photographic seeing. Much of his work since the early 1970s utilizes photographs appropriated from a stream of media sources such as cinema, television, newspapers, magazines, advertising, and industrial archives. It frequently interprets photography's untoward influence over how the world is perceived by subverting conventional relationships between photographic images, technologies, and audiences. For example, *A Movie: Directional Piece Where People Are Looking* (1972–1973), combines twenty-eight photographs from television and film sources hung in a spiral. Baldessari establishes a cinematic syntax without a narrative plot using stills of TV westerns, news pictures, and crime dramas. Arrows drawn on each photograph chart a spiral by following the direction in which people in the pictures are looking.

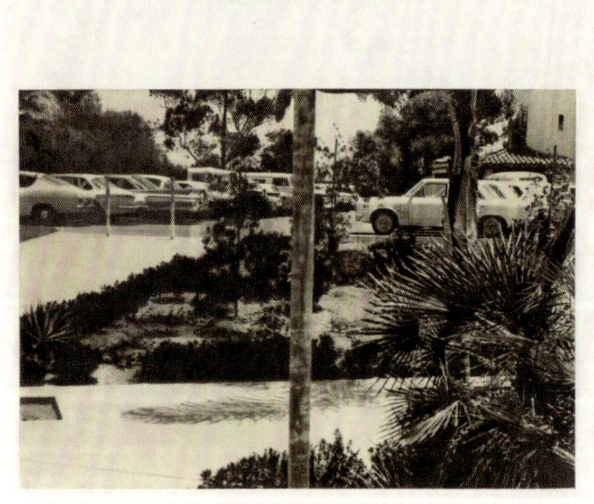



fig. 1: John Baldessari, *An Artist Is Not Merely the Slavish Announcer*, 1966–1968, photographic emulsion, varnish, and gesso on canvas, Whitney Museum of American Art, New York; Purchase, with funds from the Painting and Sculpture Committee and gift of an anonymous donor

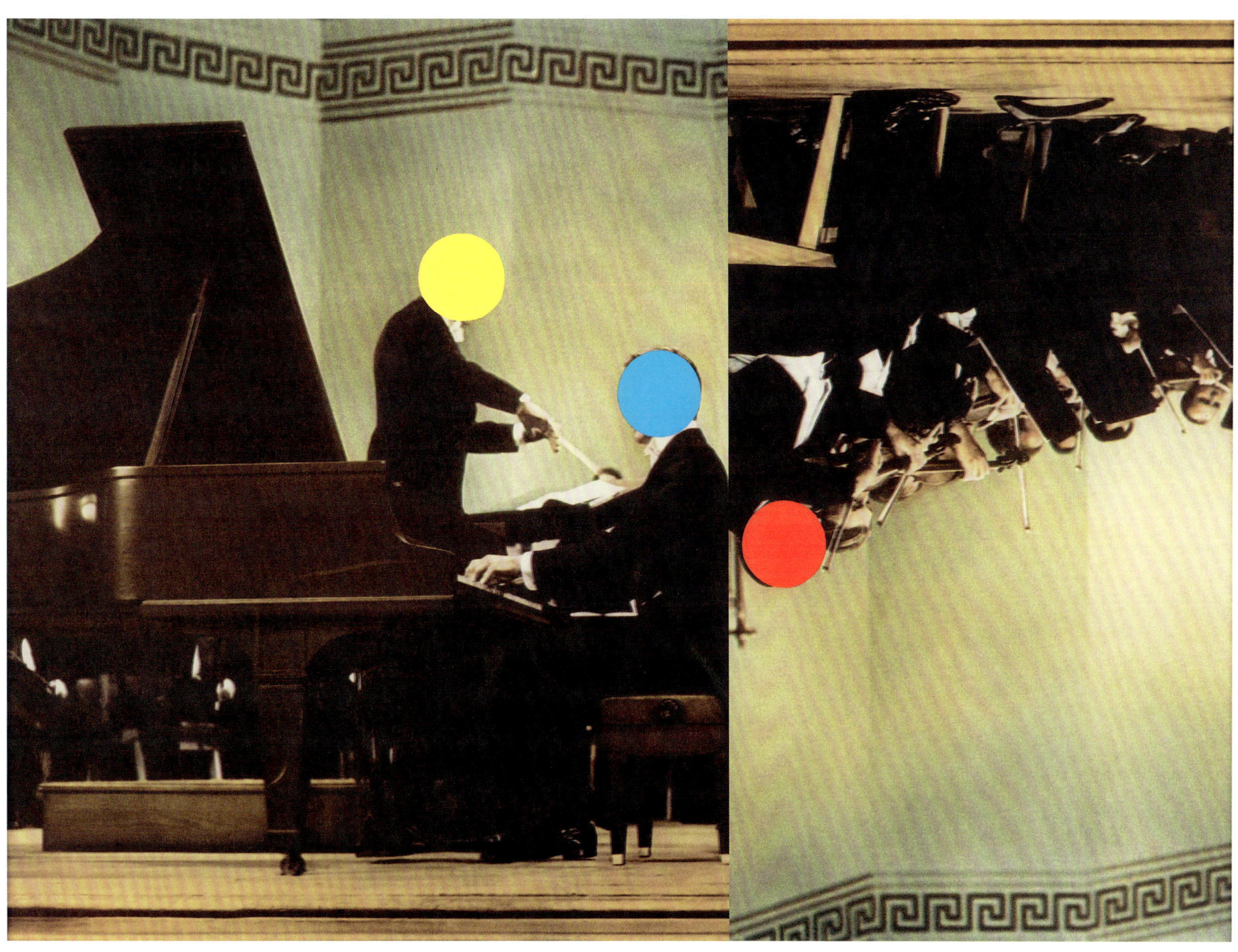

1. *Smells Like Vinyl* (Roger Merians Gallery, New York, July 6–August 18, 1995). See Holland Cotter, "Smells Like Vinyl," *New York Times*, August 4, 1995.

2. Baldessari created his own coded color scheme for the primary-colored dots, which he began to use in the mid-1980s, in which red symbolizes danger, yellow means chaos, and blue stands for perfection or harmony. The maquette for *Conductor/Pianist/Orchestra* shows a blue dot over the conductor's face and yellow on the pianist, an arrangement that was reversed on the final version. The colored dots, which obscure a figure's identity, recall his important photographic sequence *Portraits: Artist's Identity Hidden with Various Hats* (1974).

3. Klaus Hoffer, "Looking Here—and Away. Highways and Byways into Baldessari's Art," in *John Baldessari, Life's Balance: Works 84–04*, ed. Peter Pakesch (Cologne, 2005), 42.

4. *Lizards to Pianist (with Gold Sphere)* was first shown in the 1984 exhibition *Disarming Images: Art for Nuclear Disarmament* organized by Bread and Roses and circulated by the Art Museum Association of America. It toured the United States for several years. At that time Baldessari said, "I want my work to go right to the emotions." Quoted in Chalon Smith, "'Disarming Images' Puts Nuclear Age on Trial," *Los Angeles Times*, March 8, 1986.

5. The photograph at the top of *Lizards to Pianist (with Gold Sphere)* is a cropped, desaturated, and reversed version of the source image for *Conductor/Pianist/Orchestra (Red/Yellow/Blue)*. It appears to show pianist Van Cliburn in a performance conducted by Kirill Kondrashin.

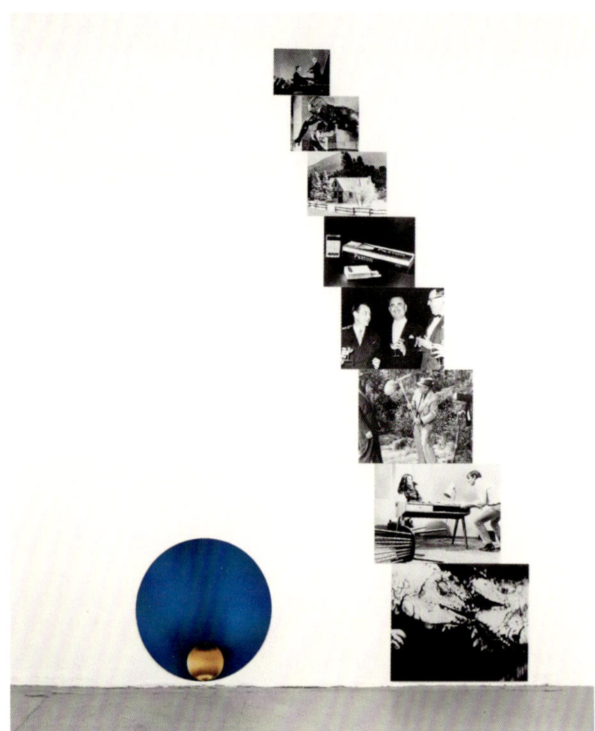

fig. 2: John Baldessari, *Lizards to Pianist (with Gold Sphere)*, 1984, eight gelatin silver prints with one chromogenic print, Courtesy of John Baldessari

In *Conductor/Pianist/Orchestra (Red/Yellow/Blue)* (1995/2007, pl. 19), Baldessari deconstructs the key elements of a concert by inverting the orchestra in vertiginous imbalance with its conductor. The ensemble can no longer follow its leader. Baldessari made a smaller maquette for this work in 1995 for a group exhibition inspired by record album cover art; the final version was not realized until 2007.[1] He painted his trademark colored dots on the photograph, obscuring the faces and identities of the conductor, pianist, and principal violinist. By flipping the right section of the picture, Baldessari disrupts any sense of spatial continuity, purposefully disorienting the viewer and shattering our presumptions about the original photograph. It becomes a graphic rebus as the mind works to reassemble disjointed pieces based on title and visual fragments, only to be thwarted again by the color-coded dots that obscure any real meaning to be derived from the original representation.[2] "Baldessari wages a battle against our innate habits of seeing by means of content as well as form," writes Klaus Hoffer. "He says about his pictures that they are 'lessons in seeing'—first in discovering, then in discarding 'what's important' to us, what the eyes look for first as if this were a matter of course."[3]

Baldessari's photographic works often address the myths of contemporary media culture and their relationship to broad themes in history, psychology, commerce, art, and music. In 1984, he created an innovative construction of seven black-and-white photographs stacked precariously next to a variegated blue form surrounding a symbolic gold sphere. *Lizards to Pianist (with Gold Sphere)* unspools a teetering cinematic pillar of stills, vacillating between threatening and camp images (fig. 2). From top to bottom, these progress from a primal depiction of nature (lizards cavorting) through folly (a man attacked by a B-movie creature) to a musical performance (a pianist).[4] Seemingly ready to tumble off the stack onto the gold sphere below, this final photograph of pianist Van Cliburn is the same picture that Baldessari altered in *Conductor/Pianist/Orchestra (Red/Yellow/Blue)*.[5] Once again he has recycled the photograph, shifting its context and reconstituting its meaning several times to mediate, interrogate, and repurpose a visual representation of music. BROOKMAN

# Louise Lawler
American, born 1947

<hr>

**20**

*Portrait (Twine)*, 1993/2003
silver dye bleach print
60.33 × 50.17 cm (23 ¾ × 19 ¾ in.)
Collection of Rheda Becker

<hr>

 Louise Lawler, part of the "Pictures Generation," has photographed works of art that were in the process of being installed, exhibited, sold, or enjoyed.[1] Rich in connotation and humor, her works make explicit and critique the network of connections among artists, dealers, collectors, and museum curators that together constitute the "art world." The photograph *Portrait (Twine)* (1993, pl. 20), for instance, documents a framed drawing of a ball of twine placed just to the top right of a white lampshade. As Lawler's title cheekily notes, this is a portrait of twine. But in fact, it is a portrait of a drawing of twine. Her title prompts viewers to question the work's biography.[2] With its close cropping, omissions, and inclusions, the image engages viewers in a game of visual recognition that hinges on a broader knowledge of art and its histories.

Lawler's photographs depict the sometimes-odd views of art in office buildings and collectors' homes, as well as in carefully curated museum and gallery spaces. In *Portrait (Twine)*, the awkwardly situated lamp to the left of the drawing emphasizes its placement in a private setting—one that Lawler, in turn, makes public through her photograph.[3] Little of the surrounding wall is visible, but the ball of twine is not alone: the reflection of two other works on the opposite wall can be glimpsed on the frame's glazing. The casualness of the space is suggested, too, by the drawing's somewhat slapdash framing, not perfectly centered within the mat's window.

Other photographs by Lawler further expand our understanding of *Portrait (Twine)*. For instance, *87, 63, 93/2000* (1993–2000, fig. 1), depicts the same wall, and shows the drawing installed in a bedroom alongside another framed work, in an intimate space to which few people would have access. Another view is reproduced in Douglas Crimp's seminal 1993 book on postmodern art, *On the Museum's Ruins*,

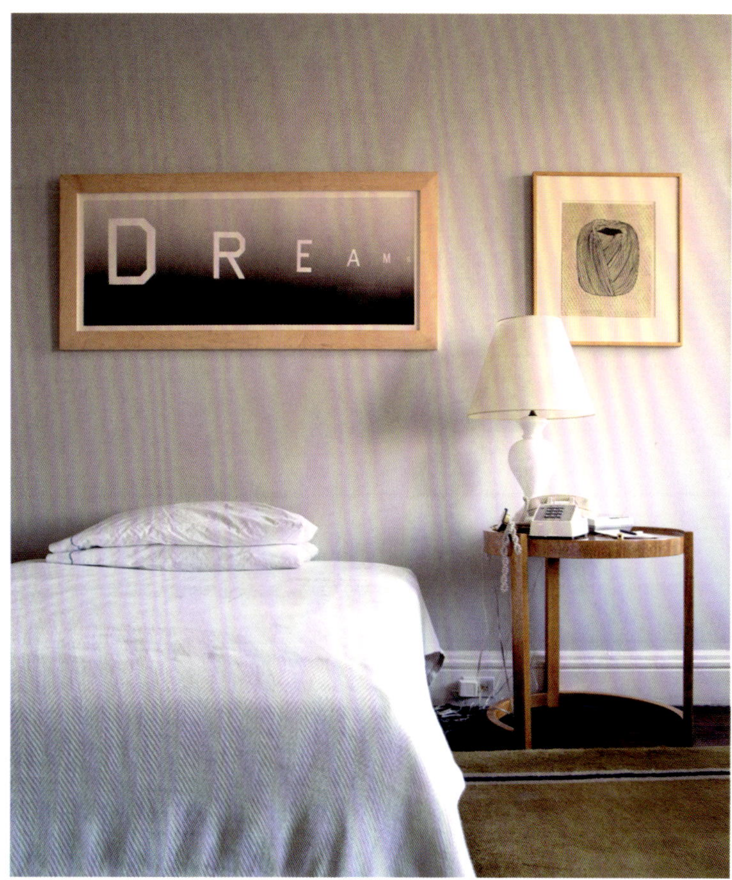


fig. 1: Louise Lawler, *87, 63, 93/2000*, 1993–2000, silver dye bleach print, Courtesy of the artist and Metro Pictures, New York

1. Douglas Crimp and Louise Lawler, "Prominence Given, Authority Taken," *Grey Room* 4 (Summer 2001): 71, and Benjamin H. D. Buchloh, "Louise Lawler: Memory Images of Art Under Spectacle," in *Louise Lawler: Adjusted* (Museum Ludwig, Cologne, 2013), 73–87.

2. Louise Lawler, "[Untitled]," 9, and Helmut Draxler, "Art into Culture," 70–72, both in *Louise Lawler: A Spot on the Wall*, ed. Hedwig Saxenhuber (Kunstverein, Munich, and Neue Galerie, Graz, and De Appel, Amsterdam, 1998).

3. See Helen Molesworth on the public/private aspect of Lawler's work in "Louise Lawler: Just the Facts," in *Twice Untitled and Other Pictures (looking back)* (Wexner Center for the Arts, Columbus, 2006), 144–145.

4. Douglas Crimp, *On the Museum's Ruins* (Cambridge, MA, 1993), 38–39.

5. *Louise Lawler: An Arrangement of Pictures*, unpaginated.

6. Rachel Wolff, "Impressive Proportions," *New York*, May 1, 2011, http://nymag.com/arts/art/features/louise-lawler-2011-5/; Lawler, "Prominence Given, Authority Taken," 73. See also Douglas Eklund, *The Pictures Generation* (Metropolitan Museum of Art, New York, 2009). On Lawler's "insider" status see Bruce Hainley, "Mata Hari Takes a Picture," *Frieze* 85 (September 2004): 80–87.

7. See Andrea Fraser, "In and Out of Place," reprinted in *Louise Lawler*, ed. Helen Molesworth with Taylor Walsh (Cambridge, MA, and London, 2013), 1–13.

on which Lawler collaborated.[4] Here Lawler dispels the mystery of the setting and the art depicted, by providing a lengthy text—including object information and exhibition and ownership histories—through which we learn that the drawing is by Roy Lichtenstein and titled *Ball of Twine* (1963), and that the work just to its left is *Dreams* (1987) by Ed Ruscha. Lawler also reveals that Lichtenstein's *Ball of Twine* hangs in the apartment of prominent art dealer Leo Castelli, who throughout his five-decade career defined how American art should be exhibited and consumed in the period after World War II. The text, reproduced alongside the peek into the room, gives a sense of the close relationships Castelli built with the artists he represented, including Ruscha and Lichtenstein. As Lawler notes, Lichtenstein gave Castelli the drawing in 1964; since then, it has been exhibited in major shows devoted to the artist and to the dealer that have helped shape the discourses on these two protean figures. Adding a humorous tone to the otherwise straightforward, factual information, Lawler notes that this "will mean more to some of you than others."[5]

Lawler herself is part of the interconnected world that she photographs. Soon after graduating from Cornell University in 1969, she started working at Castelli's New York gallery, the epicenter of the art world. There she met and befriended another gallery employee, Janelle Reiring, who along with Helene Winer from the alternative art venue Artists Space in New York founded Metro Pictures Gallery in 1980.[6] Lawler therefore navigated two very different sectors of the city's artistic milieu, from the established Castelli Gallery to the experimental Artists Space. Fusing appropriation, photography, and text, and drawing on her own intimate knowledge of the workings of the art world, Lawler playfully but potently critiques the institutions of art as only an insider can.[7] UREÑA

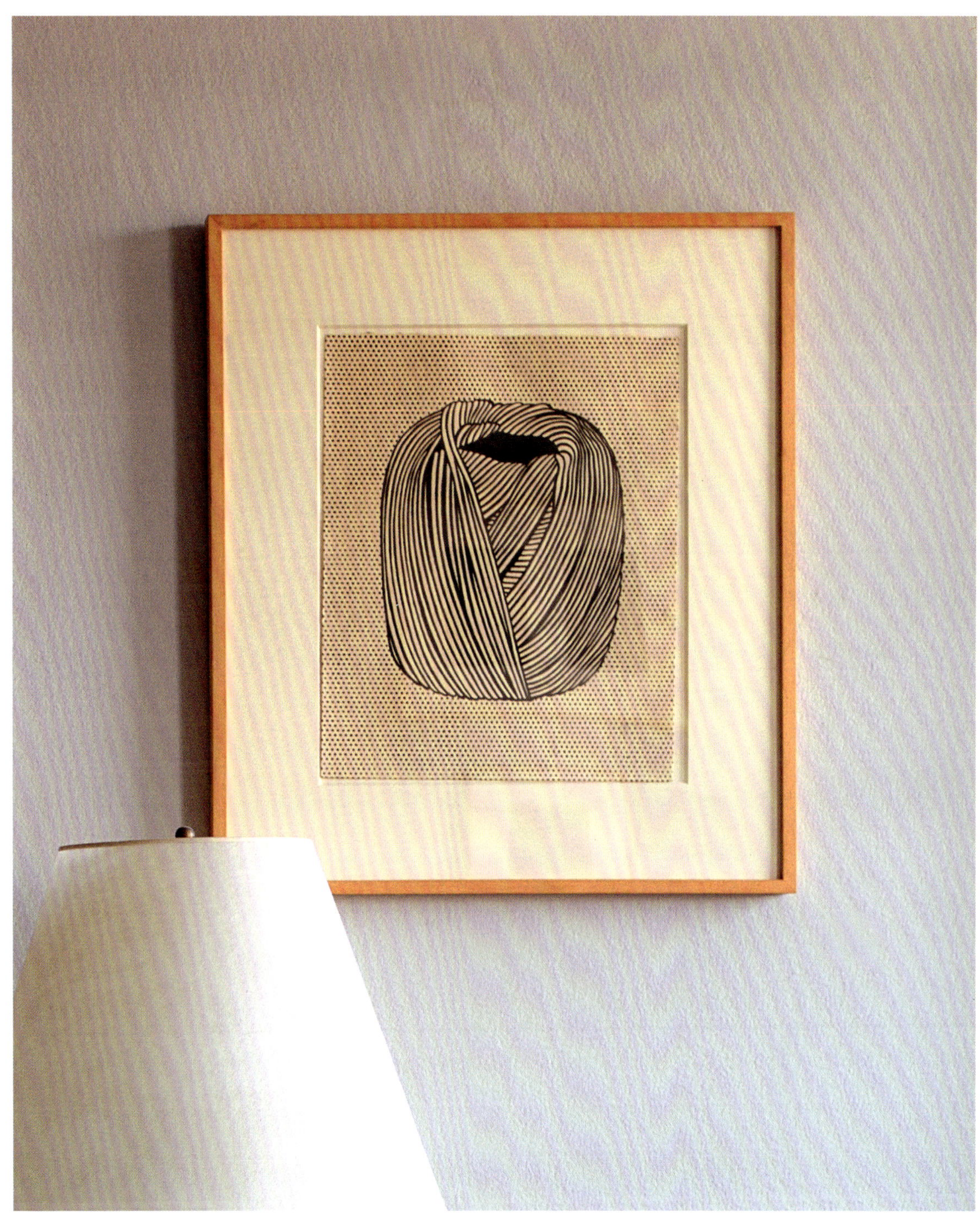

# Hiroshi Sugimoto

Japanese, born 1948

---

### 21

*Tampa, Florida*, 1979
gelatin silver print
152.56 × 182.56 cm (60⅟₁₆ × 71⅞ in.)
Promised Gift from the
Collection of Robert E.
Meyerhoff and Rheda Becker

---

### 22

*Anne Boleyn*, 1999
gelatin silver print
182.25 × 152.4 cm (71¾ × 60 in.)
Promised Gift from the
Collection of Robert E.
Meyerhoff and Rheda Becker

---

### 23

*Caribbean Sea, Jamaica*, 1980
gelatin silver print
152.72 × 182.56 cm (60⅛ × 71⅞ in.)
Promised Gift from the
Collection of Robert E.
Meyerhoff and Rheda Becker

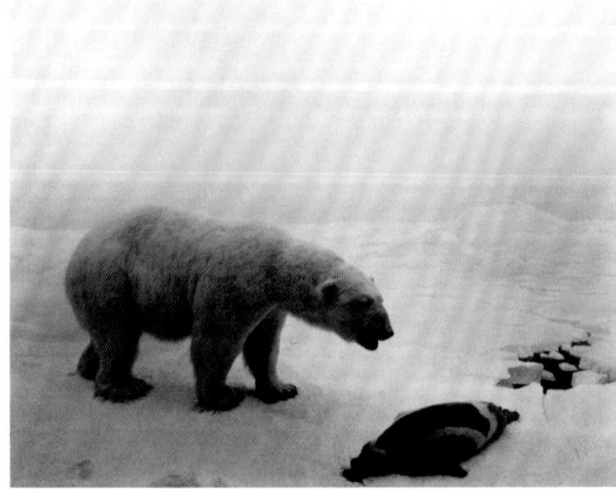

fig. 1: Hiroshi Sugimoto, *Polar Bear*, 1976, gelatin silver print,
Photograph courtesy of the artist

ON THE SURFACE, Hiroshi Sugimoto's photographs record the precise details of what we see and experience—movie theaters, oceans and sky, or mannequins in wax museums—but he frequently subverts the idea of direct representation to probe philosophical problems like temporality, wonder, and history. For example, Sugimoto's *Theater* series depicts cinema screens that reflect every frame of a feature film, symbolizing the movie's duration rather than the projected image. His seascapes are composed and printed to accentuate their abstract possibilities rather than a representational view of the ocean. And the wax museum figures that appear in his *Portraits* are isolated against black backgrounds and lit like the faces in Renaissance paintings, focusing on their illusory qualities and blurring the history of the people depicted.

Born in Japan in 1948, Sugimoto studied economic and political theory before moving to Los Angeles in 1970 to attend the Art Center College of Design, where he learned photography. He soon settled in New York, where in the late 1970s his photographic career took off. Inspired by conceptual and minimal art, as well as the photographs of Bernd and Hilla Becher, he moved toward a more theoretical practice that culminated in his groundbreaking series of cinema screens. In *Tampa, Florida* (1979, pl. 21), the historic architecture of an old-time movie palace is illuminated by a beatific glow from the screen.[1] Sugimoto set up his camera on a tripod in the balcony and opened the shutter for the length of the entire feature, a process that superimposes each frame of the movie onto a sheet of film so the screen is recorded as a white rectangle. The picture that results from this conceptual act references the underlying photographic and temporal syntax of cinema.[2] The static white glow suggests the iconic "silver screen" of Hollywood's golden age and signifies the intangible, seductive gulf between real life and a virtual world represented by movies.

For his next project Sugimoto turned his attention from the illusionistic world of cinema to the fundamental elements of air and water. *Caribbean Sea, Jamaica* (1980, pl. 23), the first in his monumental series of seascapes begun in 1980, was a breakthrough for him, as it reduced the traditional notion of a seascape to its most basic visual forms: equal rectangles of sea and sky. Untethered by any sense of gravity, the viewer has a feeling of hovering weightlessly over an expanse of calm, dark water, facing a sharply etched horizon that delineates the arc of the earth where the water meets the sky. The lower zone of tenebrous, silvery waves, their movement frozen by the camera, aligns in perfect balance with the bright sky above, which reveals just a hint of weather. There is little sense of scale or perspective as the picture drifts between the illusion of deep space and the perfectly flat photographic object. Even though Sugimoto's compositional framework is always the same in his *Seascapes,* no two are alike. Subtle changes in light, weather, time, season, and location temper their mood, creating a sense of timelessness when viewed as a group. Each picture is immutable, finite, and flat, but together as a series they present the sea as a constantly changing and endless natural phenomenon.

Precipitated by his early pictures of dioramas in the American Museum of Natural History—a series that includes deadpan shots of taxidermy animals (fig. 1) and mannequins dressed as early human ancestors—Sugimoto renewed his interest in the nature of photographic realism and its relation to theatrical space in his 1999–2000 photographs of wax figures. For his *Portraits* series he visited the Madame Tussauds wax museum in London with its collection of highly detailed, life-size representations of King Henry VIII and his consorts, modeled in part from northern Renaissance paintings by Hans Holbein the Younger and others. Before photographing these figures, Sugimoto studied the intricate lighting, flattened ceremonial space, and illusionistic effects of Renaissance portraiture to help him understand their historical context. *Anne*

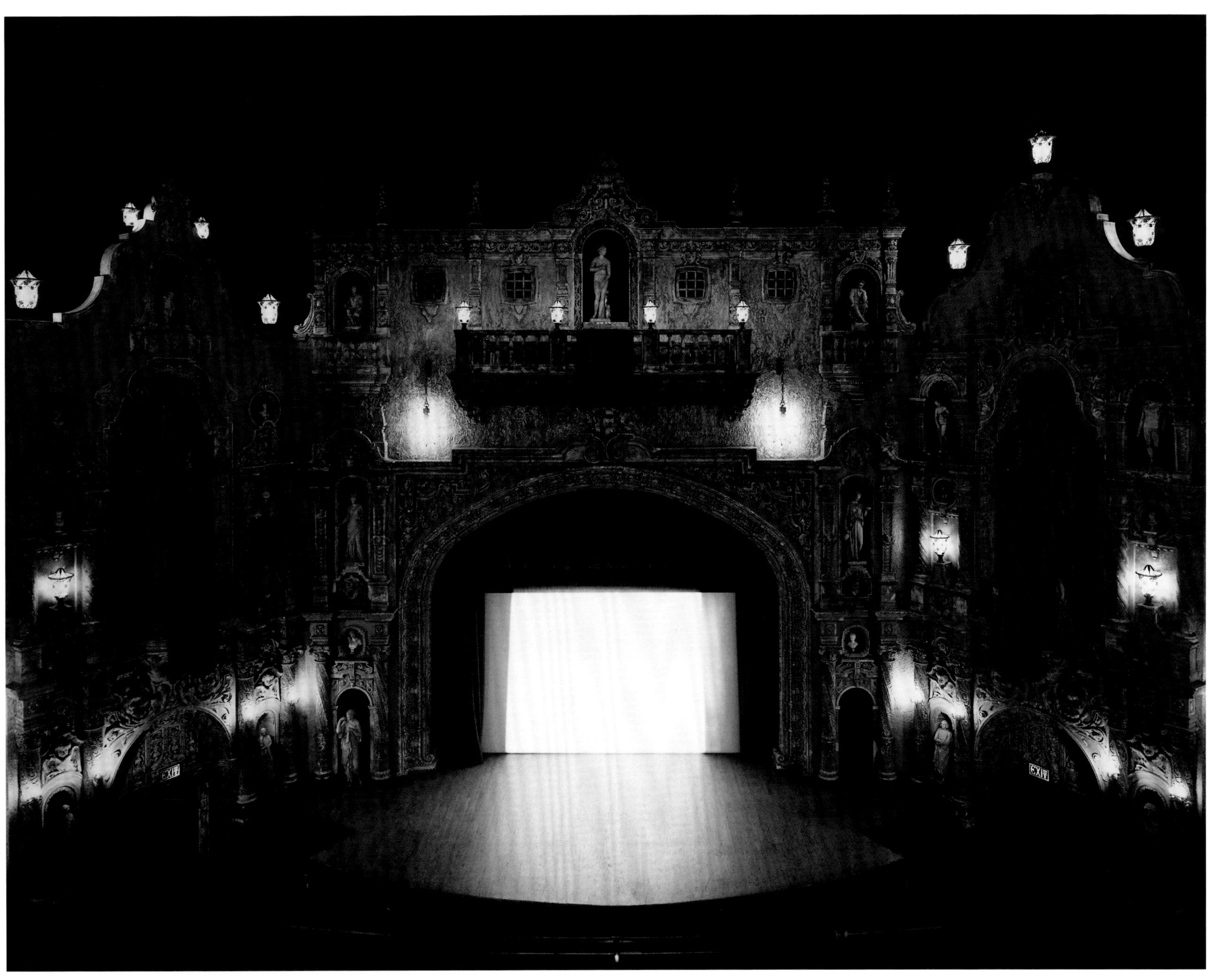

1. Designed by John Eberson and opened in 1926, the Tampa Theater's interior simulates an opulent Mediterranean-style courtyard, complete with Spanish Romanesque arches and statuary.

2. Unlike movie technology, in which individual film frames are projected one after another twenty-four times a second and the persistence of images falling on the retina allows our brains to perceive the illusion of motion, Sugimoto's camera records each frame, one atop the next, so that the exposure from light accumulates and overexposes the film, which prints as a white glow reflected from the screen.

3. Anne Boleyn became King Henry VIII's second wife in 1533 and was the mother of Queen Elizabeth I, who was crowned in 1558. Henry had his marriage to Catherine of Aragon annulled in order to marry Boleyn, a provocation that helped precipitate the monarch's split with the Catholic Church. Boleyn was subsequently executed in 1536, just before Henry's marriage to his third wife, Jane Seymour. The painted portrait by an unknown artist, now in the collection of the National Portrait Gallery, London, is oil on panel and dated to the late sixteenth century. It depicts Boleyn in almost identical clothing and jewelry as that found on her wax figure at Madame Tussauds. However, the wax figure presents an invented full-length likeness of Boleyn, who is seated and playing a lute. Although she was known as an accomplished musician, no sixteenth-century likeness shows her with a lute.

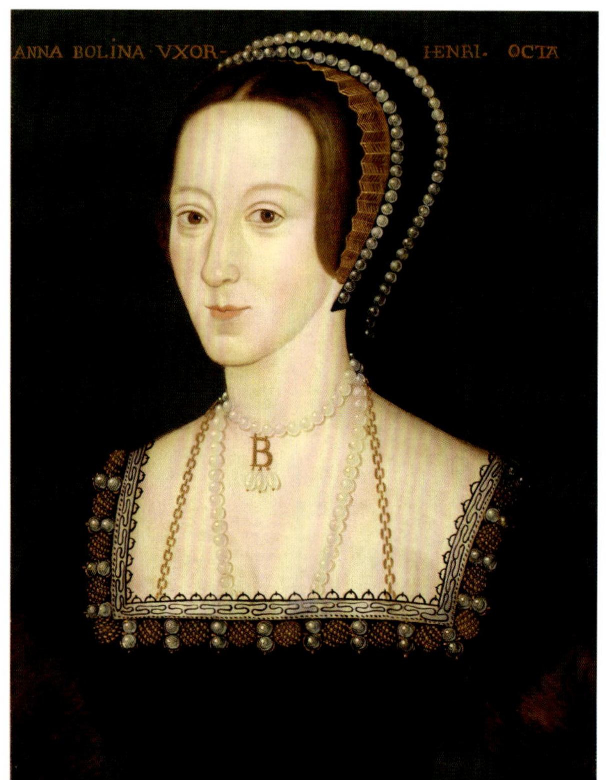


fig. 2: Unknown artist, *Anne Boleyn*, late 16th century, oil on panel, National Portrait Gallery, London

*Boleyn* (1999, pl. 22) depicts one of the most intriguing figures in British history, whose contested marriage to Henry VIII advanced the rise of the English Reformation. The wax museum figure was inspired by a late sixteenth-century portrait painted by an unknown artist years after Boleyn's execution (fig. 2).[3] Sugimoto's portrait of Boleyn, in turn, depicts a lifeless, hyperrealistic simulation where she appears, as she does in the sixteenth-century painting, in front of a flat, black background; the photograph is lit seamlessly to highlight the sumptuous manufactured surfaces of the wax figure, costume, and jewelry. By removing the figure from its wax-museum context, Sugimoto realigns it not only with Renaissance art, but also modern ideas about how historical subjects can be represented by photographers. By depicting a wax facsimile sculpted after a posthumous painting, which in turn represents just a shadow of Anne Boleyn's real life, Sugimoto's version of the "royal portrait" questions our perception of historical portraiture and playfully shows how removed it can become from history itself.

With a mix of impeccable technique, conceptual rigor, and historical allusions, Sugimoto's photographs spotlight the shifting relationships between what he depicts — his subjects — and the theoretical nature of photographic representation. He has frequently worked with the complex idea that photographs can be a kind of visual simulation or index of his subject, while also functioning as aesthetic interpretations. But rather than record the "decisive moments" of what we see, his photographs pose open-ended questions about how we see and understand the world through art, science, nature, religion, and history. BROOKMAN

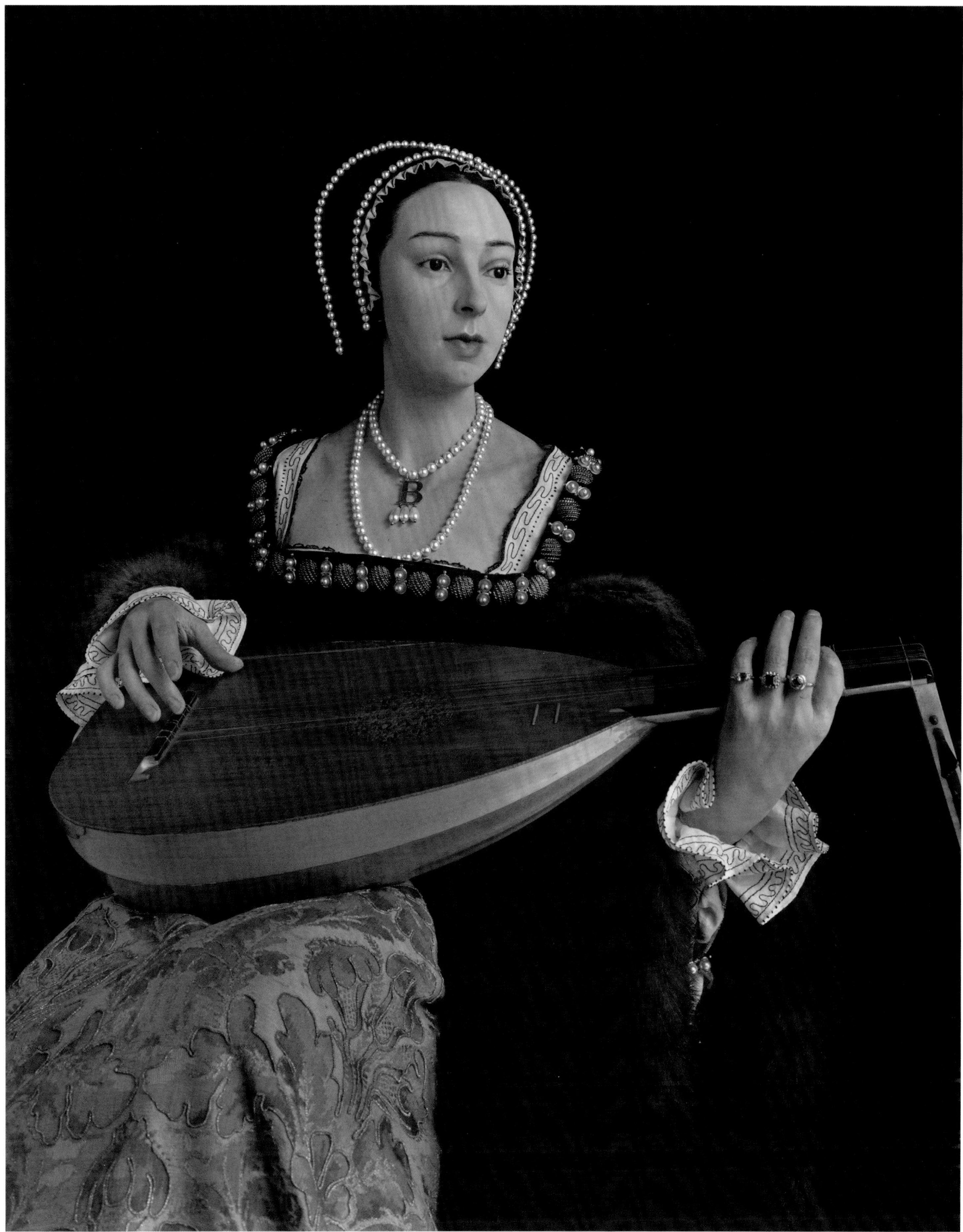

# James Welling
American, born 1951

---

**24**

*0467,* from the series
*Glass House,* 2009
inkjet print
103.19 × 145.73 cm (40⅝ × 57⅜ in.)
Promised Gift from the
Collection of Robert E.
Meyerhoff and Rheda Becker

---

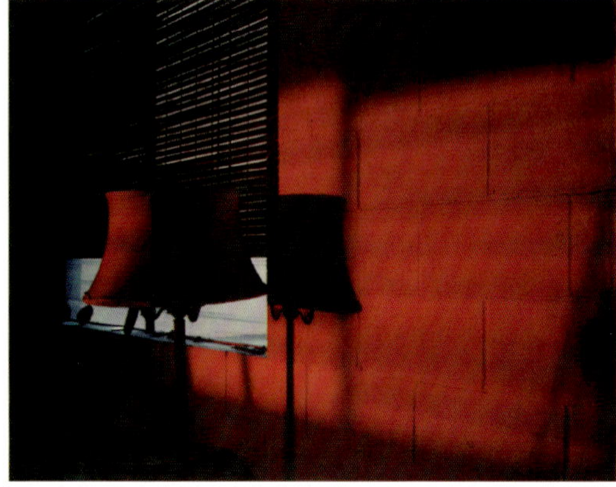

fig. 1: James Welling, *Red Dawn,* 1976, polacolor type 108 print,
Courtesy the artist and Regen Projects, Los Angeles

FOR OVER FORTY YEARS, James Welling has pursued a rich and diverse photographic practice. Employing a wide range of techniques, such as photogram and both monochromatic and color processes, he adopts heterogeneous subjects: these include incisive studies of modern and historic architecture; ruminations on particular landscapes linked to his personal history; muscular still lifes of objects, textures, and light sources; and rigorous formal abstractions. Yet throughout his work, thematic constants emerge—the interplay of light and color on form, the intensity of place coupled with memory. Welling chooses different formats to suit each project; his photographs operate at the crossroads of material and conceptual practice.

In the early 1970s, Welling studied in Los Angeles at the California Institute of the Arts (CalArts), earning an MFA in 1974. There, under the influence of his mentor, John Baldessari (pl. 19), the young artist made videos and mounted a thesis show of collages of photographs from books and magazines. Though Welling had earlier been entranced when he stumbled upon a copy of Paul Strand's 1940 portfolio of Mexico photographs, he had only dabbled in photography when he began making experimental pictures with a Polaroid camera in 1975. The prints he produced, of confined interior spaces and objects, demonstrate his early preoccupations with surface and color— inspired, in part, by a youthful admiration for the paintings of Edward Hopper—through their carefully structured compositions saturated with lush hues, achieved by heating the prints during processing (fig. 1). After purchasing a view camera, he taught himself how to develop and print. Fascinated by the "shapes of things," Welling then embarked on a probing study of architecture, denoting the contours of Los Angeles buildings with austere clarity from 1976 to 1978.[1] After moving to New York, he focused more intently on form to play with the line between representation and abstraction in series made in the early to mid-1980s that depicted aluminum foil, drapes, gelatin, and tiles. All of these works, which cultivated an open-ended ambiguity, participated in the shift embraced by his CalArts peers and others of the "Pictures Generation," such as David Salle, Matt Mullican, Cindy Sherman (pls. 17, 18), and Laurie Simmons, who variously explored the ways that images dictate our perceptions of the world.

Welling's conceptual turn, however, was particularly rooted in the parameters and history of the photographic medium itself. Throughout these years, he was also making *Diary/Landscape* (1977–1986, fig. 2). Photographing the pressed leaves, flowers, feathers, and drawings incorporated in the 1840–1841 journal of his great-great-grandparents, he later realized that his ancestors' act of flattening these delicate scraps between pages mirrored the earliest photograms of botanical specimens made contemporaneously by Anna Atkins. Paired with landscapes of his native Connecticut, Welling's project, steeped in a sense of layered history, both personal and photographic, investigated the intersection of materiality, place, and memory. Other long-running landscape projects continued to keep aspects of Welling's art anchored in New England and a sense of the past. In *Railroad Photographs* (1987–2000), he charted rail lines crisscrossing the Northeast, which, while invoking earlier precedents that celebrated them as triumphs of technology, deliberated upon their vestigial effect on the landscape in the postindustrial present. He also revisited sites important to him in his youth with *Connecticut Landscapes* (1998–2007).

In 1995, Welling moved back to Los Angeles to take up a post teaching at UCLA and began a persistent engagement with abstractions and photograms in series such as *New Abstractions* (1998–2000), which used paper strips to create illusory architectonic spaces, and *Flowers* (2004–2011), in which he employed black-and-white photograms of botanical specimens as negatives, enlarging them on chromogenic paper and manipulating color filters to create vibrant prints of the floral shapes (fig. 3).

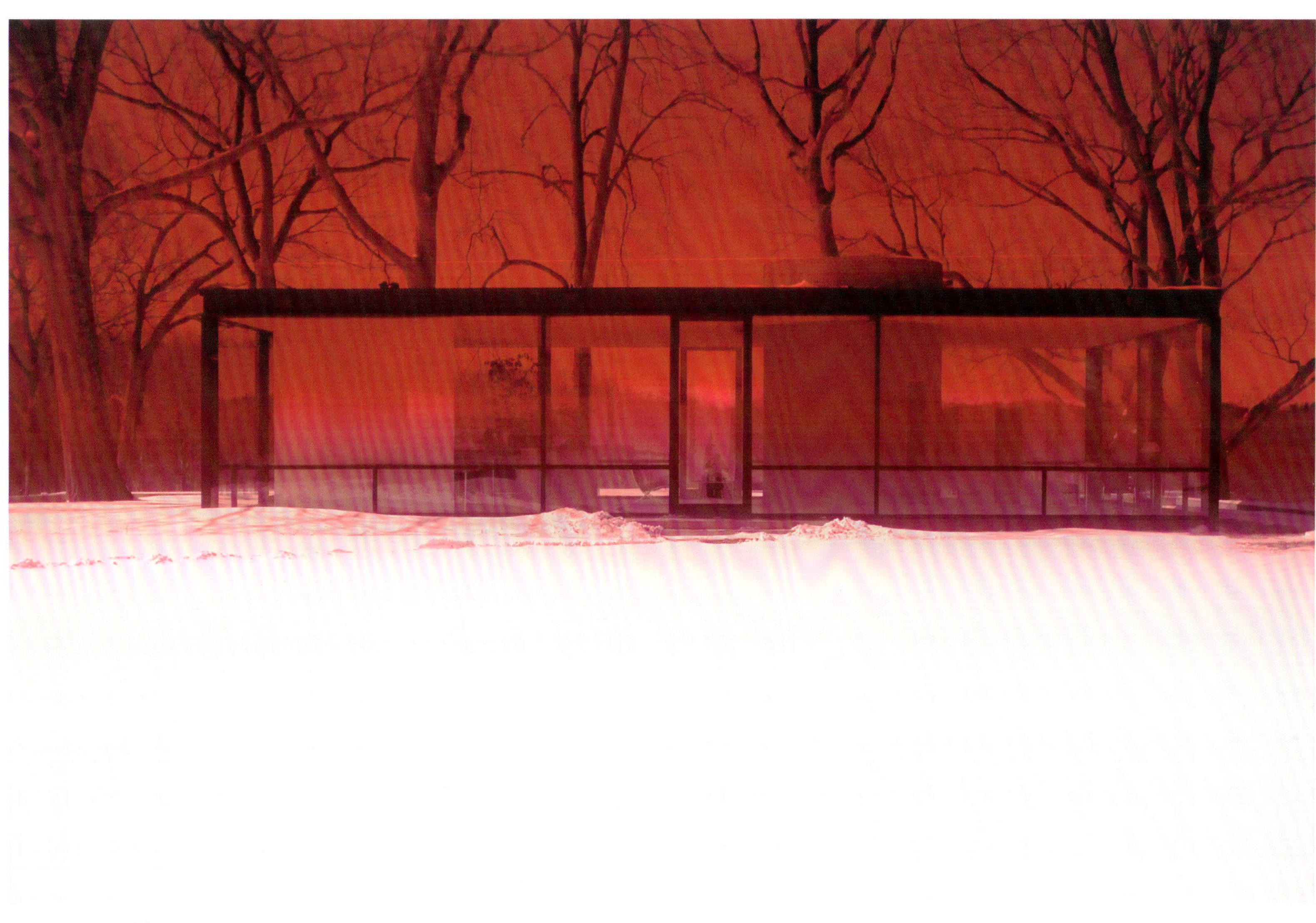

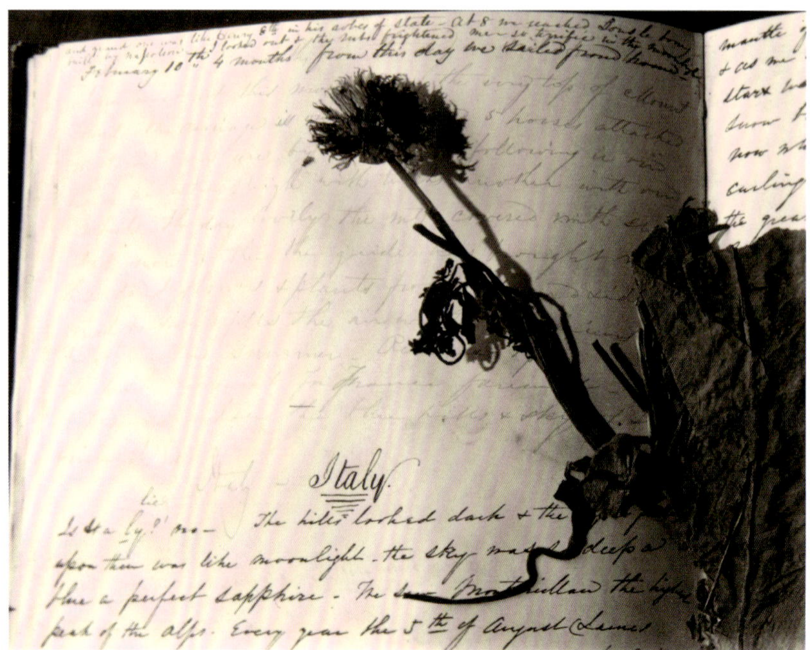

fig. 2: James Welling, *A10*, 1977, gelatin silver print, from the series *Diary of Elizabeth and James Dixon (1840–41)/Connecticut Landscapes*, *1977–86*, The Art Institute of Chicago, Comer Foundation Fund

Indeed, color grew more and more central to his work in Southern California. In *Hexachromes* (2005), Welling sought to demonstrate how the color receptors in human eyes function. Photographing a plant by making many exposures using different colored filters on the same piece of film, he created a rainbow effect from the shadows moving across the plant's form between each exposure.

These manifold practices converged in *Glass House*, Welling's extended study of Philip Johnson's modernist glass-walled residence built in 1949 and sited on forty-seven acres in New Canaan, Connecticut. Though Welling initially began the project in 2006 as a commission for *New York* magazine, he photographed the house several times over the next three years for his own purposes. Continually revisiting this land-mark further fostered his longstanding commitment to Connecticut's geography. The house also appealed to Welling's knowledge of architectural history: for Johnson had not only intended the house's transparent walls to connect the structure to the landscape, blurring the boundaries between inside and outside, but also understood its modernism to be shaped by architectural precedents, from classical design to nineteenth-century iron-and-glass pavilions and, finally, Ludwig Mies van der Rohe's Farnsworth House, which Welling had also previously photographed.[2]

In addition to their historical heft, Welling's *Glass House* photographs speak to his captivation with the union of light and color. As with *Flowers* and *Hexachromes,* Welling employed multiple filters with his digital camera—clear, colored, or fogged plastic; clear or tinted, uneven glass; and a diffraction filter, which caused bursts of light—to remake the modernist icon into something beyond itself.[3] From different areas of the picture plane, Welling's prints variously emanate incandescent blues, yellows, greens, or reds, seemingly divorced from naturalistic hues. Rejecting the idea that his colors are artificial, however, Welling commented that, as he "became sensitized to unnat-ural colors, I realized that they were not unnatural—I just hadn't noticed them. Becom-ing attuned to color has led me to think that we actually see more color than we normally perceive." Johnson's architecture became a means for Welling to "liberate color," making a sustained commentary on the reverberation of color in human perception.[4]

1. "On Photography and Influence: James Welling in Conversation with Eva Respini," in *James Welling: Monograph*, ed. James Crump (New York, 2013), 120.

2. Noam M. Elcott, "Reflections in Glass Houses," in *James Welling: Glass House*, ed. Denise Bratton (Bologna, 2010), 69.

3. "James Welling—As Told to Arthur Ou," *Artforum*, January 26, 2010, www.artforum.com/words/id=24743.

4. "On Photography and Influence: James Welling in Conversation with Eva Respini," 124.

5. "James Welling—As Told to Arthur Ou."

6. "I am repeating the history of the Claude glass by putting colored filters in front of my lens." "A Conversation with Sylvia Lavin, Los Angeles, February 28, 2010," in *James Welling: Glass House*, 28.

Welling's views of the Glass House appear as if color has been poured into the negative space around the architecture. In *0467* (2009, pl. 24), vermilion envelops the house and magenta glows within its confines. Though punctuated by the dark, irregular forms of the trees and the controlled lines of the house's structure, the incarnadine hues create a sense that the viewer is seeing *through* the image, much as the glass house itself can be seen through as "a lens in the landscape," as Welling describes it.[5] Welling conceives of his filters as a present-day version of the "Claude glass," an eighteenth-century optical device (named after the painter Claude Lorrain) consisting of a convex piece of dark or colored glass that reflected a scene in subdued colors to reveal its tonal values for landscape artists. Welling's picture thus resonates with this historical act of aesthetic looking—similar to the Atkins echo in *Diary/Landscape*—but the darkness and reductive scale of the Claude glass has instead been inverted and writ large in the radiant color of the print.[6]

Yet more than that, the house is a vehicle for Welling's material practice. In the physical act of making the photograph, he was gazing through numerous translucent layers: the glass walls of the building, which both reveal and reflect the landscape around and through it; the camera lens; and, most significantly, the layers Welling imposed with the tinted filters. In *0467*, he embeds a trace of this act of looking by recording his reflection, melded with his tripod, in the doorway of the house—it is one of the few prints in the series in which his figure is visible. Effectively placing himself, at one with lens and filters, at the almost perspectival vanishing point of the composition, Welling is a ghostly figure, standing at the threshold between visibility and invisibility. Fusing together the strands of his decades-long scrutiny of light, color, and form, the *Glass House* series is a luminous meditation on the ability of the photographic medium to channel the potency of place intertwined with history and serve as an emblem of the experience of perception in the present. WAGGONER

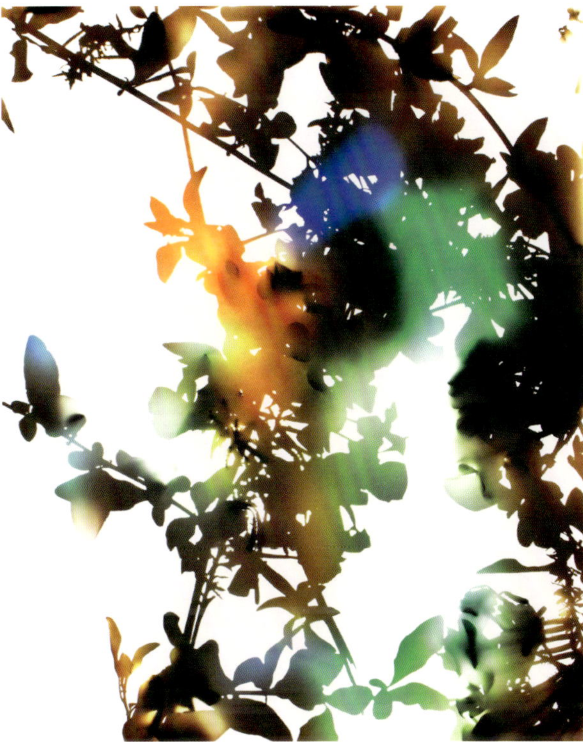

fig. 3: James Welling, *21*, 2006, chromogenic print, Courtesy the artist and Regen Projects, Los Angeles

# Vera Lutter

German, born 1960

---

25

*World Trade Center 7, III:*
*October 30, 2007*, 2007
gelatin silver print
174.94 × 124.46 cm (68⅞ × 49 in.)
Promised Gift from the
Collection of Robert E.
Meyerhoff and Rheda Becker

---

FROM THE MOMENT she arrived in New York City in 1993 as a thirty-three-year-old art student, Vera Lutter was entranced with her new home. Although she found the country "largely foreign" and her neighborhood "really bad," the city itself was intoxicating and liberating. "I was overwhelmed by the sheer magnitude of the place and the speed,"[1] she later asserted, the "mix of people and culture…the general energy, the light, and the ways the city presents itself.…New York was absolutely new to me, and I was profoundly inspired by it all."[2] Many other artists before and since have been moved by New York City, but few have devised as strikingly original a method of depicting it—one that mimics its scale, embodies its monumentality, and rivals its ambition yet also turns our perceptions of both it and photography inside out.

Born in Kaiserslautern, a small town near Frankfurt, Germany, Lutter came to maturity during the "difficult…volatile, and aggressive" decades of the 1960s and 1970s when "anxiety and violence were in the air at all times."[3] After graduating from the Akademie der Bildenden Künste München, she received a fellowship to study in New York. Although she intended to focus on sculpture, "something magical happened to me when I came to New York." She inherited a lease on a commercial loft on Eighth Avenue: "From the twenty-seventh floor, I had a breathtaking view of the busy Garment District center…and of course the top of the Empire State rose above everything else. The loft faced east and the morning sun would shine in, an incredible golden red glow that would wake us up." In the evening, she made "it a ritual to be home by midnight to watch the lights of the Empire State Building switch off"; she and her roommate even made "bets on which colors would be lit on different nights." Overwhelmed by "the spirit of novelty and observation," she determined to capture the experience of living in that space.[4] She drew on her background in conceptual art, turning the loft itself into a giant camera obscura by blackening the windows, save for one small pinhole—the "seeing eye"—which projected an inverted image of the outside world onto the opposite wall where she hung large sheets of photographic paper. To insert "a certain rawness that is so typical for New York, despite its charms," she determined to work in black and white; to maintain the directness and immediacy of her original experience, she decided to exhibit the laterally reversed negative image and not make positive prints.[5]

For the next three years, Lutter focused exclusively on depicting New York, working in the Financial District, Gramercy Park, Fulton Landing, and Columbus Avenue, striving to make pictures that both "repeated and transformed" her experiences.[6] She quickly discovered that each of her photographs embodies several complex and interdependent variables: time, movement, light, and space. Because her exposures are long—almost always four, six, or eight hours and often extending over several days or even weeks—people, moving objects, and fleeting incidents are recorded as ghostly presences or not at all. She also realized that because her photographs collapse many hours into one picture and are denied the specificity of a single moment, they assume a timeless universality. And with their elevated vantage point, their absence of people and cars, her views of the deserted city are also uncannily silent, as if observed in a dream or by an omniscient power.

Starting in 1998 she looked beyond New York for subjects, exploring other cities around the world as well as industry and modes of transportation, but she always circled back to her adopted home, most notably in a series of pictures made from the World Trade Center in 2007. These photographs are, of course, about not just New York City but also the devastating attacks of September 11, 2001. Deeply attuned to the anxious tenor of the time, Lutter rose to the challenge of paying homage to the victims of one of the most tragic events in American history while simultaneously acknowledging the profound impact those attacks had on the psyche of the city and the nation. As indicated

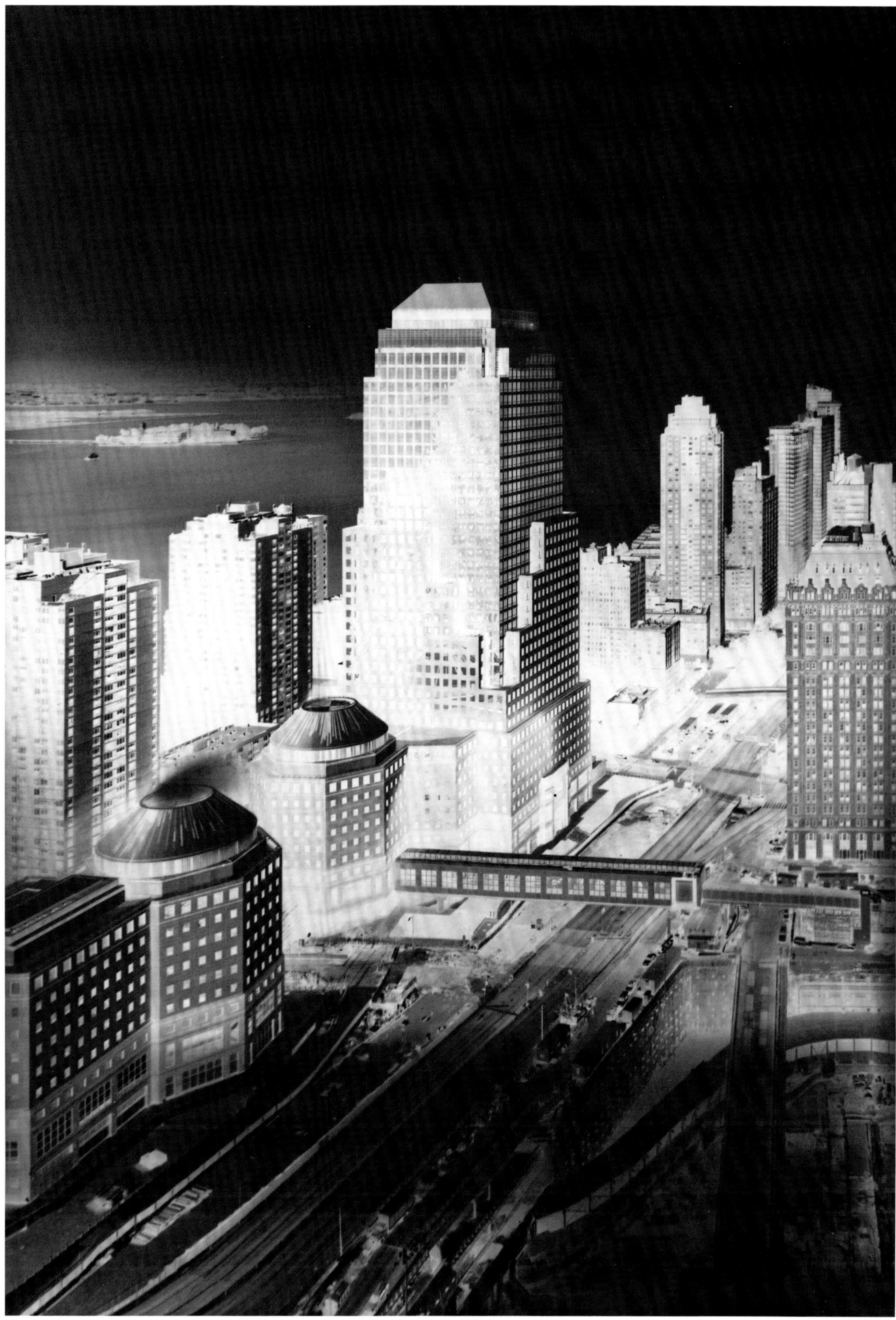

1. Lutter as quoted by Edith Newhall, "Turning Rooms into Camera," *Artnews*, March 2009, 104.

2. Vera Lutter in conversation with Marvin Heiferman, "Vera Lutter," *Gagosian Gallery Quarterly*, February–April 2015, http://www.gagosian.com/now/vera-lutter.

3. Newhall, "Turning Rooms into Cameras," 102.

4. Heiferman, "Vera Lutter."

5. Heiferman, "Vera Lutter."

6. Peter Wollen, "Vera Lutter," *Bomb* 85 (Fall 2003): 48.

7. See Glenn Collins, "9/11's Miracle Survivor Sheds Bandages: A 1907 Landmark Will Be Restored for Residential Use," *New York Times*, March 5, 2004.

by her title she erected her camera in 7 World Trade Center, the second building to bear that name and address. The original structure was damaged by debris when the nearby North Tower of the World Trade Center collapsed on September 11. With inadequate water pressure for its fire suppression system, the inferno ignited by the wreckage burned throughout the day and 7 World Trade Center collapsed at 5:20 p.m. when a critical internal column buckled. The second incarnation of 7 World Trade Center opened in May 2006, only months before Lutter secured permission to photograph from its windows. Looking south over the void at Ground Zero, Lutter focused on 200 Liberty Street (formerly known as One World Financial Center), the tallest building in the center of the picture. Designed by César Pelli and opened in 1985 as part of the World Financial Center, it was kitty-corner to the former World Trade Center. Although it and the nearby Winter Garden Atrium sustained significant damage in the 9/11 attacks as fiery debris and explosions shattered many windows, it was rebuilt. Across the street, along the righthand edge of Lutter's photograph, stands 90 West Street, designed by the renowned turn-of-the-century architect Cass Gilbert and opened in 1907, only a few years before his celebrated Woolworth Building. With its Gothic Revival style, gargoyles, and mansard roof, 90 West Street was also severely damaged during 9/11 when flaming debris rained down on it, gouging the exterior, melting the decorative copper balustrade, and sparking fires that ravaged the interior for days afterward. Unlike other more modern buildings in the area, 90 West Street may have survived because its older terracotta and granite construction materials acted as fireproofing.[7] After extensive renovation, it reopened in March 2005.

Lutter's somber picture highlights two of the architectural survivors of 9/11 — one built at the dawn of New York's modernity, the other at its dusk — and speaks of the profound sadness and devastating loss many experience on viewing the site. But she also transforms the view, presenting a world that has been turned inside out not only by terrorism but also by her own artistic process. Laterally reversed and geographically challenging, her picture shows a city where east has become west and west has become east, disorienting anyone who knows it and obscuring traditional points of reference, much as terrorism itself does; even Ellis Island, the symbol of American democracy, seems to have moved from the southwest tip of Manhattan to the southeast. As tones are reversed and light becomes dark, dark becomes light, all our expectations of how a city should look are undermined as the colossal buildings lose mass and are rendered as nebulous voids. Coupled with Lutter's lofty, commanding point of view, her elegiac picture assumes an ethereal, otherworldly, even postapocalyptic feel. But there is also a sense of metamorphosis. Although a deep, ambiguous shadow obscures much of Ground Zero itself, old buildings have been reclaimed, new ones constructed, and the windows in these and many of the other structures seem to pulsate with light and life, transforming the always hard, relentless, constantly changing New York from an emblem of modernity into one of resilience, even resurrection.  GREENOUGH

# Thomas Demand

German, born 1964

---

26

*Sink*, 1996
chromogenic print
53.02 × 56.52 cm (20⅞ × 22¼ in.)
Promised Gift from the
Collection of Robert E.
Meyerhoff and Rheda Becker

---

27

*Daily Nr. 2*, 2008
dye imbibition print
93.03 × 74.61 cm (36⅝ × 29⅜ in.)
Promised Gift from the
Collection of Robert E.
Meyerhoff and Rheda Becker

---

28

*Clearing*, 2003
chromogenic print
192.09 × 495.3 cm (75⅝ × 195 in.)
Promised Gift from the
Collection of Robert E.
Meyerhoff and Rheda Becker

---

IN ANOTHER LIFE, Thomas Demand might have been an author—perhaps one like Franz Kafka, whose stories of protagonists struggling against incomprehensible powers feel both utterly real and dreamlike. Demand is, of course, not a writer but a visual artist who has spent more than twenty years borrowing already existing photographs, usually from newspapers and the media but also postcards, cell phones, and other ephemera, and making life-size sculptural reconstructions of them out of colored paper and cardboard, which he then carefully lights and photographs. He is not a traditional sculptor or photographer for he does not utilize sculpture's material presence, its tactility, or its ability to redefine our sense of space and scale; nor does he exploit photography's supposed documentary veracity, its capacity to freeze a moment of time, or its immense descriptive capabilities. Instead, his unsettling pictures of empty rooms and commonplace objects—always devoid of people, denuded of details, and eerily silent—show that his real fascination lies in the gap between truth and fiction, the real and the fabricated. Like a novelist, he draws on the events of our time, especially those that have been seared into our minds through pictures in the media. Yet he strives not to elucidate our understanding of those incidents but to cause us to reflect on how pictures themselves have informed our perception of the world. And like a novelist, he creates pregnant scenes that suggest a compelling narrative whose story remains unclear, for he aims, as he says, to construct a "fragile balance" between proposition and fact. "Think of the most beautiful novels," he suggests, "where the imagination of the reader is triggered…that doesn't happen when every little thing is written out."[1] As we become seduced by his scenes and seek to unravel their narratives, we perceive that his true subject, as he puts it, is "memory and how we share mediated experiences to construct our identities with images."[2]

Born in Munich, Demand grew up in Germany during the politically anxious postwar decades of the 1960s and 1970s when the silence that had existed since the war about the Nazi legacy was finally broken with the 1961 Adolf Eichmann trial and the 1963–1965 Frankfurt Auschwitz trials. These years were also marked by the student riots of the late 1960s, the killing of eleven Israeli athletes at the 1972 Munich Olympics, which Demand cites as his first conscious memory, and the terrorist activities and subsequent suspicious deaths of the socially active, far-left-wing members of the Baader-Meinhof group in the 1970s.[3] But Demand, the son of two painters and the grandson of an architect, was also deeply influenced as a young adult by minimal and conceptual art. Ed Ruscha's work made a strong impression on him, especially his wry photography books published in the 1960s and 1970s, whose banal subject matter—gas stations or parking lots—and ironic, deadpan, and decidedly anti-art style signaled a new approach to photography that forced viewers to critically analyze what they see everyday. Steeped in this fraught but experimental milieu, Demand first enrolled at the Akademie der Bildenden Künste München in 1987, where he focused on church and theater design, and later at the Kunstakademie in Düsseldorf, where he trained as a sculptor. There he began to work consistently with paper both because of its ubiquity (it was a "common merchandise which absolutely everyone has experience of using") and its emblematic power (it was "the material of ideas").[4] Although Bernd Becher taught at the Kunstakademie at this time, Demand did not study with him but instead taught himself how to photograph in 1989 to record the fragile paper models that he was making. In 1993, though, when he was studying at Goldsmiths College in London and imbibing its interdisciplinary approach, he made a simple but radical change in his practice: he began to make models only for the purpose of photographing them. He also decided to use as source material not actual objects—buildings, for example, as he had previously done—but rather photographs, in order to see "what happens…if instead of using my

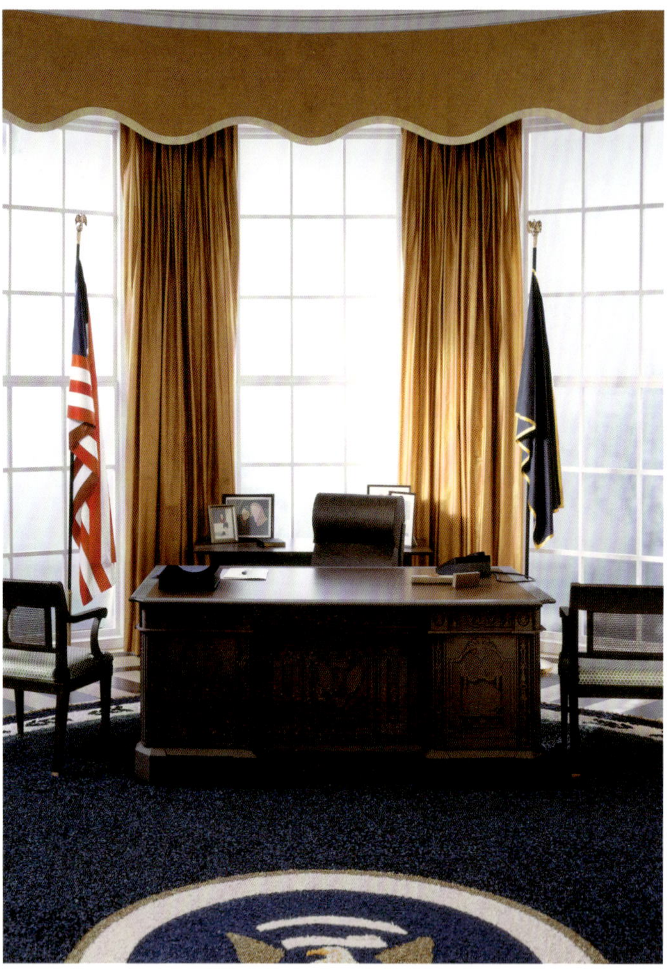

fig. 1: Thomas Demand, *Presidency I*, 2008, chromogenic print, National Gallery of Art, Washington, Gift from Agnes Gund and Jo Carole and Ronald S. Lauder

own experience I use somebody's else's."[5] To further obfuscate the question of originality (the appropriated source image, his laboriously constructed model, or his photograph), he also made it a habit to destroy his models after photographing them.

With this leap, Demand immediately discovered his style and approach, which have varied little in the intervening years. He also found his subject matter, at first focusing on celebrated incidents often known to us largely through the media. Some of Demand's photographs are based on iconic pictures of dramatic moments from German history that transpired many decades earlier, such as the 1944 bombing of Adolph Hitler's headquarters. Others are derived from international events, such as the 2013 Boston Marathon bombing, and made shortly after the incidents themselves, so that, as Demand asserted, they would be "so close to the real event that my picture of it and the media coverage would become indistinguishable."[6] Still more are of charged, instantly recognizable political spaces, such as the Oval Office (fig. 1). Many of the pictures that he chooses to copy, such as the Boston Marathon bombing, focus on mundane aspects of those incidents highlighted by the media—for example, the backyard of the home of one of the bombers, Tamerlan Tsarnaev—and mimic the seemingly random style of photojournalists hungry to capture any image linked to a celebrated story. In order to explore what he describes as "the diffuse shadow realm such events inhabit in our collective memory," he intentionally excludes key details from his works: no soldiers inspect the damage to Hitler's headquarters, no stars adorn the flag in the Oval Office.[7] Devoid of explicit facts, Demand's pictures not only bring to the fore photography's

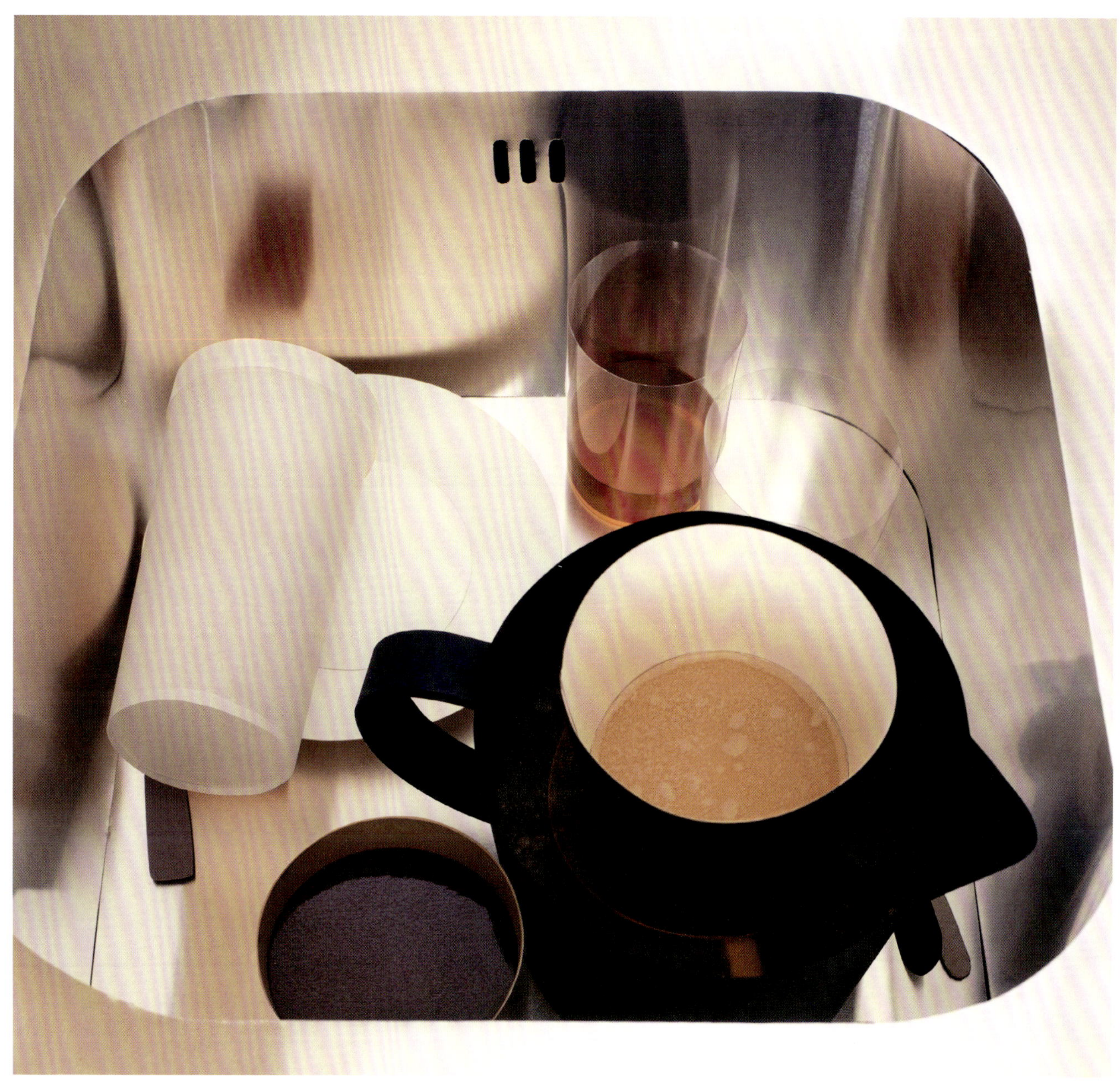

26

1. "A Conversation with Thomas Demand," *Ocula*, June 17, 2015, https://ocula.com/magazine/conversations/thomas-demand/.

2. Ken Weingart, "An Interview with German Fine Art Photographer Thomas Demand," September 22, 2015, PetaPixel, http://petapixel.com/2015/09/22/an-interview-with-german-fine-art-photographer-thomas-demand/.

3. Roxana Marcoci, "Paper Moon," in *Thomas Demand*, ed. Roxana Marcoci (Museum of Modern Art, New York, 2005), 10.

4. Thomas Demand, Beatriz Colomina, and Alexander Kluge, *Thomas Demand* (Serpentine Gallery, London, 2006), 90.

5. "A Conversation with Thomas Demand," *Ocula*, June 17, 2015.

6. Marcoci, *Thomas Demand*, 22.

7. Thomas Demand, "A Conversation between Alexander Kluge and Thomas Demand," *Thomas Demand*, 86.

inherent unreliability, especially in the digital age, but also cause us to see all images as oscillating between documentation and construction, truth and fiction, reality and memory.

Revealing the blurry lines between personal and collective memory, Demand has also explored more mundane, less fraught pictures, such as *Sink* (pl. 26). Based on a photograph of dirty dishes in a friend's sink, the picture initially appears more plausible than many of his others. With its simple geometric forms filled with luminous liquids that are reflected in the dazzling, stainless steel sink, the picture seems almost like an advertisement for modern living. Then we notice the roughly cut edge of the cardboard ringing the sink, the less-than-watertight seal around its bottom, even its unnatural cleanliness, and realize that this is a picture more about the *idea* of a sink than an image of a real, functioning one: a picture about a world of surface, not substance. Demand expanded this subject in more-recent photographs based on offhand snapshots made with his cell phone of empty coffee cups or cigarette butt receptacles (pl. 27, *Daily Nr. 2*). Recognizing that the majority of the pictures we talk about now are drawn not from the mainstream media but from personal images that people post on social media, he determined to highlight the ways in which photography has become for so many an almost compulsive, diarylike practice. He calls the pictures *The Dailies*, a title taken from the daily rushes of film left on the cutting-room floor and a nod to the potential stories that might be found in these throwaway images. For the first time in his career, Demand also printed the *Dailies* photographs using the labor-intensive, outmoded dye imbibition (dye-transfer) process. Producing intensely saturated colors with a rich tonal range and great spatial depth, this process renders his photographs even more lifelike and immediate—we can almost feel, for example, the texture of the sand surrounding the cigarette butts.

*Clearing* is one of Demand's most spectacular works and one of only two pictures he has made of nature (pl. 28). To create it he constructed a model embedded in a steel frame that was 50 feet long, 18 feet high, and 32 feet deep, then glued 270,000 pieces of die-cut paper onto the cardboard trees and bushes. He lit the scene using a 10,000-watt klieg light to make it appear that he had captured the moment when the sun had broken through a forest's canopy. Construction was not his only challenge: pitting the real against the artificial, he based his model on a photograph of the park in Venice where the Biennale is held, and installed his 6 × 16 foot print in front of the exact location where the original photograph was made (see "Picturing a Collection, Presenting a History," p. 12, fig. 7). In addition, Demand's point of view is skewed. Although the work seems to allude to German romantic landscape painting, Demand does not give his viewers easy access to the scene; unlike Caspar David Friedrich, he presents no person seen from behind experiencing the sublimity of nature. Instead, Demand's viewer is perched high in the trees, in a spot that those of us with our feet on the ground would have a hard time reaching. With its lush colors and evocative imagery, but inaccessible point of view and ersatz reality, the picture both attracts and destabilizes us, and seems to suggest that the ability to find spiritual union with nature is just another remnant of the past—a reconstructed memory and an illusion, albeit a glorious one. **GREENOUGH**

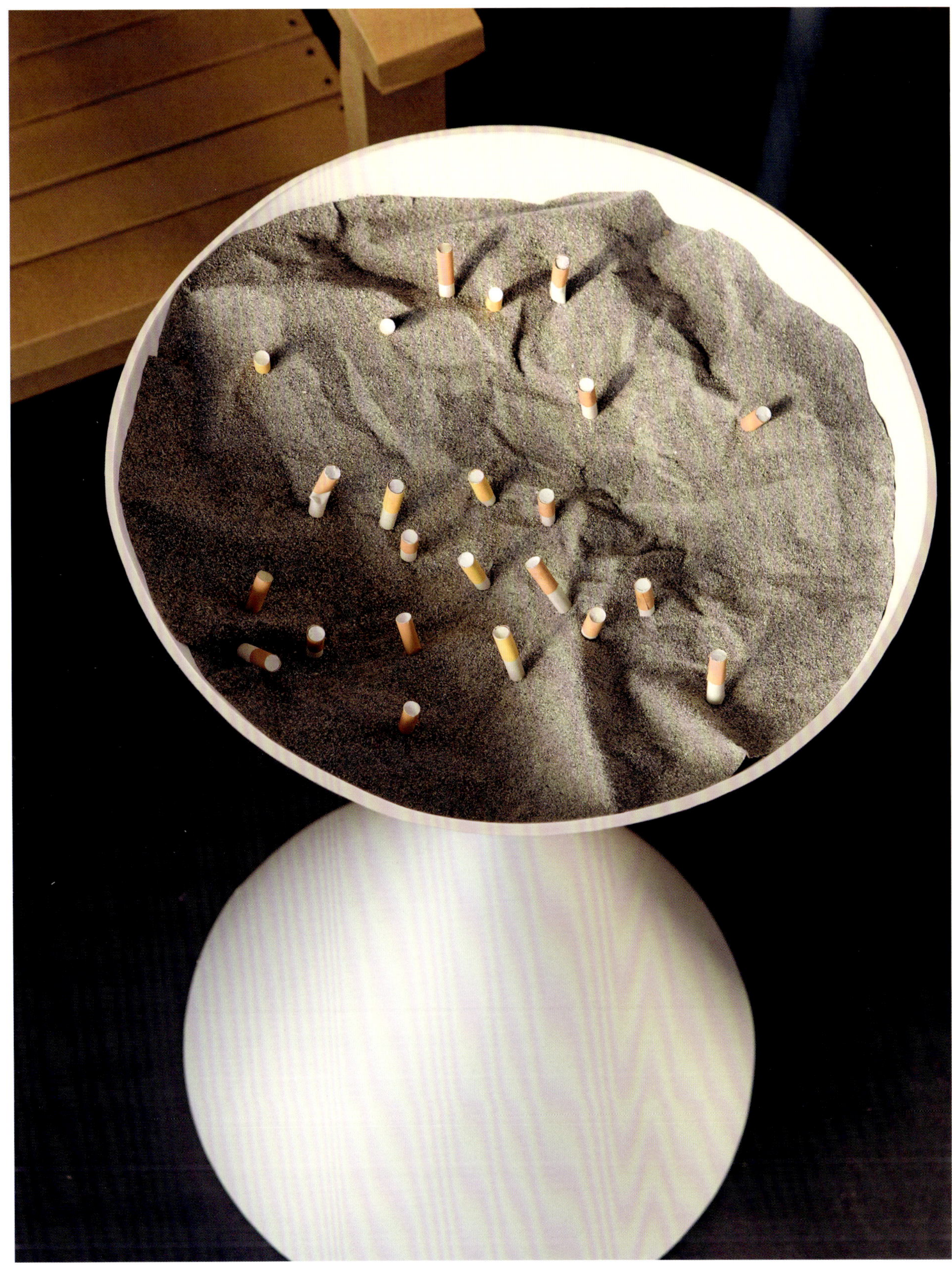

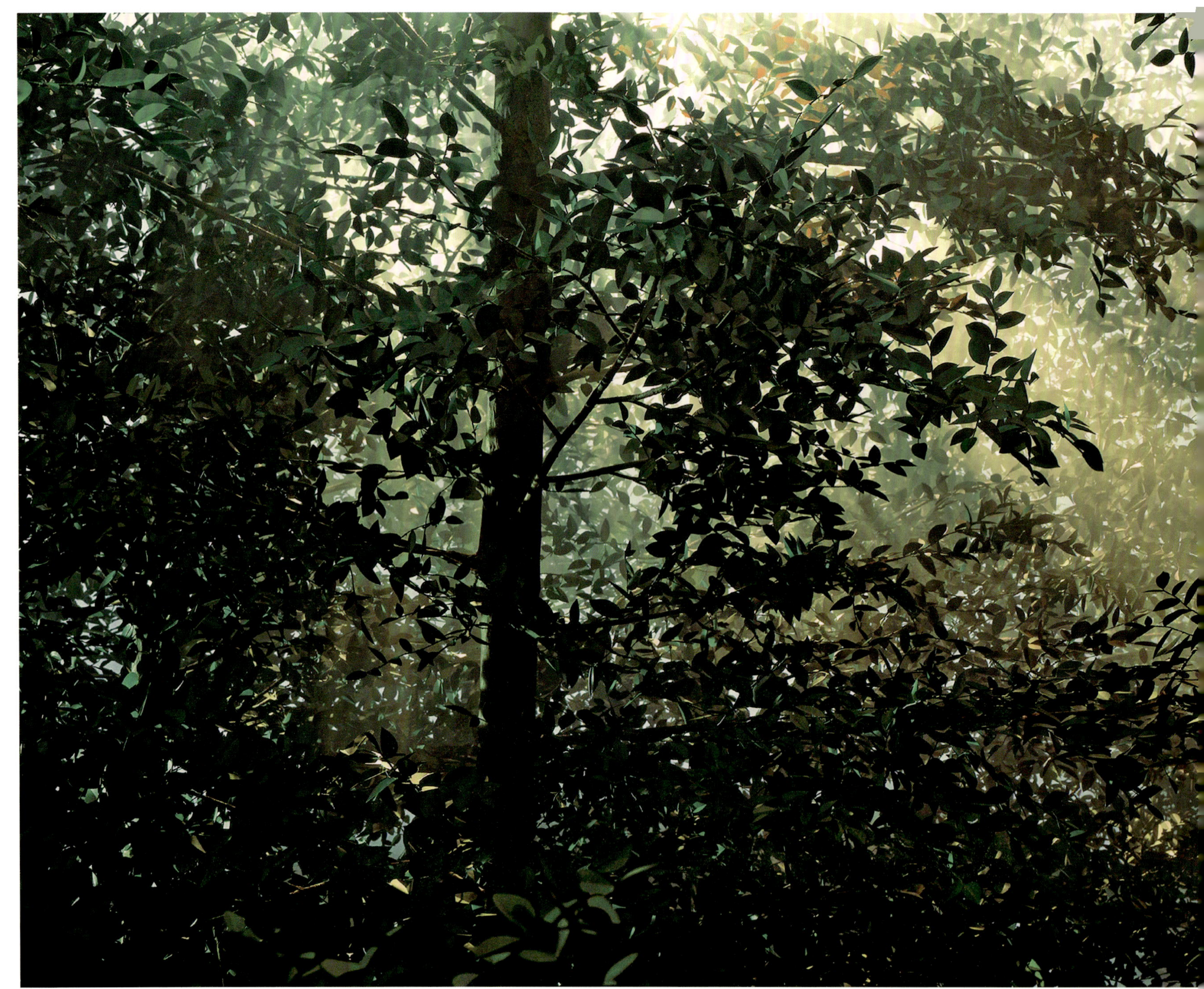

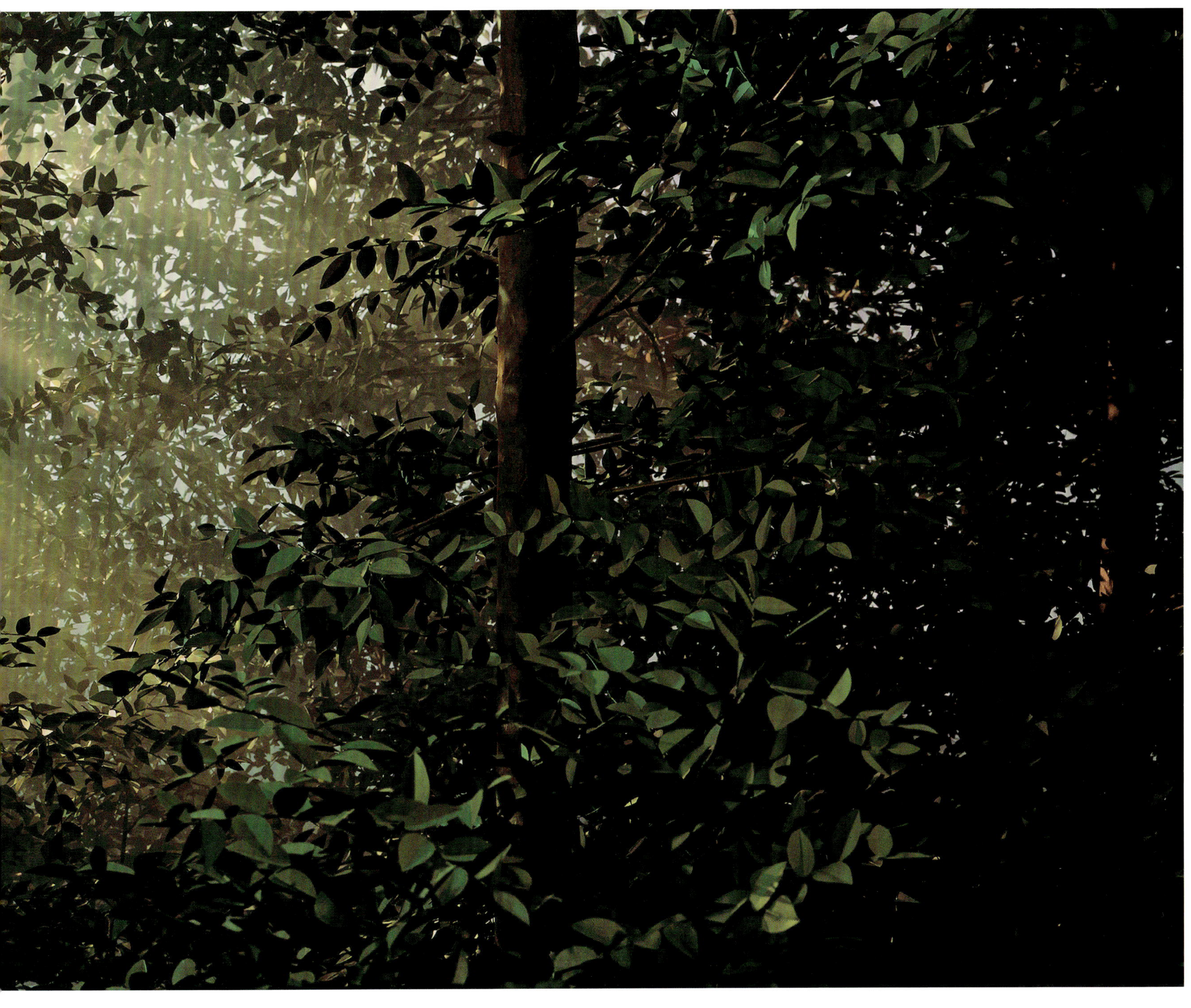

# Anselm Kiefer

German, born 1945

---

29

*Vanitas*, 2007
mixed media with oil paint,
emulsion, shellac, plant material,
and soil on gelatin silver print
191.14 × 140.97 cm (75¼ × 55½ in.)
Promised Gift from the
Collection of Robert E.
Meyerhoff and Rheda Becker

---

FOR MORE THAN FORTY YEARS, Anselm Kiefer has made provocative, elegiac, and experimental art that confronts the difficult issues of his generation—German national identity, history, and the Holocaust—while simultaneously exploring more universal concerns of war, religion, and the politics of survival. Drawing inspiration from a wide variety of figures and subjects from across the centuries, including ancient Jewish mystical writings, Egyptian, Greek, and Nordic mythology, Richard Wagner, and the twentieth-century poets Paul Celan and Ingeborg Bachmann, among many others, Kiefer has created an art that reaches both backward and forward in time, as sweeping and ambitious as it is monumental and moving. With a sophisticated understanding of the visceral and metaphorical resonances of materials, he folds the literal building blocks of our time (concrete, lead, steel) into his own shamanistic vocabulary, merging them with natural and fabricated elements (dirt, stones, flowers, trees; clothes, toys, industrial parts) to create dense, layered, three-dimensional paintings, books, and sculptures. A collector of both ideas and objects, Kiefer has constructed two huge studio complexes that function as building sites where he creates his large and multifaceted installations. One, La Ribaute, is situated on an eighty-six-acre plot near Barjac in southern France; the other is in a vast abandoned department-store warehouse in Croissy-Beaubourg, outside of Paris, where he stores a plethora of materials and objects—stacked concrete casts of shipping containers, twelve-foot lead battleships, World War II airplanes, even a monumental model of a decommissioned nuclear cooling tower—for use in his art.

His unconventional approach to materials has also prompted an equally innovative exploration of photography. With its fixed one-point perspective, its rootedness in a specific time and place, and the questions it raises about representation and truth, photography has both fascinated and bothered Kiefer since his student days. Born in southern Germany shortly before the end of World War II, he grew up amid the destruction of a ruined culture. When he went to art school in the 1960s, he, like so many other conceptual artists of the time, used a camera to document a series of performances he conducted in 1969. Dressed in his father's World War II uniform, he photographed himself assuming the Nazi salute in France, Switzerland, and Italy for a series of pictures titled *Occupations*. Although his actions, and the subsequent display and publication of the photographs, were hugely controversial—since 1945 it has been illegal to assume the gesture in Germany—Kiefer's intent was both to force Germans to examine their recent history and to question how one could be a German artist in the wake of Hitler and National Socialism.

His relationship with photography has been anything but straightforward and obvious; he has challenged and undercut it, questioning its reliability, as often as he has exploited it. In the 1970s, he made photographs of staged scenes for use in his hand-made books, drawing on the medium's innate ability to convey a story through a series of pictures. Yet as the sequences progress, he undermines photography's narrative power and its implied truthfulness by painting pictures or words on top of his prints, covering them with sand or other substances, or gluing reproductions over them to obscure their imagery. Since the early 1980s, he has made thousands of photographs that he pastes onto his canvases or other supports so that, as he asserts, he can begin with a "recognizable image."[1] Thus, photography itself—its vision, temporality, and physicality—is the foundation of his pictures. Often his photographs are pictures of empty, barren landscapes taken with a wide-angle lens that emphasizes the camera's decidedly fixed, one-point perspective and exploits its capacity to create a plunging sense of space. Yet because Kiefer recognizes that photography has its limits, as it records "only the instant the shutter was open," while he seeks in his art to "present a history,"[2] he

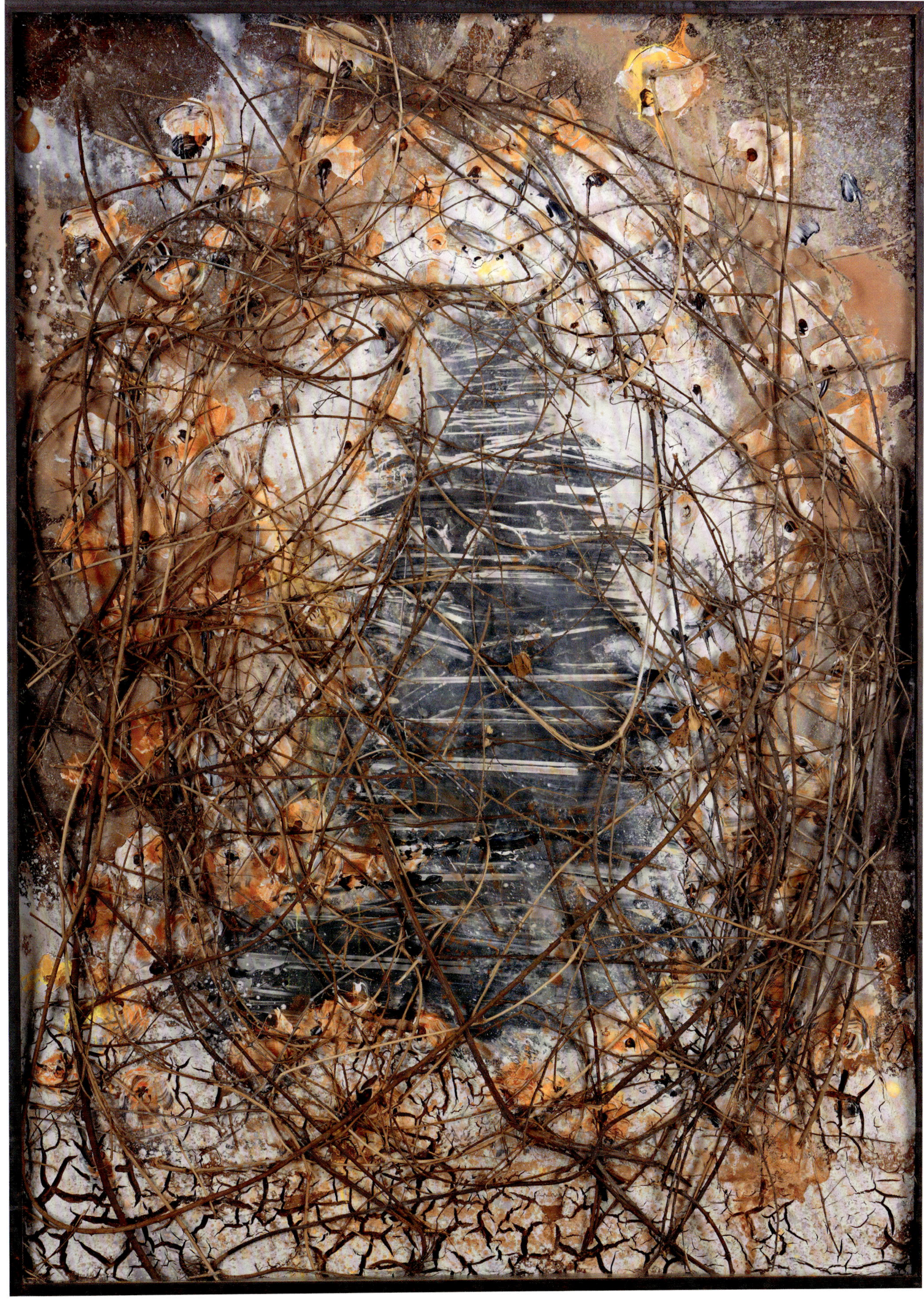

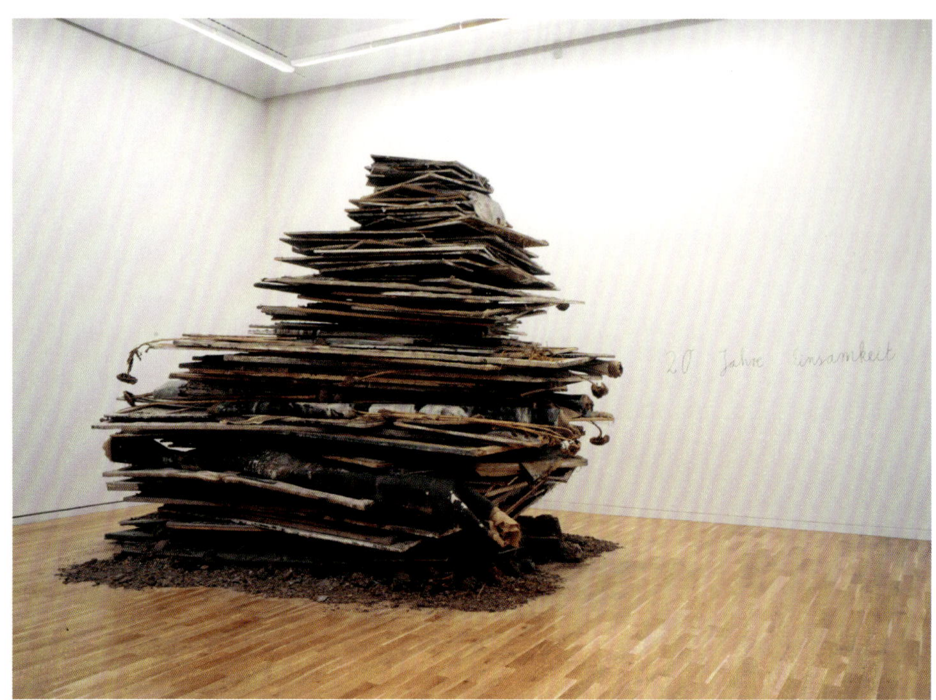

fig. 1: Anselm Kiefer, *20 Years of Solitude,* 1971–1991, mixed media, Kunstmuseum Wolfsburg

slathers layers of oil, acrylic, emulsion, lead, clay, ash, or other substances on top of his photographs, destroying their specificity and veracity while intensifying the allusive, metaphorical qualities of the final piece. The result, he says, is an "inverted archaeology."[3] Sometimes parts of the silvery gray photographic emulsion peek through the other materials, contributing a spatial, temporal, and pictorial ambiguity as well as a slick, almost industrial aura to the picture, in sharp contrast to the often organic forms over it. At other times, the photograph is entirely obliterated. Yet in both cases, the camera's original articulation of the space remains, creating a curious amalgam—a picture that emphatically announces itself as a painting yet hints at its genesis in the alchemy of photography.

As an artist who repeatedly recycles ideas and images, Kiefer has also exploited photography's reproducibility and the opportunity the negative gives the artist to return to an idea years later. In one of the most dramatic gestures of his career, in 1991 he created an enormous sculpture consisting of a pile of discarded paintings— some rolled, some on stretchers, all covered with dirt, dried sunflowers, leaves, straw, and stones. He titled the work *20 Years of Solitude* (1971–1991, fig. 1) and exhibited it in New York in 1993, along with several handmade books, most with blank pages stained with semen. Staggering and disturbing, the piece—part funeral pyre, part artistic totem—marked a moment of profound change for Kiefer, who had recently moved from Germany to France. Unable to leave this piece behind, Kiefer has revisited it several times in the intervening years through the negatives he took of it. In the mid-1990s he painted on top of a print of it, obliterating all evidence of the sculpture's installation in the gallery and emphasizing instead its singular nature and monumentality; in another print, he again obscured the background and collaged a second photograph of the sea on top, as if to suggest the sculpture's affinity with nature (fig. 2).

He returned to the subject yet again in several works from 2007 and 2008, this time surrounding the photograph of the sculpture with branches, emulsion, clay, oil paint, and paper collage mimicking flowers, probably poppies. Branches—some-

1. Albert P. Albano, "Reflections on Painting, Alchemy, Nazism: Visiting with Anselm Kiefer," *American Institute for Conservation of Historic and Artistic Works* 37, no. 3 (Autumn/Winter, 1998): 350–351.

2. Martin Gayford, "'I Like Vanished Things': Anselm Kiefer on Art, Alchemy and His Childhood," *The Spectator*, September 20, 2014, www.spectator.co.uk/2014/09/meet-everyones-favourite-post-catastrophic-romantic-anselm-kiefer/.

3. Götz Adriani, ed., and Bruni Mayor, trans., *The Books of Anselm Kiefer, 1969–1990* (New York, 1991), 12.

times blasted and burned, sometimes delicate and encircling—have figured prominently in Kiefer's art throughout his career. Their dual nature as symbols of death and destruction as well as sheltering, maternal protection was inspired by his childhood memories of playing in the woods near his parents' home where the family hid during the intense bombing of World War II. Flowers—representing evanescent beauty, fertility, and perishability, and especially poppies, with their associations of memory, forgetfulness, death, and veterans—are also common subjects in his art. By lacing the flowers and branches together, he intertwines beauty, fragility, and salvation with death and oblivion, wrapping them all around the monument of art.

Kiefer titled most of these 2007 and 2008 reflections on his sculpture *20 Years of Solitude*, like the original itself. Yet he called one *Vanitas* (pl. 29), alluding to the genre of still-life painting that flourished in the Netherlands in the sixteenth and seventeenth centuries. Like Kiefer's work, *vanitas* (from Latin, "vanity") paintings usually contain objects symbolizing the inevitably of death and the transience of earthly accomplishments, and they often include emblems of the arts, wealth, resurrection, and eternal life. For an artist such as Kiefer, who layers memory with myth, who is mindful of his own enormous acclaim and its fleeting nature, and who is, above all else, concerned with the tenuousness of endurance, with moral culpability, and with redemption, it is a fitting title. GREENOUGH

fig. 2: Anselm Kiefer, *20 Years of Solitude*, 1993, white gouache on gelatin silver prints, cut, torn, and tipped together, The Art Institute of Chicago, Gift of Susan and Lewis Manilow

# Vik Muniz

American, born Brazil 1961

---

### 30

*Marilyn Monroe, Actress,
NY City, May 6, 1957, After Avedon
(Gordian Puzzle)*, 2007
chromogenic print
190.82 × 189.39 cm (75 ⅛ × 74 ⁹⁄₁₆ in.)
Promised Gift from the
Collection of Robert E.
Meyerhoff and Rheda Becker

---

### 31

*Noon Rush Hour on Fifth Avenue,
1949, After Andreas Feininger
(Pictures of Paper)*, 2009
gelatin silver print
166.37 × 130.81 cm (65 ½ × 51 ½ in.)
Promised Gift from the
Collection of Robert E.
Meyerhoff and Rheda Becker

---

FOR MORE THAN THIRTY YEARS, memory and matter have been key components of Vik Muniz's art. When he arrived in the United States from his native Brazil in 1983, he spoke no English and had little artistic training beyond some work for an advertising company. Yet he immersed himself in the New York art world and quickly received attention for his innovative sculptures that reveal his deep-seated interest in both the physical qualities of materials—their texture, luminosity, mass, and weight—and their metaphoric power. As he photographed his sculptures, he became fascinated with the way photographs depict other works of art and, more broadly, with visual perception and reproductive techniques. In 1996, he merged these interests following a trip to Saint Kitts. There he befriended children whose parents worked on sugar plantations. When he returned to New York, he "could not help thinking," he later wrote, "about the sad metamorphosis most of my little friends were bound to experience" when they, like their parents, began to work the "long, backbreaking hours of labor at the sugar-cane plantation for a meager, survival-based salary."[1] Striving to convey the children's exuberance while simultaneously suggesting their ominous fate, he used snapshots he had taken to create portraits of them out of sugar, the very material whose cultivation had drained the life from their parents. He then photographed the results and destroyed the drawings. The sugar seen in his photographs appears glowing and effervescent, but when coupled with the images of the children, it also alludes to its grueling production and the history of colonialism and exploitation.

At this time, Muniz, who worked in a frame shop that sold reproductions of artworks, became intrigued with the question of originality. From his earlier experience in an advertising agency, he had learned that "the rule was not to use any new idea that hadn't been tested by an artist before."[2] He put this idea into practice in another early series, *The Best of Life* (1988–1990). After spending several years studying a book of Pulitzer Prize–winning photographs that had been published in *Life* magazine, he lost the volume. In order to assess how accurately he remembered the images, he drew some of them from memory: Neil Armstrong's photograph of Buzz Aldrin walking on the moon, or Nick Ut's image of a naked child in Vietnam burned by napalm, for example. Seeking to incorporate the memories of others into his art, he asked friends to recount their impressions of the photographs and then folded their recollections into his pictures. His depictions omitted details (and even laterally reversed some of them) but always captured the essential emotional power of the originals. After photographing his drawings, he then printed them as halftones, the same process used when they were first reproduced in *Life*. Blurry and suggestive, Muniz's final prints reveal not only his own memory of the pictures but also the ways in which these images have been seared into the collective cultural memory.

This practice of replicating other works of art using unusual but often quotidian materials—dust, junk, or chocolate syrup—continues to inform his work to the present day, making the tactile qualities of his art, as the historian Germano Celant notes, as important as the final photograph itself.[3] Striving to give photography the "materiality and tangibility" that "have always belonged to painting," Muniz selects an image and then highlights its potential physicality by breaking it down into pieces.[4] In the process, he also brings attention to both its fragility and cultural resonance, whether his source works are as widely recognized as Richard Avedon's *Marilyn Monroe, actor, New York, May 6, 1957* (1957, fig. 1) or less well known, such as Andreas Feininger's *Lunch Hour on Fifth Avenue* (1949, fig. 2).

In 2007, *New York* magazine commissioned six artists to commemorate the fiftieth anniversary of Richard Avedon's iconic photograph of a seemingly forlorn Marilyn Monroe. Avedon, a superstar photographer of the postwar period whose portraits of

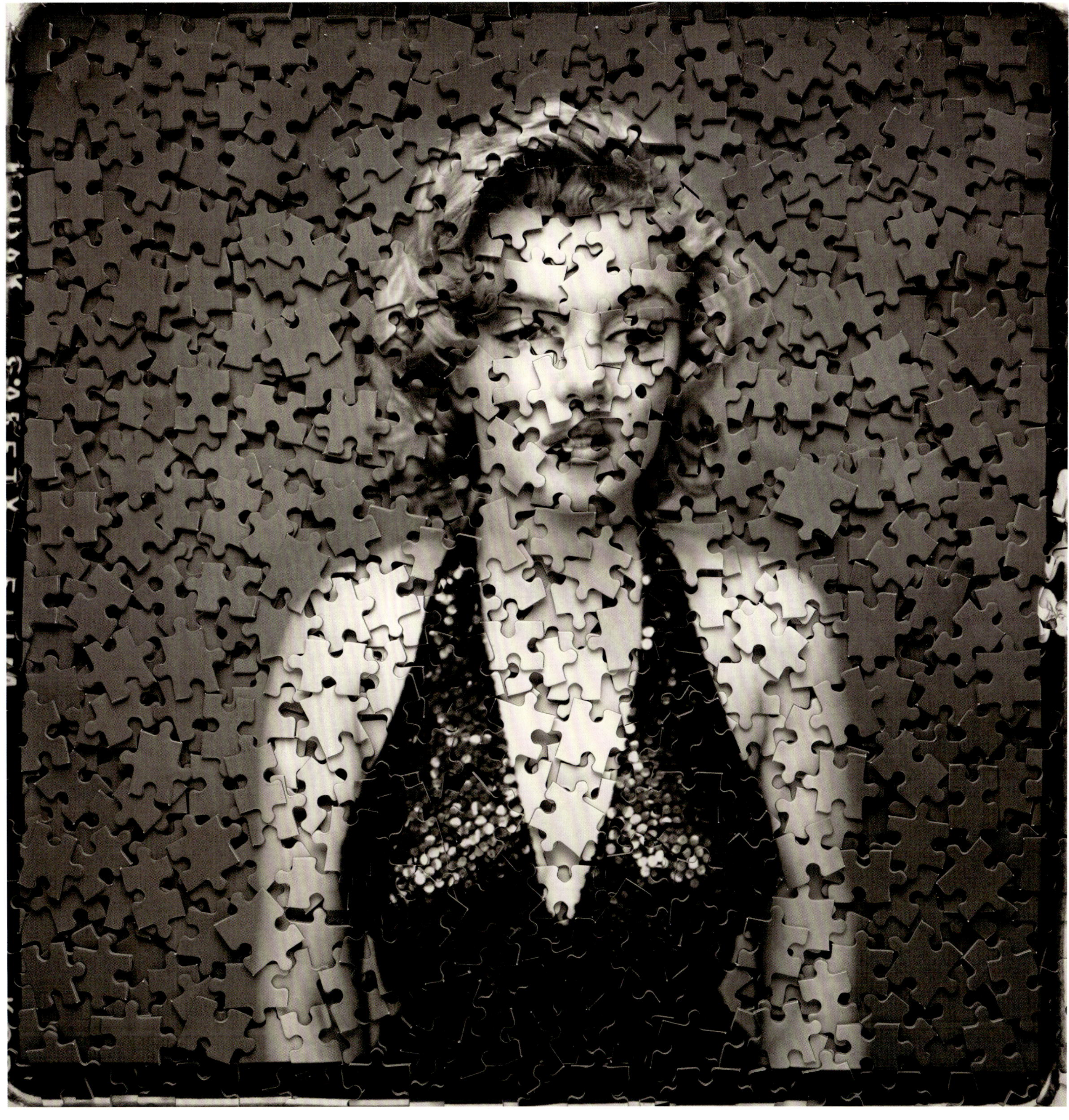

celebrities and models regularly graced the pages of the United States' foremost magazines, including *Harper's Bazaar* and *Vogue*, was hired in 1957 to take promotional photographs for Monroe's latest film, *The Prince and the Showgirl*. Although the film's story was innocuous—a romantic comedy about a prince who becomes entangled with a showgirl—there was considerable drama behind the scenes, with conflicts between Monroe and her new husband, Arthur Miller, who was under investigation by the House Un-American Activities Committee, and costar Laurence Olivier and his wife, Vivien Leigh, who suffered a miscarriage during the filming. For most of the session with Avedon, Monroe, attired in a slinky, sequined halter dress, dutifully played the role of movie star and sex symbol that accorded with her public persona. But by the end of the evening when the performance was over, the showgirl vanished and the strain of being in the spotlight resurfaced. "She sat in the corner like a child, with everything gone," as Avedon later recounted. He approached her, but "wouldn't photograph her without her knowledge of it.…I came with the camera, I saw that she was not saying no."[5] With her implied permission, in this unguarded moment, portraitist and sitter, in complicity, brought about a new subject—the "melancholy heroine" or "mere mortal."[6] In retrospect, the photograph has come to be seen as providing an insightful glimpse into the pain and tragedy that lay behind each of Monroe's alluring and ebullient performances.

Muniz shares this view of the photograph, which he has described as "a picture of Norma Jean, not Marilyn," contrasting her birth and screen names. While other artists working on the *New York* magazine commission restaged or altered the portrait, Muniz, as he always does, chose to relate "the material and the idea."[7] Making ten puzzles out of Avedon's photograph, he positioned the pieces one on top of the other, rotating each segment at a different angle. In this way, he hoped to "subvert the traditional order of a puzzle, since the image is independent of the arrangement of the pieces and how they fit with one another."[8] The result is that Monroe's skin now appears as if dented or pockmarked. Her tousled hair, makeup, halter dress, and facial expression are marred by the sharp protrusions and rounded indentations of the puzzle pieces, yet the overall image is recognizable. As he dissects her into pieces—much as the public did during her lifetime and in the years since—Muniz cuts through Monroe's (or Norma Jean's) superficial, cosmetic facade, granting her not only physicality and presence but also humanity.

Muniz's interest in the materiality of the photographic image also prompted him to undertake his series *Pictures of Paper*. In 2005, Kodak announced that they would no longer make black-and-white photographic paper, sparking a panic among photographers, which intrigued Muniz. What was it about the loss of this paper that led so many to stockpile it, especially when black-and-white images could be printed through digital means?[9] In *Pictures of Paper*, he explores this question by constructing pictures from carefully cut pieces of plain paper, replicating the shape and tone of the black, white, and gray areas of earlier photographs. One of the photographs from this series, *Noon Rush Hour on Fifth Avenue, 1949, After Andreas Feininger (Pictures of Paper)* (2009, pl. 31), is, as its title indicates, based on a picture of New York City made fifty years earlier by Andreas Feininger, son of a German painter and a recent immigrant to the United States (fig. 2). Often using a telephoto lens, Feininger photographed New York's skyline and streets, compressing buildings and people into a previously unimaginable gridlock and succinctly capturing the bold, brash, and bustling pace of New York City as it emerged after the war.

In *The Best of Life*, Muniz had relied on memory to recall the originals, resulting in works that do not correspond exactly with their sources. But with Feininger's *Lunch Hour on Fifth Avenue* he followed the source much more closely. From the precise

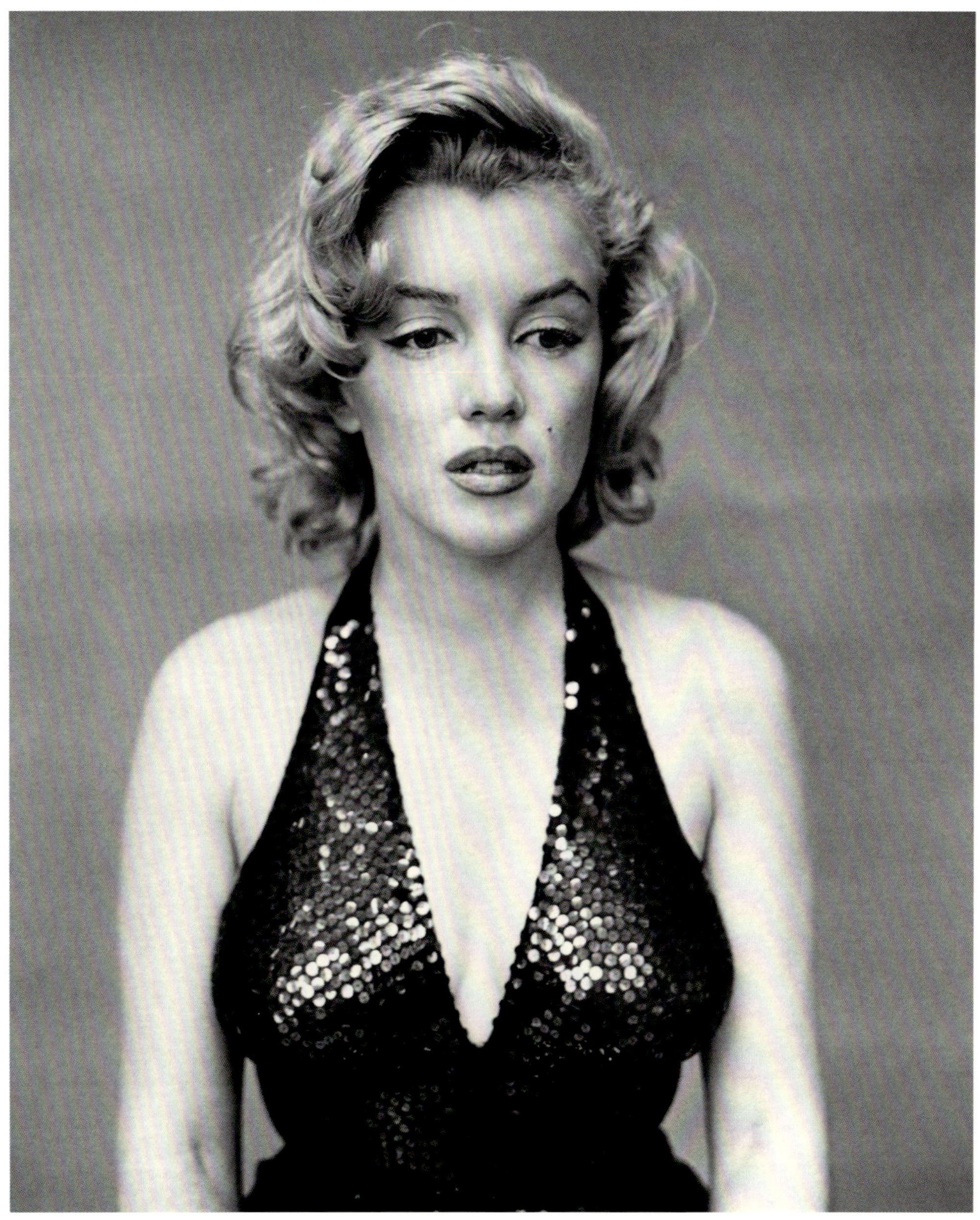

fig. 1: Richard Avedon, *Marilyn Monroe, actor, New York, May 6, 1957,* 1957, gelatin silver print, printed 1980, Promised Gift from the Collection of Robert E. Meyerhoff and Rheda Becker

1. Vik Muniz, "Crystals, Grains, Dirty Negatives," in *Reflex: A Vik Muniz Primer*, ed. Lesley A. Martin (New York, 2005), 59–60.

2. Muniz, "The Art of Selling What Is Not for Sale," in *Reflex: A Vik Muniz Primer*, 93.

3. Germano Celant, "Mimesis of Mimesis: Vik Muniz," in *Vik Muniz*, ed. Germano Celant (Museo d'Arte Contemporanea, Rome, 2003), 13.

4. Juan Uslé, "'In Top Hat, or Crystal Glass,' A Conversation," in *Vik Muniz*, ed. Fernando Francés (Centro de Arte Contemporáneo de Málaga, 2012), 278.

5. Richard Avedon in *Richard Avedon: Darkness and Light*, directed by Helen Whitney (1995), 00:40:45.

6. Maria Morris Hambourg and Mia Fineman, "Avedon's Endgame," in *Richard Avedon Portraits* (Metropolitan Museum of Art, New York, 2002), unpaginated; Colin Westerbeck, "Beyond the Photographic Frame," in *On the Art of Fixing a Shadow: One Hundred and Fifty Years of Photography*, ed. Sarah Greenough (National Gallery of Art, Washington, and Art Institute of Chicago, 1989), 374.

7. Muniz, quoted in "The Title of This Photograph Is *Marilyn Monroe, Actress, New York City, May 6, 1957*," *New York*, May 14, 2007, http://nymag.com/news/features/31523/ (published online October 4, 2007).

8. Muniz, "Quebra-cabeças górdios," in *Vik Muniz, Obra Completa 1987–2009: Catálogo Raisonné*, ed. Pedro Corrêa do Lago (Rio de Janeiro, 2009), 664. Translated from the Portuguese by Leslie Ureña.

9. Muniz, "Imagens de papel," in *Vik Muniz, Obra Completa 1987–2009*, 646.

10. Muniz in Charles Ashley Stainback, "Cranium Envy, or Trompe L'Oeil for the Image Conscious," in *Vik Muniz: Seeing Is Believing*, ed. Charles Ashley Stainback (International Center of Photography, New York, 1998), 17.

11. Feininger, *The World through My Eyes* (New York, 1963), 34; for Muniz's replacement of one work for another, see Celant, "Mimesis of Mimesis," 13. For more on Muniz and illusion, see Richard Leydier, "Vik Muniz: L'Enfance de l'art," in *Art Press* 304 (Spring 2004): 22–26.


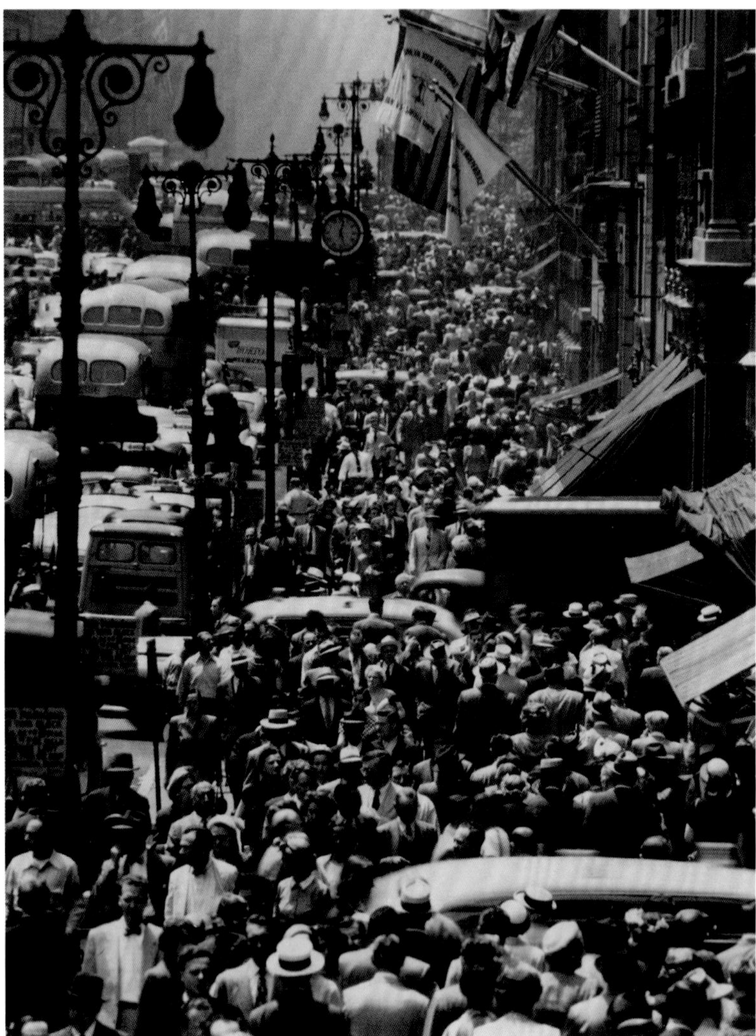

fig. 2: Andreas Feininger, *Lunch Hour on Fifth Avenue* (detail), 1949, gelatin silver print, Getty Images, Premium Archive

positioning of the flags to the exact time on the clock, even the stifling feeling of the hordes of people brushing up against one another as they make their way down one of New York's most famous thoroughfares, Muniz's pieces of paper replicate the vibrancy and oppressiveness of the city street seen in Feininger's photograph. But Muniz also infuses a sense of depth and three-dimensionality that is not present in the original by layering the pieces, rebuilding Feininger's work using all of the tones of a carefully gradated black-and-white photograph, starting with a rich black then progressing to lighter shades of gray to white. His materialization of the object thus draws the viewer's eye to the picture's nonrepresentational characteristics — the shades of gray, the dappled light, the shadows — rather than to particular figures, cars, or flags that punctuate the original image, transforming an already chaotic picture into a disorienting abstraction, a vision of a city fractured and dissolving before our eyes.

Muniz relishes "destabiliz[ing] the viewer's notion of what a photograph is."[10] In doing so, whether through the puzzle pieces that break down and rebuild Marilyn Monroe or the accretion of paper meant to depict "New York at its worst," as Feininger had put it, Muniz brings viewers into the realm of illusion and makes them question the very notion of originality.[11] GREENOUGH / UREÑA

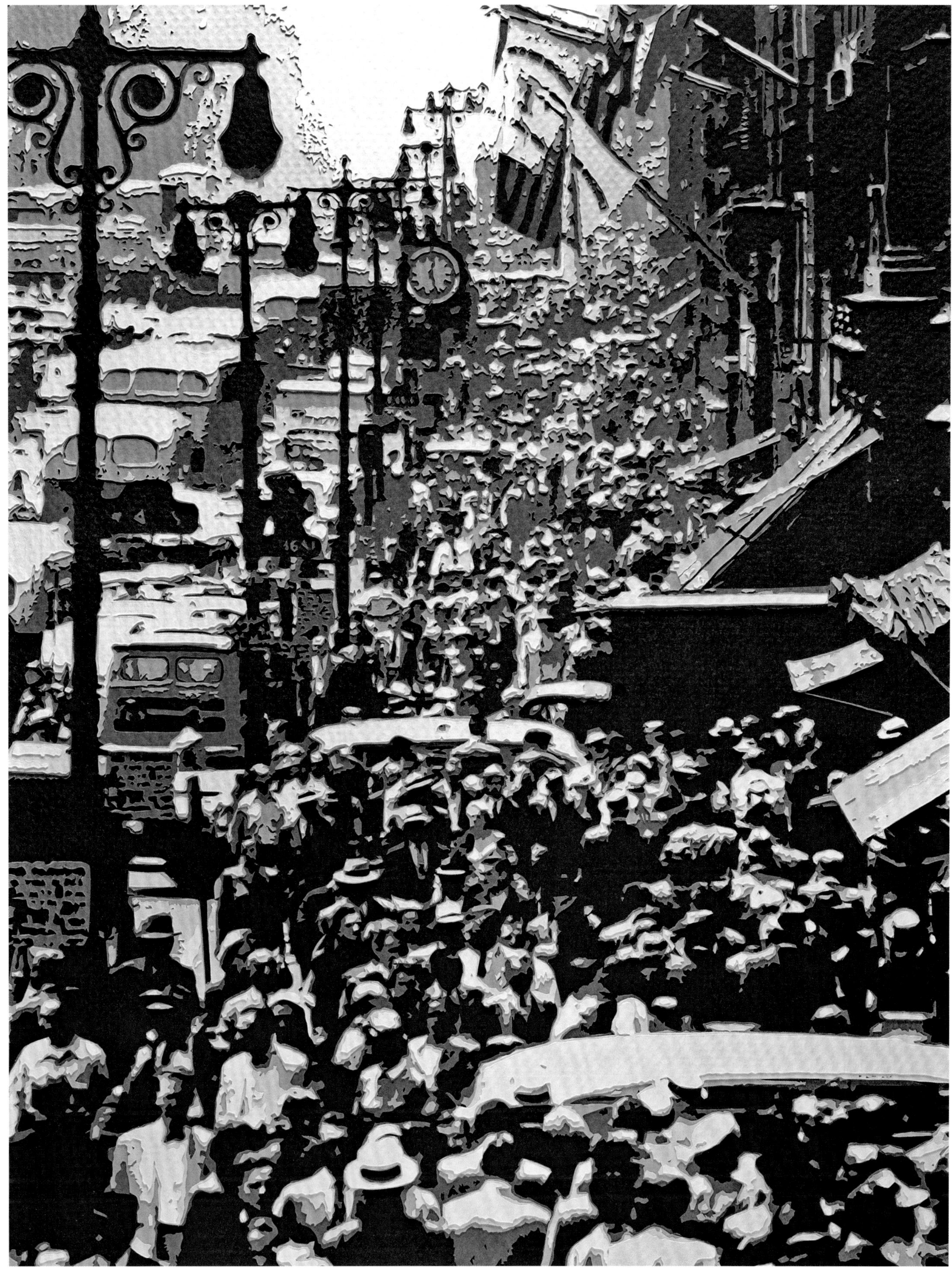

# Jeff Wall

Canadian, born 1946

32

*Hotels, Carrall St., Vancouver, summer 2005*, 2005
transparency in light box
244.48 × 302.26 cm
(96 ¼ × 119 in.)
Promised Gift from the
Collection of Robert E.
Meyerhoff and Rheda Becker

 economics, identity, architecture, and art, Jeff Wall questions our reliance on photographs to instantly convey information and promote a culture of consumption. Appropriating the glossy production techniques of mass media, he uses large-scale light boxes to elicit a highly detailed and pervasive photographic experience that mimics the immediacy of shopping-mall advertising and the narrative characteristics of movies. Wall's subjects are frequently dramatized to accentuate the contrast between documentary truth and fiction, a style he calls "near documentary." Working slowly to construct imagined tableaux on the grand scale of history painting, Wall frequently incorporates into his photographic process actors, props, and lights on a constructed set or an outdoor location. These are all techniques from film production, employed to create still pictures that reference the grammar of cinema. However, in a nod to more traditional forms of street photography, he sometimes depicts everyday city and landscape scenes as he encounters them to focus on found symbols for the economic and political structures that influence community well-being.

Wall, who is Canadian, was trained in both art and art history at the University of British Columbia in Vancouver and the Courtauld Institute of Art in London. He often refers to historical sources in his work, connecting themes from art, history, literature, and critical theory with contemporary social topics such as race, identity, immigration, war, economics, and the environment. While his illuminated transparencies frequently display the formal precision and saturated palette of high-end advertising, they also exemplify Wall's dramatic experiments with photographic representation. *The Destroyed Room* (1978, see "Picturing a Collection, Presenting a History," p. 13, fig. 8), depicts the contents of a brightly lit, upper-class bedroom blasted chaotically across a stagelike space constructed in his studio, apparently the outcome of some unseen rampage. He questions the presumption of documentary truth by fabricating this beautifully intricate scene and connecting it to narrative and metaphorical subjects found in nineteenth-century romantic painting. Wall's picture is based on Eugène Delacroix's *The Death of Sardanapalus* (1827, see "Picturing a Collection, Presenting a History," p. 13, fig. 9), which depicts a defeated Assyrian king overseeing the destruction of all his wealth, including his women and horses. Owing to its scale, backlit theatrical construction, and overtly narrative subtext drawn from art history, *The Destroyed Room* signaled a radical shift away from both documentary and conceptual photography of the 1960s and 1970s.[1]

Completed almost thirty years later, *Hotels, Carrall St., Vancouver, summer 2005* (pl. 32) presents a seemingly ordinary view of urban redevelopment: a street and two old rooming houses in the city's urban Downtown Eastside neighborhood. A candy-colored yellow trash chute snakes down the facade of the Pennsylvania Hotel, signaling the renovation of a building first opened in 1906. Historic Carrall Street has long been an important north-south axis in the city, running through Chinatown and bridging downtown Vancouver by connecting False Creek to the south with the harbor on the north shore. Bordering on a tough, low-income district since the 1960s, Carrall Street became the focus of local attention in 2005 when the city authorized development of a greenway to connect Chinatown to the northern neighborhoods and facilitate community revitalization and historic preservation.

In Wall's picture, Carrall Street has the appearance of a banal urban thoroughfare, easy to pass by without a second glance. Regarding his portrayal of Vancouver's urban locale, Wall says, "In my pictures I try to perceive it as the actual environment in which we live, as the result of all our labors and errors."[2] To do this, he packs his picture with information: he shows the street-level storefronts boarded up to secure the building for construction, with spools of razor wire to protect the scaffold in front. Tiny figures milling around a distant pub signal the only sign of life on the street. Like a war zone,

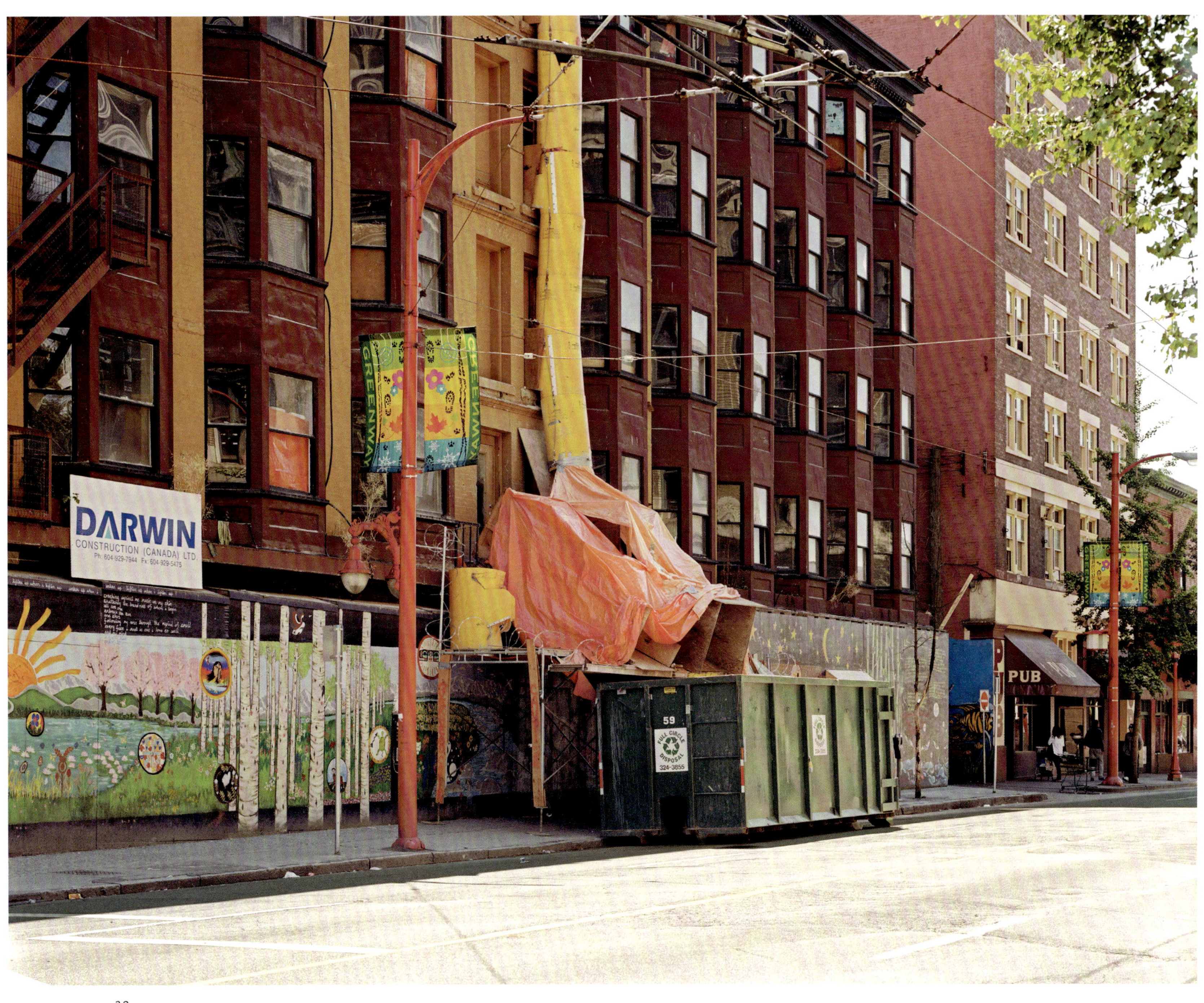

DARWIN
CONSTRUCTION (CANADA) LTD.
GREENWAY
PUB
59
FULL CIRCLE
DISPOSAL
324-3055

1. Although he had created earlier works, Wall considers *The Destroyed Room* to be his first successful light box. See *Jeff Wall: Installation of Faking Death* (1977), *The Destroyed Room* (1978), *Young Workers* (1978), *Picture for Women* (1979) (The Art Gallery of Greater Victoria, 1979). Referencing the study of art history in his catalog introduction, "To the Spectator," he wrote, "I think of the field in terms of the theoretical issues posed by the historical development of the means of production of representation or signification. My work depends on this continuous study," 4.

2. Jacques Herzog, Jeff Wall, and Philip Ursprung, *Pictures of Architecture, Architecture of Pictures: A Conversation between Jacques Herzog and Jeff Wall, Moderated by Philip Ursprung* (Vienna, 2004), 25.

3. Jeff Wall, "The Storyteller," in Jeff Wall, Robert Linsley, and Verena Auffermann, *Jeff Wall: The Storyteller* (Museum für Moderne Kunst, Frankfurt, 1992), 7. Wall based this idea on Walter Benjamin's essay "The Storyteller: Reflections on the Work of Nicholai Leskov," 1936, in Benjamin, *Illuminations: Essays and Reflections* (New York, 1969), 83–109.

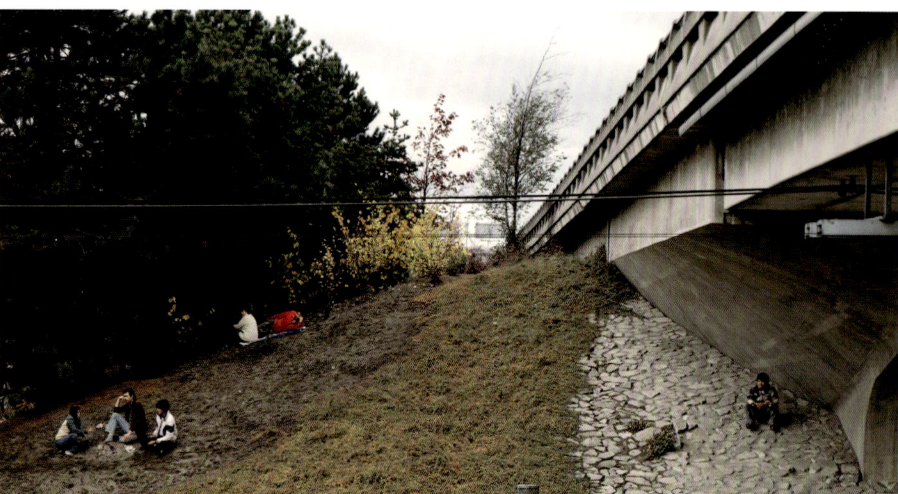

fig. 1: Jeff Wall, *The Storyteller*, 1986, transparency in light box, Courtesy of the artist

the barriers suggest trouble or danger, yet bursts of sunny colors punctuate the scene, injecting a sense of transformation or resurgence. Lampposts are painted bright red, echoing the colored tarps covering the chute, which empties into a green dumpster. Rainbow-colored banners hang from the posts to promote the greenway and are printed with icons for the four seasons. A cheerful, childlike mural painted on the main barrier describes a beautiful green marshland adjacent to an untouched harbor with pink flowering trees and an orange sun rising over mountains to the east; a grove of white birch trees woven with symbols of the First Nations people who inhabit this imagined wonderland completes a visual narrative of how Carrall Street might have appeared in the years before white settlers arrived in 1862. Ironically, these recollections of a rural arcadia that adorn the barricade now protect the construction of urban public housing for those left behind in Vancouver's modern economic boom.

This complex mix of images depicting real and invented worlds disrupts the flow of time and could be read as an allegory about the evolution of the landscape and the people who inhabit it. With another ironic twist, Wall highlights a large sign above the mural that advertises Darwin Construction (Canada) Ltd., the company that is renovating the hotel to provide single-room occupancy facilities for Vancouver's transient and homeless population. Signifying the financial, physical, and historical "evolution" of Carrall Street, this matrix of symbols suggests a cautionary tale about the effects of development.

*Hotels, Carrall St., Vancouver, summer 2005* takes on added meaning when considered in light of Wall's ongoing focus on Vancouver's evolving social and physical landscape. Earlier works, such as his large 1986 light box, *The Storyteller* (fig. 1), which depicts First Nations people camped beside a concrete highway bridge, also explored the relationship between native communities and land development. On the left margin of this picture, seated under intrusive communication and electrical wires that bisect the composition, a woman speaks excitedly to a small group gathered around a fire. For Wall, this storyteller who communicates face to face with her audience signifies "the process in which marginalized and oppressed groups reappropriate and re-learn their own history."[3] Paradoxically, *Hotels, Carrall St., Vancouver, summer 2005* tells of an imaginary Aboriginal landscape from the past superimposed on the urban space that displaced it. Now the hotels are being rebuilt to help accommodate people expelled by prior development. Here Wall himself becomes a storyteller whose innovative approach calls attention to the conflicting histories that define his own community. BROOKMAN

# Catherine Opie
American, born 1961

---

33

*Lawrence (Black Shirt)*, 2012
inkjet print
88.27 × 68.26 cm (34¾ × 26⅞ in.)
Promised Gift from the
Collection of Robert E.
Meyerhoff and Rheda Becker

---

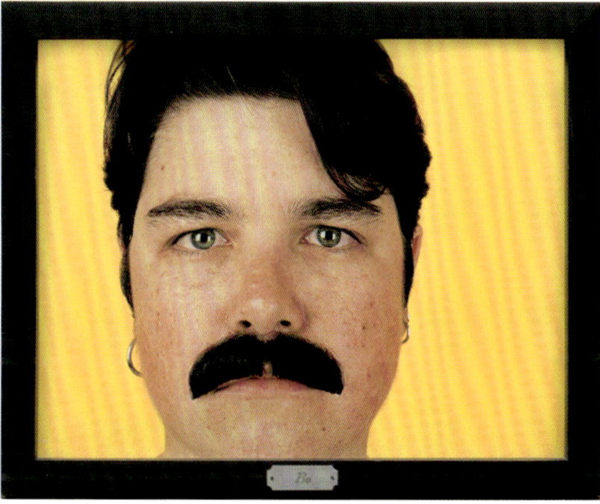

fig. 1: Catherine Opie, *Bo*, 1991, chromogenic print and wood frame with metallic nameplate, Courtesy the artist and Regen Projects, Los Angeles

CATHERINE OPIE'S personal perceptions of gender, home, family, friends, and community have been a significant source of inspiration in her work. She is best known for her remarkable self-portraits and photographs of lesbian and gay friends, sometimes in gender-challenging drag, shot in the early 1990s. Posed in front of brightly colored backgrounds, her subjects enacted new personas (such as her self-portrait as alter ego "Bo") that confronted viewer assumptions about traditional gender roles, questioning social and cultural stereotypes (fig. 1). Frequently grappling in her work with the core concepts of belonging, transformation, and identity, Opie humanized her band of outsiders by presenting them in powerful poses under strong and expressive illumination. This strategy, borrowed from fashion photography, models the subjects' features and moderates their outward appearance. Her later portraits of friends and artists, such as *Lawrence (Black Shirt)* (2012, pl. 33), made about twenty years later, follow a similar aesthetic approach. Opie draws us in to establish symbolic connections with her subjects through expressive poses, high-key lighting, and shallow, opaque spaces borrowed from Renaissance and baroque portraiture.

Throughout much of her career, Opie has also photographed landscapes and architecture to assemble a more intricate picture of the natural and social world outside her own studio and community. Based in Los Angeles, she has pictured a wide range of familiar subjects across America—from the modernist arches of Southern California freeways, the forbidding gates of Beverly Hills homes, and the lonely panoramic chill of West Coast strip malls to the prosaic urban architecture of cities like St. Louis, Minneapolis, and Chicago. She has also expressed a fascination with recurring shared rituals like ice fishing, surfing, and high school football. She photographed her childhood home in Sandusky, Ohio, to reexamine her roots, and she created informal and personal documentary studies of lesbian couples and families in domestic settings while on a road trip across the United States.

But Opie always returns to portraiture, the hub from which many spokes radiate in her work. For example, a series of studio portraits of children made in 2004, shortly after she had a child of her own, retraced her early images of solitary figures against colored backgrounds. While she began to represent a wider variety of people in her work, including children, adolescents, and surfers, her images often portrayed them as individuals whose openness to the camera and connection to a particular community parallel her own early photographs of lesbian and gay friends. The combination of these portraits and her photographs about urban and suburban alienation gives this work a particular resonance; people appear disconnected from their empty, dehumanizing surroundings.

Opie's later portraits and allegorical groupings, created in 2012 and 2013, often depict artists and writers in her circle of friends, including Ron Athey, John Baldessari, Jonathan Franzen, Mary Kelly, Glenn Ligon, Kara Walker, and Lawrence Weiner, among others. These photographs convey a sense of her subjects' gaze, work, and creativity. By isolating figures in the photographic frame against dark backgrounds and under carefully rendered studio lighting, she maps their appearance and physiognomy in great detail to express something of their character. By referencing the symbols of earlier art, she opens up these portraits to new interpretations beyond the codes of gender and family that framed many of her earlier works. "With their moody black backgrounds, extreme lighting, and arch compositions, these works foreground their citations of Baroque religious paintings," writes art historian David Getsy. "In *Anthony & Michael* we have a Pietà, and Weiner could be a doge. *Kate & Laura* could be offering an Annunciation or a temptation."[1] When first exhibited, these works were combined with a series of hauntingly beautiful, almost abstract landscapes that punctuated the display of portraits. These

1. David J. Getsy, "Catherine Opie, Portraiture, and the Decoy of the Iconographic," in *Confronting the Abject*, ed. Amy Honchell and Jeremy Ohmes (Chicago, 2015), 15.

landscapes can be read as contemplative spaces that contrast the beauty and time-lessness of nature with the mortal issues of everyday lives.

*Lawrence (Black Shirt)* depicts conceptual artist Lawrence Weiner caught in an intense moment of philosophical reflection. His figure emerges from blackness. The deep folds of his dark shirt are hardly separated from the obsidian background, only just revealing his shoulders and arms. In stark contrast, Weiner's vulnerable bare chest pokes from his unbuttoned shirt, which is crowned by his brightly lit face, white collar, and full white beard. His right hand is silhouetted against the black ground and pushed forward, fingers perfectly positioned in a lateral tug against a vertical shaft of raking light that delineates his features. Weiner balances a cigarette between fingers, which accents the stillness of his face and beard and suggests that smoking is an integral part of his personality. A lustrous ring on his third finger echoes several bright buttons and a small pendant hanging by a chain from his neck, diverting attention across the middle of the image to his eyes, which gaze intently away from Opie's lens. Like the painted portraits of noblemen by Bellini, Holbein, Rembrandt, or Tintoretto, Weiner's enigmatic psyche emerges from darkness, projecting an air of exposed mystery and ethereal creative intensity.

Weiner's own art is rooted in written language. Believing that the linguistic depiction of an object or idea is analogous to its physical representation, he presents only typographic texts that spell out in words the concept of a work of art. In some ways, Opie's portrait of the artist provides a divergent experience by delivering a highly detailed visual description of Weiner's physical being. Yet, by isolating the figure in a seemingly empty, flat space, without any illusion of depth, she presents him with a directness and economy of style that echoes his own textual art. By aligning the black background with his black shirt she compresses any illusion of depth in which to situate the figure, accentuating the artist's features as well as the picture's surface.

From her impeccable lighting, which models Weiner's corporeal form, to her balanced observation of his static pose, which anchors the figure in its frame but does not grant intimate access, Opie brings together the physical and symbolic attributes of her subject. While she shares with her audience a contemplative look at Weiner's personality, it is the tension between this and her references to art history that situates *Lawrence, Black Shirt* in the context of her recent portraits. **BROOKMAN**

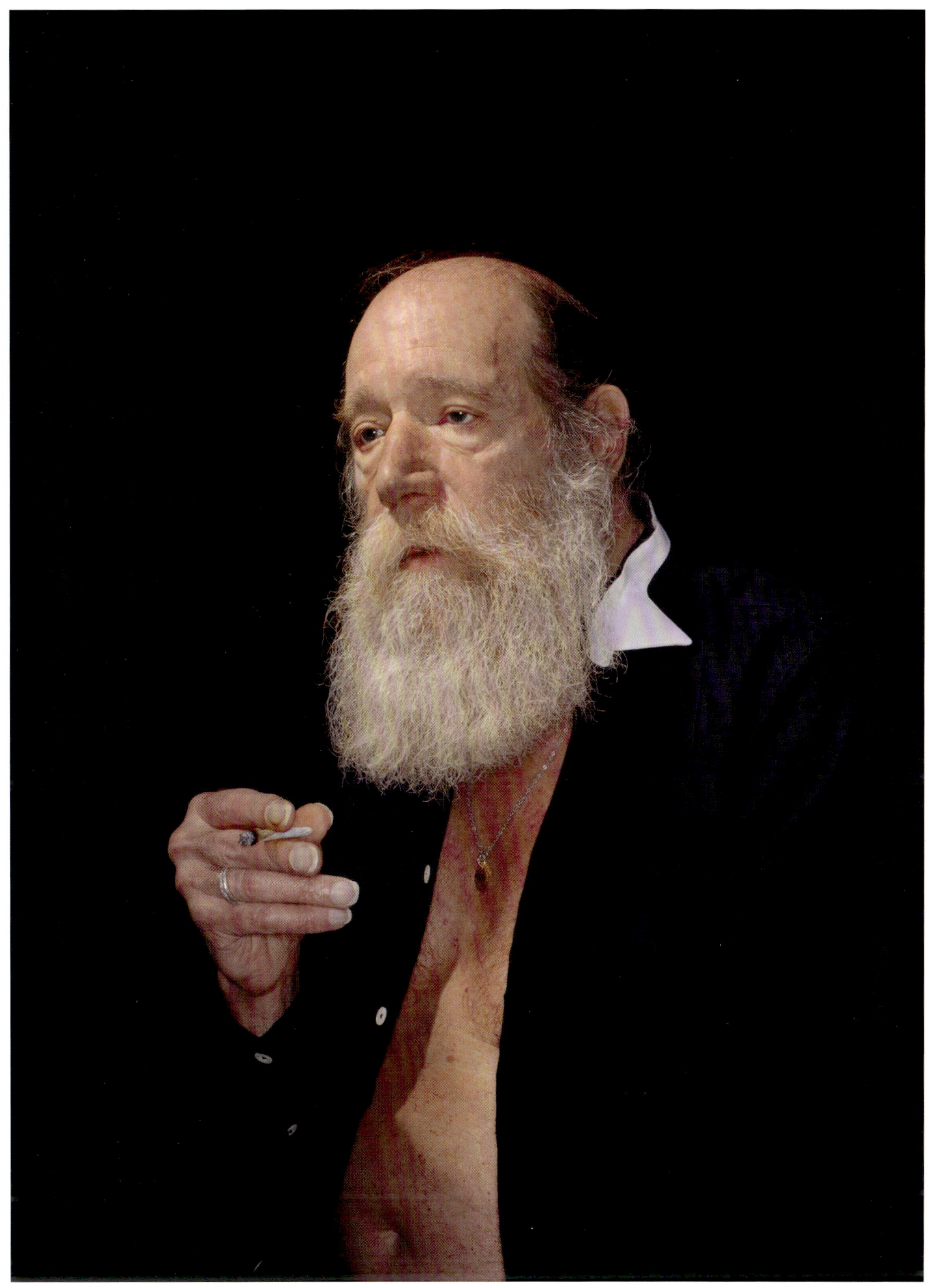

# Marina Abramović

Serbian, born 1946

---

34

*The Kitchen I*, from the series
*The Kitchen, Homage to
Saint Therese*, 2009
inkjet print (color fine-art
pigment print)
222.25 × 162.56 cm (87 ½ × 64 in.)
Promised Gift from the
Collection of Robert E.
Meyerhoff and Rheda Becker

---

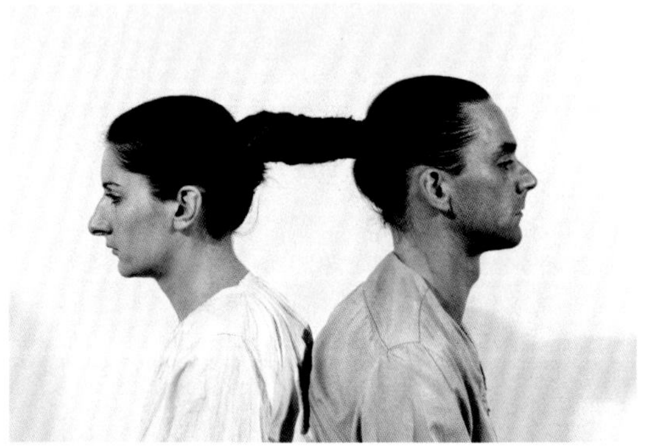

fig. 1: Ulay and Abramović performing *Relation in Time*, Studio
G7, Bologna, Italy, 1977, gelatin silver print, Courtesy Marina
Abramović Archives

ONE OF THE EARLIEST artists to adopt performance as her means of expression, Marina Abramović has devoted her career of over forty years to the art of duration and the body. Part of a wave of artists, including Chris Burden, Vito Acconci, and Valie Export, who explored the possibilities of performance in the 1970s, Abramović is unusual in that she has steadfastly continued making work in this vein long after her contemporaries moved on to other media. Her first performance, *Rhythm 10*—in which she repeatedly stabbed knives between her fingers for an hour—took place in 1973. Since then, in her groundbreaking collaborations with Ulay (her partner of thirteen years) and in her solo endeavors, she has conceived numerous pieces that are often treacherous, even potentially life threatening. In lengthy presentations, Abramović taxes her mental concentration, seeking to place her mind fully and unequivocally in the present, and tests her physical endurance to the extreme. Using her body as a vehicle, she creates performances that challenge her spectators, either as observers or, at times, participants who interact with her. Her work questions the very nature of art and its relationship to the audience.

Abramović's life story, which is intertwined with her art, is no less dramatic. Born in Belgrade in the former Yugoslavia, she wanted to be an artist from an early age. While studying at the Academy of Fine Arts in Belgrade, she made works that centered on sound before beginning to probe the limits of her body. In 1974, in Naples, she memorably performed *Rhythm 0*, in which audience members were allowed to do anything to her for a period of six hours using any of seventy-two objects she had placed on a table, such as a gun, scissors, hammer, grapes, and a rose. The year after, Abramović met the German artist Ulay (Frank Uwe Laysiepen) in Amsterdam just before her performance of *Lips of Thomas*, in which she carved a five-pointed star on her abdomen and flagellated herself, among several other acts. She soon moved to the Netherlands to be with Ulay, beginning a fruitful artistic and romantic partnership. Living together and traveling in a van for several years, they collaborated on many performance pieces that emphasized their interactions. These included *Imponderabilia* (1977), where the two stood naked opposite one another in the narrow entrance to the Galleria Communale d'Arte Moderna in Bologna, so that visitors had to pass between them; *Relation in Time* (1977, fig. 1), in which they sat back to back with their hair twisted together for a period of seventeen hours; and *Nightsea Crossing* (1981–1987), repeated twenty-two times at different venues, where the pair simply sat still in chairs for hours, facing each other across a long table. In 1988, Abramović and Ulay turned their separation into its own act, *The Great Wall Walk*, in which they walked the Great Wall of China—from opposite ends—until, after ninety days, they met in the middle.

After her breakup with Ulay, Abramović embarked on a solo career, performing pieces such as *Balkan Baroque* (1997), intended as a statement on her family and heritage as well as the violence occurring in her native country, during which she spent hours scrubbing butchered cow bones with a brush. After moving to New York, her first major piece in the United States was *The House with the Ocean View* (2002): she lived without food for twelve days on a platform at the Sean Kelly Gallery (fig. 2). For her 2010 retrospective, *The Artist Is Present,* at the Museum of Modern Art (the first ever mounted there for a performance artist), she performed another work of long duration: she sat silently in a chair, without breaks, when the museum was open to the public. Any visitor could sit in the empty seat across from her.

Though less known for her other work, Abramović has nevertheless made a wide range of multimedia art. *The Kitchen* (2009) is a series of photographs and videos that incorporate many of the themes that have fascinated Abramović in her performance pieces, from the physical (ritual, repetition of action, and pain) to the

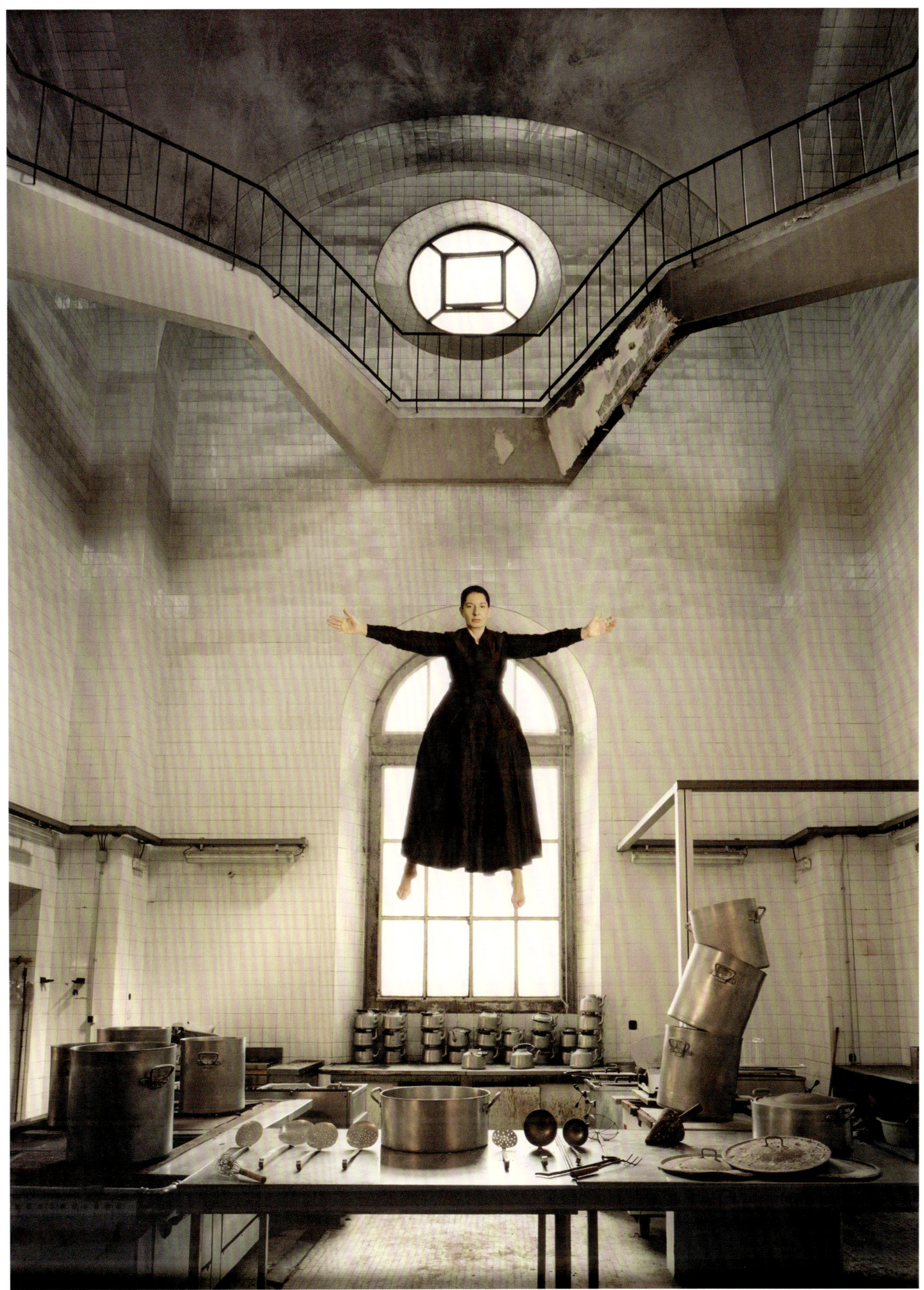

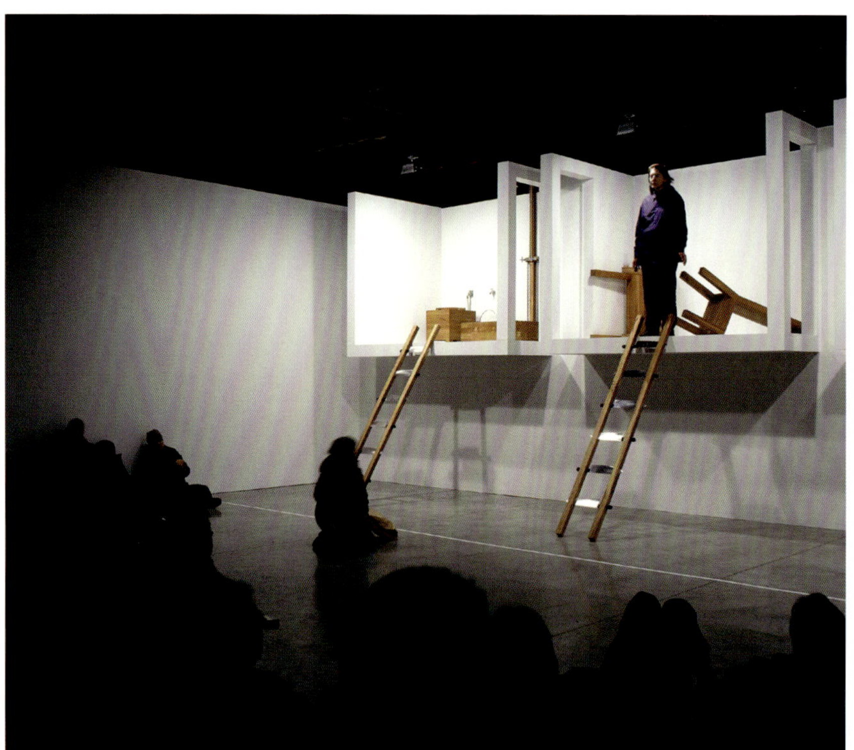

fig. 2: Abramović performing *The House with the Ocean View*, Sean Kelly Gallery, New York, 2002, Courtesy Marina Abramović Archives

mental (concentration, contemplation, and ecstasy). The series was staged in an abandoned convent in Gijón, Spain, built between 1946 and 1956, whose kitchen had been used by nuns to prepare food for students, and which is now part of the cultural arts center Laboral Ciudad de la Cultura. Its architecture is austere and imposing, vast and empty. In one video, *The Kitchen V: Carrying Milk,* Abramović stands for almost thirteen minutes in front of a luminous window. She holds a small pan of milk filled to the brim, which gradually begins to spill and drip down her dress as her hands start to shake. Recalling seventeenth-century Dutch paintings such as Johannes Vermeer's *The Milkmaid,* Abramović's action—a simple ritual of daily life elongated in duration— is transformed into a sacramental act.

*The Kitchen I* (2009, pl. 34), printed on a large scale, also brings together the everyday and the spiritual. Though she is in the cavernous yet humble space of the kitchen, Abramović pictures her body suspended in the air, echoing an earlier performance piece, *Luminosity* (1997), in which she, naked, appeared to be floating against a wall, spotlighted in a square of light.[1] Yet in *The Kitchen I,* Abramović's choice of clothing takes on a vivid symbolic meaning, with the heavy, long, and dark-colored gown suggesting the weight of history and the austerity of religious habits. As the title makes clear, Abramović deliberately channels the sixteenth-century Saint Teresa of Ávila, who described her ecstasy as a force that overwhelmed her, making resistance impossible, even overtaking her in the kitchen: "I say that often, it seemed to me, the body was left so light that all its weight was gone, and sometimes this feeling reached such a point that I almost didn't know how to put my feet on the ground."[2] Saint Teresa's account accords with Abramović's own description of the feeling of otherworldliness she experienced during her performance pieces:

> The moment you really go through the door of pain, you enter to
> another state of mind. This feeling of beauty and unconditional
> love, this feeling of there is no kind of borders between your body

1. In *Luminosity*, Abramović achieved the effect by sitting on a hidden bicycle seat. In *The Kitchen I*, she used a pulley system.

2. Saint Teresa of Ávila, *The Collected Works of Saint Teresa of Ávila*, volume I, trans. Kieran Kavanaugh and Otilio Rodriguez (Washington, 1976), 134–135.

3. Marina Abramović in *Marina Abramović: The Artist Is Present*, directed by Matthew Akers and Jeff Dupre (2012), 1:18:34.

4. Stephen Lucas, "Marina Abramović's Kitchen," *Dazed*, 2009, http://www.dazeddigital.com/artsandculture/article/5849/1/marina-abramovics-kitchen.

and environment. You start having this incredible feeling of lightness and harmony with yourself. You suddenly become like a, like a holy, I can't explain."[3]

Abramović's hovering body imparts a sense of time slowed and arrested, suggestive of her durational works, and her expression conveys her inner state of contemplation. The iconic power of her pose transmits a heightened sense of her physicality at one with the monumentality of the space, indeed erasing the borders between her body and environment as she floats in lightness and harmony.

Beyond referencing Western religious narratives, the *Kitchen* series also resonates for Abramović with her personal past. Though the convent kitchen seems immense and impersonal, and the implements arrayed on its shiny metal surfaces indicate its former use to feed a large community, the space nevertheless conjures feelings of warmth and nostalgia for her:

> The kitchen was the centre of my world. The kitchen was the place where I would tell my grandmother my dreams. The kitchen was the place where she would tell me stories, and the kitchen was the place where all the secrets were told. It was a kind of place where the spiritual world and the daily world met and mixed.[4]

The kitchen is thus a site of revelation, just as it was for Saint Teresa, intermingling the sacred and the elemental, laying bare the mysteries of life and sustenance.

*The Kitchen* consciously calls out to the visual heritage of Renaissance art. Abramović's exploitation of the dramatic proportions of the architecture in the framing of the picture, and her placement of herself at the center, evoke the colors and compositional symmetry prized in Renaissance painting, ranging from the soft jewel tones and simple pictorial storytelling of Giotto to the muted chiaroscuro of Francisco de Zurburán. The glow of light from the windows, which bathes the tile of the kitchen all the way into its upper recesses in a golden hue and makes the metal of the kitchen implements gleam, recalls the use of light to symbolize spirituality in these historical precedents. The incandescence silhouettes Abramović's figure, making her dress the darkest point of the picture and connecting her to the line of the shadows of the balcony above. Though situated at the perspectival vanishing point of the composition, Abramović instead soars triumphant, a female recasting of Leonardo da Vinci's Vitruvian man. Joining individual and communal visual memory, the personal and the archetypal, the quotidian and the sacred, Abramović's *The Kitchen I* is numinous, asserting the force of its presence and potently visualizing a yearning for a sense of belonging and a state of transcendence. **WAGGONER**

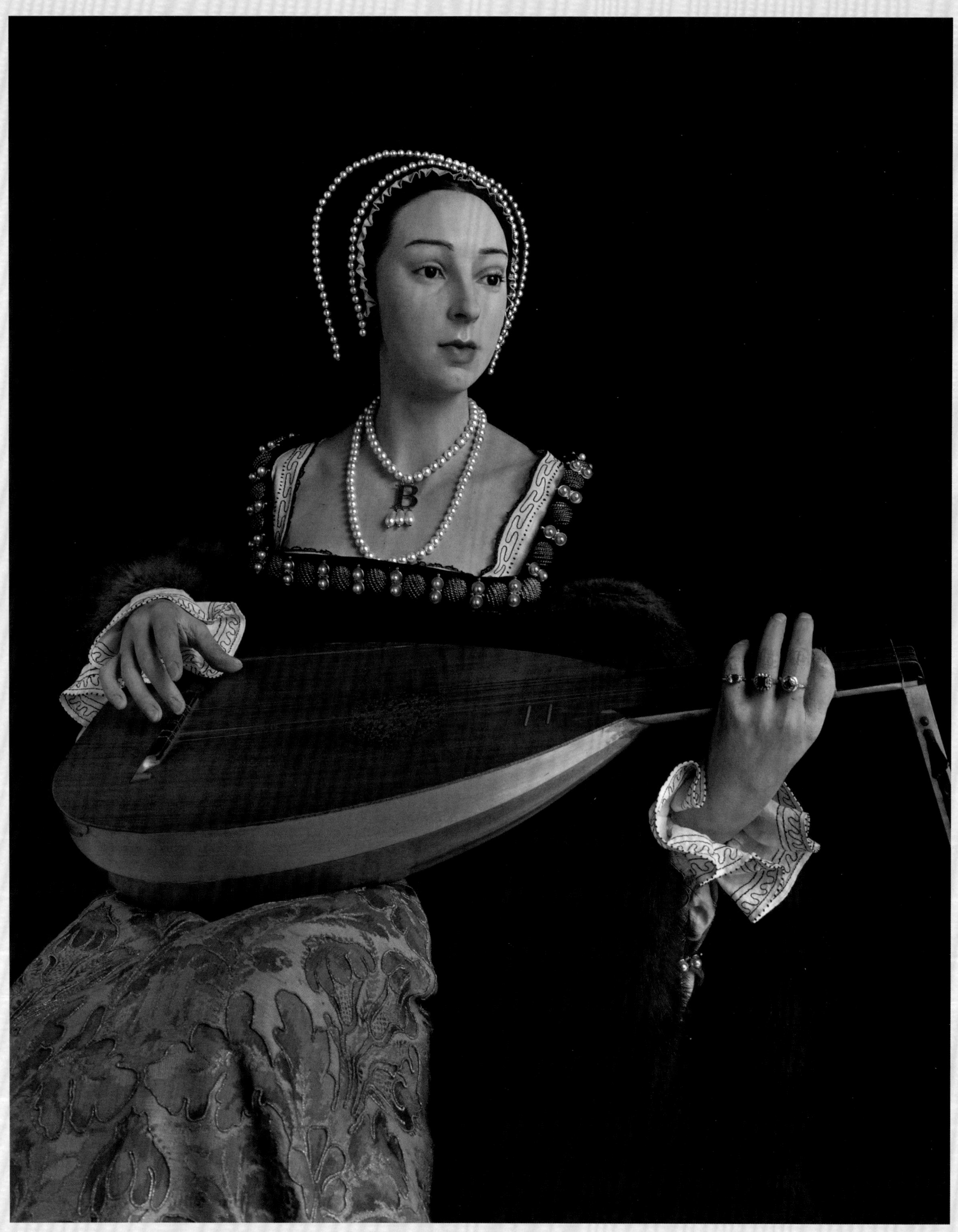

# Photography Credits